POWERS OF DARKNESS

Clinton E. Arnold

Principalities

& Powers

in

Paul's

Letters

INTERVARSITY PRESS
DOWNERS GROVE, ILLINOIS 60515

InterVarsity Press is the book-publishing division of InterVarsity Christian Fellowship, a student movement active on campus at hundreds of universities, colleges and schools of nursing in the United States of America, and a member movement of the International Fellowship of Evangelical Students. For information about local and regional activities, write Public Relations Dept., InterVarsity Christian Fellowship, 6400 Schroeder Rd., P.O. Box 7895, Madison, WI 53707-7895.

All Scripture quotations, unless otherwise indicated, are from the HOLY BIBLE, NEW INTERNATIONAL VERSION. Copyright ©1973, 1978, 1984 International Bible Society. Used by permission of Zondervan Publishing House. All rights reserved.

Cover illustration: Roberta Polfus

ISBN 0-8308-1336-5
Printed in the United States of America

Library of Congress Cataloging-in-Publication Data
Arnold, Clinton E.
    Powers of darkness: principalities and powers in Paul's letters/
Clinton E. Arnold.
        p.   cm.
    Includes bibliographical references.
    ISBN 0-8308-1336-5
    1. Powers (Christian theology)—History of doctrines—Early
church, ca. 30-600.   2. Occultism—History.   3. Bible.   N.T.
Epistles of Paul—Criticism, interpretation, etc.   I. Title.
BS2655.P66A76   1992
235'.4'09015—dc20   91-33075
                                                                              CIP

15	14	13	12	11	10	9	8	7	6	5	4	3	2	1
04	03	02	01	00	99	98	97	96	95	94	93	92		

*To Jeffrey and Dustin
with the prayer
that the Lord would strengthen them
with his power
to resist the evil one
and tell others of his love.*

Abbreviations

BAGD   W. Bauer, W. F. Arndt and F. W. Gingrich. *A Greek-English Lexicon of the New Testament and Other Early Christian Literature.* 2d rev. ed. by Frederick Danker. Chicago: University of Chicago Press, 1979.

OTP   *The Old Testament Pseudepigrapha.* 2 vols. Edited by James H. Charlesworth. New York: Doubleday, 1983, 1985.

PGM   *Papyri Graecae Magicae: Die Griechischen Zauberpapyri.* 2 vols. Edited by Karl Preisendanz. 2d rev. ed. by A. Heinrichs. Stuttgart: Teubner, 1973-74. English translation now available in *The Greek Magical Papyri in Translation.* Edited by Hans Dieter Betz. Chicago: University of Chicago Press, 1986.

P. Oxy.   *The Oxyrhynchus Papyri.*

All citations from the Old Testament and New Testament are taken from the New International Version unless otherwise noted.

All citations of Old Testament pseudepigraphal documents are taken from James H. Charlesworth, ed., *The Old Testament Pseudepigrapha,* 2 vols. (New York: Doubleday, 1983, 1985), unless otherwise noted.

All citations of the Dead Sea Scrolls are taken from Geza Vermes, *The Dead Sea Scrolls in English,* 2d ed. (New York: Viking Penguin, 1975).

All citations of the Greek Magical Papyri *(PGM)* are taken from Hans Dieter Betz, ed., *The Greek Magical Papyri in Translation* (Chicago: University of Chicago Press, 1986), unless otherwise noted.

Preface

I do not like to think about evil. It grieves and frightens me. I would much rather ignore it and discuss something pleasant.

I think many Christians feel the same way, especially when it comes to discussing the notion of evil spirits and Satan. *Christianity Today* devoted its August 20, 1990, issue to this topic (for which I contributed one of the articles). The editor commissioned artist Michael Annino with the task of creating a suitable image of the devil for the cover, an image that would strip away the devil's disguise as "an angel of light." Annino did a good job, perhaps too good. Many readers wrote letters to the editor complaining bitterly about the horrific figure. The managing editor of the magazine was correct in observing that this "is not a pretty subject"!

Ultimately we cannot ignore the topic. Evil imposes itself upon us and those we love. And if we want help from the Bible for dealing with the problem of evil, we must be willing to take seriously what the Bible takes seriously: the intense involvement in life of a figure named Satan and his powers of darkness. Far too long the Western church has given neither sufficient nor serious attention to this topic. My Asian and African students tell me this repeatedly. They acknowledge a tremendous debt to the Western church for rich biblical teaching that has been passed on to them, but they cannot understand why so little has been offered on this topic. For them the issue of developing an appropriate Christian perspective on spirits is a foundational concern.

The Bible does indeed have much to say on this topic, especially the letters of the apostle Paul. This book is written for those who want to explore the extent of Paul's teaching on the evil unseen realm. Paul has far more to say on this topic than many realize. In recent years, despite the flood of popular publications dealing with "spiritual warfare," very little has been written from a biblical-theological perspective. It is my hope that this volume may provide a helpful beginning.

Initial credit for the appearance of this book must be given to Andy Le Peau, editorial director of InterVarsity Press, for convincing me that I should work on this project now rather than later. I also want to express my deepest thanks to Dr. W. Bingham Hunter, dean of Talbot School of Theology, who encouraged me to pursue this task and did all he could to support me along the way.

During the summer of 1990, I shared some of this material with a few groups of Rumanian Christians in Transylvania. While they expressed much appreciation for what they learned, I felt myself the greater beneficiary. They helped me a great deal in clarifying my thoughts in part three, especially the discussion on "The Powers and Society."

I owe many other people a public acknowledgment of my gratitude for their contributions to this project. Above all, I would like to thank my wife, Barbara, not only for her helpful suggestions for improving the manuscript, but also for her faithful partnership in the work of the ministry. Dr. Michael J. Wilkins gave me constant encouragement throughout the process. During the summer of 1989, as my department chairperson, he helped me clear my schedule to continue work on the manuscript. The Biola University Research Committee also supported the project with a grant. Tim Peck, my teaching assistant, carefully read a large portion of the manuscript, which resulted in numerous improvements. It remains for me to thank Dr. Joel Green, editor of *Catalyst,* for permission to use substantive portions of my article " 'Principalities and Powers' in Recent Interpretation."

Three other people were very important to this project: Dr. Robert Saucy, for the many fruitful discussions on this topic and matters pertaining to the kingdom of God; Dr. Robert Yarbrough (Wheaton College), my teaching partner in Rumania, for reading the manuscript and offering critical interaction and encouragement; and Dr. I. Howard Marshall (University of Aberdeen) for first suggesting in 1986 that I write a popular treatment on this theme.

Introduction

In 1992 Salem, Massachusetts, commemorated the 300th anniversary of the city's infamous witch trials. More than 400 persons were accused of being witches in the inquisition. Of these, 150 were jailed, 14 women and 5 men were hung, and one supposed witch was crushed to death under several tons of rock.

Today, as visitors tour an 1845 stone church converted into Salem's Witch Museum, the museum narrator greets them with, "Welcome to the Witch Museum. Do you believe in witches? Millions of our ancestors did."

Many people today find it incredible that our forebears gave credence to these ideas. How could anyone possibly believe that "witches" have actual supernatural powers, that spell-casting can work, and that evil spirits wreak all kinds of terror in peoples' lives? For most, these beliefs were rendered obsolete with the rise of the scientific age and the spread of educational opportunity for everyone.

Now, three centuries after the witch trials, no threat of a similar inquisition is looming, and I hope that that threat never will loom. But there is an upsurge of interest in witchcraft and the occult throughout the West. Note, for instance, the following advertisement that appeared in a recent tabloid:

> I will cast a spell for you. I can cast a spell to make one love another, or cause a person to change his mind about a relationship, or bring two people together. I can do all these things because

I have the combined powers of my mother who was a sorceress and my father, one of the most powerful warlocks who passed on his secrets to me moments before he moved on to a different world. My magical powers are beyond your imagination. I can cast a spell in your behalf regarding a relationship, your financial situation, future events, or whatever is important to you. I have the power and I use the power.[1]

This announcement is typical of a number of occultic advertisements that appear regularly in tabloids throughout the United States.

This burgeoning interest in the occult is not a local fad but a trend in Western society. The growing fascination in the occult of the sixties became what the eminent history of religions scholar Mircea Eliade termed an "occult explosion" in the seventies.[2] He notes, "As a historian of religions, I cannot fail to be impressed by the amazing popularity of witchcraft in modern Western culture and its subcultures. . . . The contemporary interest in witchcraft is only part and parcel of a larger trend, namely the vogue of the occult and the esoteric from astrology and pseudospiritualist movements to Hermetism, alchemy, Zen, Yoga, Tantrism, and other Oriental gnoses and techniques."[3] Then came the New Age movement, a definite "explosion" in its own right during the eighties and continuing vigorously into the nineties.[4] The movement received a strong impetus from the publicity it received from a number of entertainment celebrities who popularized its teachings. The religious vocabulary of the West expanded with a barrage of neologisms such as "channeling" (getting in contact with a spiritual entity), "spirit guide" (a spiritual entity who provides information), "cosmic consciousness" (the perception that all in the universe is "one") and "astral flight" (soul travel during meditation or the night).

It is difficult to gauge the size of this growing "movement" since it is loosely organized. Its current popularity can best be seen by perusing the shelves of any bookstore. Increasing space is given to the literally thousands of New Age publications. Businesses and corporations are hosting more and more "human potential" seminars based on New Age principles.[5] The New Age concept of channeling has grown increasingly popular, especially in Southern California. A *Los Angeles Times* poll revealed that more women in West Los Angeles are consulting channelers than psychologists or counselors.[6] In a recent cover story, entitled "New Age Harmonies," *Time* magazine summarized the surprisingly rapid acceptance and popularity of the movement in many sectors of Western society.[7]

The New Age movement is characterized by a monistic world view that has much in common with classic Hinduism. Monism is the belief that the entire universe is a living unified whole. God permeates the entire universe, and in a sense every person is a part of God. God and humanity are therefore one. What is needed, according to this view, is a change in our consciousness to heighten our level of awareness into our essential unity with the divine. The New Age movement also has a lively belief in the realm of spirits and thus practices forms of divination and magic (under the euphemism "channeling"). For this reason some evangelical analysts have described the heart of the New Age religion as occultism.[8]

Given this rise in occultism, expressed also in the form of the New Age movement, we need to ask if the church is alert and ready to face this fresh challenge? Is the church prepared to effectively handle the spiritual problems that will surface in ministering to people who have opened their lives to the direct and immediate influence of the realm of Satan?

There are some encouraging signs. Many evangelical seminaries and Christian colleges are offering courses in spiritual warfare (or the equivalent) and, almost invariably, these courses have turned out to be the most popular courses among the students.[9] Quite a number of books and articles have also appeared, treating topics on spiritual warfare, demon possession, counseling the demonized, and the New Age movement. Regrettably, the Christian community has not been well served with material dealing with a biblical perspective on demons, principalities and powers, and the nature of the church's conflict with the powers of evil. I hope that this book can be a helpful first installment on developing a biblical perspective on the powers of darkness.

But is this topic relevant for everyone? Certainly not everyone in the church has had contact with professing Satanists or witches, with New Age advocates, or with those deeply involved in the occult. Furthermore, this topic is rather frightening. Why spend time exploring the varied dimensions of evil, especially in terms of demons and evil spirits? Would it not be better to avoid this topic altogether and spend the time meditating on the positive aspects of our Christian life?

I believe this topic is important for all Christians because it touches us in a profound way, regardless of whether we have had any involvement in the occult. The Bible teaches not only that evil spirits exist, but also that they are actively hostile to all Christians; their perverse instigations adversely affect our day-to-day life and the lives of those around us. The Bible consequently provides us with vital information, information designed to give Christians an appropriate perspective on these malicious forces and how to deal with their activity against us.

My personal interest in this theme originated during the course of my doctoral studies. Nestled in my office high in a tower of the sixteenth-century King's College of the University of Aberdeen (Scotland), I banged away on a keyboard, researching and writing on the biblical concept of power. I was not far into my research before I realized that it was nigh well impossible to study the power of God without studying the opposing sphere of power, the kingdom of Satan. The end result was a dissertation entitled, "The Power of God and the Powers of Evil in Ephesians," a study of this theme in one New Testament letter.

Not only in Paul's letter to the Ephesians, but also throughout the New Testament, Christ is portrayed in terms of a struggle with the powers of darkness. Jesus confronted the demonic in his earthly ministry, dealt a decisive blow to the kingdom of evil on the cross, continues to wage war against the hosts of Satan through the church, and will finally vanquish Satan and his forces once and for all after his Second Coming. Christ's conflict with the powers of evil surfaces as a major theme in New Testament theology. Surprisingly, this theme has been terribly neglected in the exegetical and theological study of the New Testament. Why? I am not certain. It may be due partly to the Western post-Enlightenment world view that has interpreted the New Testament references to evil spirits as outmoded primitive myth.

The grip of our common Western world view provides yet another reason for this book. In contrast to people in Africa, Korea, China, and other parts of the non-Western world, we have grown up disbelieving in the realm of spirits, demons and angels. Most Westerners, if asked, "Do you believe in evil spirits?" would say no. This is also true of many Christians in the West, although we display some double-mindedness on the issue. Many Christians would affirm a belief in demons because they are mentioned in the Bible (and perhaps because some missionaries have come home with tales about dealing with the demonic). In actual fact, however, the spirit realm may have no more a part of a given Christian's world view than it does of that person's non-Christian neighbor. It is tough to break the all-pervasive influence of one's culture. If the realm of spirits and angels is a dominant part of the biblical world view, it should thus be a dominant part of a Christian world view in our age.

In the following pages I hope to show precisely what role evil spiritual powers had in the world view of one of Christianity's most brilliant and inspired thinkers, the apostle Paul. Comprising about one-quarter of our New Testament, Paul's letters constitute an important source for building a Christian world view today.

PART I
First-Century Belief in the Powers

PAUL PREACHED THE GOSPEL AND PLANTED CHURCHES AMONG people who believed in the existence of evil spirits. This fact had an impact on how he preached the gospel and on what he taught those new Christians in his letters.

The belief in spirits crossed all religious, ethnic and geographical boundaries. The Jews, Greeks, Romans, Asians and Egyptians all believed in spirits who populated the heavens, the underworld and the earth. Many were thought to be good spirits, or gods, who were worthy of worship and could be trusted. Others caused people to tremble in fear because they were believed to be wicked and injurious. Everyone, however, agreed on one thing: The supernatural realm exercises control over everyday life and eternal destiny.

Our goal in this section will be to uncover the world view of the populace—the kind of people who were becoming Christians and to whom Paul ministered. What specifically did the average person believe about gods, spirits, demons and the like? This task is not easy. Most of the Greek and Roman literature that we have comes from the educated elite and, with the finest rhetorical craftsmanship, presents philosophical understandings of existence that are often quite removed from what common folk believed. Fortunately, some literature gives us a glimpse into the folk belief. Scholars are increasingly recognizing the value of papyri, inscriptions and archeological evidence for piecing together a picture of folk belief. We will begin by taking a look at an aspect of first-century life that many scholars believe gives us the greatest insight into the beliefs of the populace about the spirit realm—magic.

1
Magic and Divination

*O*NE OF THE CLEAREST WINDOWS FOR SEEING WHAT ORDINARY PEOPLE BE-lieved about supernatural powers in the New Testament era is the realm of magic and divination. Magical beliefs and practices were a part of all religious traditions (and even came to have a share in Christianity!).

In Western culture we have come to think of magic as harmless trickery in the context of entertainment. When we speak of magic during the period of the New Testament, however, we must realize it was not the art of illusion. Magic represented a method of manipulating good and evil spirits to lend help or bring harm. Magical formulas could be used for such things as attracting a lover or winning a chariot race. Black magic, or sorcery, involved summoning spirits to accomplish all kinds of evil deeds. Curses could be placed, competitors subdued, and enemies restrained.

These practices were widespread and reflect the common views, or "folk belief," of the age. Magic was not something separate from organized religion. It was an important part of the official religions, though in many cases, not a sanctioned part. For example, the cult of Artemis did not have an official magician attached to the cult. Nevertheless, this goddess was invoked in magical formulas, the ornamentation on her cultic statue was interpreted magically, and magical words were even inscribed on her image. Many of the people who worshiped Artemis also practiced magic.

Scholars have learned much about Hellenistic magic in recent years. Virtually hundreds of papyrus texts have been discovered over the past century in addition to numerous magical amulets, lead curse tablets *(defixiones)* and a variety of other magical sources. Arthur Darby Nock, the famous classics scholar, strongly underscored the value of these sources for providing insight into the folk belief of the time. He advised his fellow scholars that "we may and must make use of the magical papyri in our attempt to reconstruct the religious attitude of the mass of mankind in the Roman world."[1]

While virtually all of the magical papyri that have been discovered were found in Egypt, this does not imply that people practiced magic only in Egypt. The climate and conditions of Egypt were well suited to the preservation of papyrus materials. In fact, our papyrus fragments of the Greek New Testament were found in Egypt. Although the country was indeed famous in antiquity for being a hotbed for prolific magical activities, there is plenty of evidence that magic was practiced throughout the Mediterranean world.

Many accounts about magical practices exist in the literature of the first century. Even in our own New Testament, Luke tells us about magical activity in Palestine, Cyprus, Asia and Northern Greece, which we will discuss later. In addition, the thousands of magical amulets, gems and *defixiones* (lead curse tablets) uncovered by archeologists were discovered in all of the Mediterranean lands. Whereas most of the papyrus texts date from the second century A.D., the texts recorded on the more durable materials (stone, metals, etc.) date throughout the Hellenistic period (beginning c. 330 B.C.). All these texts are basically of the same character and encompass much of the same vocabulary. They are also based on the same assumptions regarding the spirit world—people and situations can be influenced by invoking the help of supernatural, powerful spirit-beings.

The supernatural nature of magic may be seen clearly by looking at the content of a few magical recipes. We will take a close look at three magical recipes that provide a good overview of the nature of magic and its close connection to the realm of spirits and demons, principalities and powers. A typical magical formula consisted of three parts:

1. Instructions for a magical rite.
2. A list of the proper names to invoke.
3. A statement of the command.

A Protective Charm

The first text we will examine is a short recipe for a protective charm (or amulet) to be worn like a necklace. The purpose of this amulet was to protect the wearer from harmful or evil spirits.[2]

While there is no need to perform a magical rite with this charm, there are specific instructions on how the amulet is to be fashioned: "Onto lime wood write with vermilion this name. . . . Enclose it in a purple skin, hang it around your neck and wear it."

The second part of the recipe gives a series of magical names to be written on the charm: *"epokopt kopto bai baitokarakopto karakopto chilokopto bai"* (in some of the texts that I cite below, such magical names will be summarized by "magical names"). Although these words are transliterated from the Greek and are unintelligible to us, they were no more intelligible to most Greek readers. They are magical words, probably the names of the spirits who are supposed to make this magical charm effective. Often magical names were invoked together with the names of known gods and goddesses, such as Hekate, Artemis, Selene, Kore, Kronos, Aphrodite and others. All of the magical texts show an incredible amount of syncretism; that is, the mixing together of various elements from different religious beliefs and practices. Any name thought to be laden with supernatural power could be invoked. Hence, one will find Greek, Egyptian, Persian, Phrygian and Roman deities all invoked in the same text.

The third part of the text contains the command that the spirit agents are being summoned to fulfill: "Guard me from every daimon of the air, on the earth and under the earth, and from every angel and phantom and ghostly visitation and enchantment." This representative example is what is called *apotropaic* magic; that is, the "warding off" of demons and harmful spirits.

In the magical papyri the Greek word *daimōn* did not necessarily signify an evil or harmful spirit. Although in this magical recipe the term is plainly used to refer to the spirits who could inflict harm, by itself the word has no moral connotations. In the classical era before the New Testament age, the word *daimōn* had been used for the gods (such as Apollo, Dionysus and Hermes) and for supernatural beings regarded as somewhat lower than the gods. Increasingly it was used of the supernatural intermediaries (between the gods and humanity) and of the spirits of nature. Many regarded the *daimones* (plural form) who filled the air to be the disembodied souls of the dead, especially heroes. Influence from the East, especially Persian and Jewish thought, resulted in the Greek word *daimōn* taking on an increasingly evil connotation in its common use. Both *daimōn* and the related word *daimonion* are consistently used to refer to an evil spirit in the New Testament.³ Throughout this book the term *demon* will be used in reference to evil spirits and *daimōn* will be used in its neutral sense.

This magical text illustrates fear and dread of the spirit realm felt by the general populace. This magical recipe also illustrates the fact that people believed evil powers populated all of creation, including the air, the earth and the underworld. Magic provided a means for dealing with the fear of this reality.

Numerous accounts could be given to depict the great fear of demons among people in antiquity. It was believed these evil beings could even threaten to bring death. One ancient writer gives an account of a certain wise man, or shaman, endowed with a knowledge of the magical arts who could exhibit a certain measure of control over these hostile forces. Apollonius of Tyana became a well-known wonder worker throughout the Mediterranean world. He lived during the time of Paul, and Flavius Philostratus chronicled his life about a century later. This work is very important for giving us further insight into the folk belief of the time.

On one occasion Apollonius of Tyana encountered a woman whose sixteen-year-old son had been possessed by a demon for two years. She was aware of his possession because of her son's altered behavior and because the demon allegedly revealed itself to the woman using the boy's voice. The demon claimed to be the ghost of a dead person who hated women and was in love with the boy. The mother, understandably anguished over her son's tormented condition, explained to Apollonius all the symptoms. Among other things, she observed that "the boy does not even have his own voice, but speaks in a deep, hollow tone, the way grown-up men do, and when he looks at me, his eyes don't seem to be his own." The mother explained to Apollonius that whenever she had tried to bring the boy to him, the demon would threaten to throw the young man into a crevice or off of a precipice and kill him. Apollonius confidently responded to the woman by supplying her with something like an amulet or a magical recipe that would prevent the demon from killing the boy.⁴

A Love Potion
The second text provides us with a vivid illustration of how magic involved the direct assistance of supernatural beings to perform a

given request. This recipe, recorded on a papyrus scroll discovered in Egypt, reveals how a certain lovesick Theodorus attempted to gain the affection of a woman named Matrona.[5] The intent of the recipe is stated simply: "Let Matrona love Theodorus for all the time of her life." This type of "love potion" is commonly called an *aphrodisiac*. There is virtually no magical rite for Theodorus to perform, but the text does presuppose that he has obtained some of her hair. The recipe is quite expansive, however, in invoking the help of the underworld gods and spirits. The formula continues:

> I entrust this charm to you, underworld gods, to Pluto *uessemigadon ortho baubo,* to Kore, Persephoneia, Ereschigal, and to Adonis *era . . . puonrth* and to underworld Hermias Thoth *phokentazepseu* and to mighty Anubis *cherichtha kanchene . . . th,* keeper of the keys of the gates of Hades, and to the underworld gods and to the untimely dead, lads and lasses.

The final phrase, "to the untimely dead, lads and lasses," lends some insight into a common interpretation of a segment of the spirit realm by the ancients. Many in the Greco-Roman world believed people who were heroes or who had suffered an untimely death became disembodied spirits after death. They would customarily take on a rather evil disposition and could bring harm to someone if commanded to do so through a curse.

The text goes on to invoke two additional goddesses (Hekate and Artemis) and uses many more magical names. It is also very clear that the conjurer expects these supernatural beings to accomplish his stated intent to make Matrona a devoted lover of Theodorus. The formula is quite explicit:

> I adjure all ghosts [Greek=*demonas*] in this place to come to the assistance of this ghost. Raise yourself up for me from the repose that keeps you and go out into every district and every quarter and every house and every shop, and drive, spellbind Matrona . . . that she may not have intercourse vaginal, anal, or oral with anyone else, nor be able to go with any other man than Theodorus . . . and never let Matrona . . . be able to endure or be healthy or find sleep night or day without Theodorus.

In this particular case the conjurer is not exactly sure which "demon" will be compelled to perform the task. The spell continues: "Do not turn aside from hearing me, ghost [Greek=*demon*], whoever you are, and raise yourself up for me, for I adjure you by the lady Hekate

Artemis *demon damno damnolukake damnippae damnomenia damnobathira damnobathiri damnomenia dameamone*, tail-swallower, night roamer." Here it appears that the conjurer is threatening a "demon" by the goddess of the underworld, Hekate Artemis, and certain magical names. Thus, Hekate Artemis will enforce his request because she is believed to respond to these magical names and the epithets that are ascribed to her. Other magical texts even give instances of hymns to be sung to the deities, which would render them more receptive to the requests of the petitioner. In this text the implication for the "demon" is clear—there is now no choice but to respond to the request of Theodorus. The "demon" is thus manipulated by the conjurer.

A Spell to Inflict Harm

The last example is a rather horrific piece of black magic that has an elaborate rite. It is a recipe for inflicting great harm on an enemy.[6] The rite is to proceed as follows:

Take a lead lamella [thin, metal plate] and inscribe with a bronze stylus the following names and the figure [depicted in the papyrus text], and after smearing it with blood from a bat, roll up the lamella in the usual fashion. Cut open a frog and put it into its stomach. After stitching it up with Anubian thread and a bronze needle, hang it up on a reed from your property by means of hairs from the tip of the tail of a black ox, at the east of the property near the rising of the sun.

Following this is an invocation of supernatural beings and the statement of the devilish command to the powers:

Supreme angels, just as this frog drips with blood and dries up, so also will the body of him [a space to insert the name of the victim] whom [a space to insert the name of the victim's mother] bore, because I conjure you, who are in command of fire *maskelli maskello*.

It is important to understand that the conjurer is not invoking the good "angels" surrounding the Christian or Jewish God, Yahweh. In the Hellenistic era pagans used the term "angel" *(angelos)* for supernatural beings and messengers. Here the idea of a supernatural assistant or servant is what is in mind.

Various parts of this magical rite seem rather strange and nonsensical to us. Indeed, for the person who performed the rite, a rational explanation for the details may have defied explanation, but it was believed to work! There was, however, a somewhat rational basis for certain aspects of the magic rite. Magic was based partly on a system of correspondences. Animals, plants, herbs, precious stones and metals were believed to be associated with or to symbolize various gods and demons; therefore, they could be used to attract or repel the presence and influence of these supernatural beings. Moreover, the use of written symbols functioned in much the same way. The seven vowels of the Greek alphabet, for instance, were used in magical texts to represent the seven planetary deities.

These three magical texts give us a glimpse not only of the nature of magic, but also of some fundamental assumptions behind magic: Gods, spirits, angels and demons do exist; they are involved in everyday life; and, most important, they can be manipulated.

Numerous words, names and titles are used in the magical texts to refer to the wide array of spirit beings. From all religious traditions during the New Testament era, people seem to have used a broad vocabulary for the spirit realm. While much of Paul's vocabulary for the principalities and powers can be found in the magical papyri, he was probably drawing more specifically from the vast reservoir of terminology in the demonology and angelology of first-century Judaism (see chapter four). Pagan readers would have clearly understood what Paul was talking about when he referred to principalities and powers since they shared many of the same terms and concepts with Judaism.

The Uses for Magic

Magic is often described in terms of *white* and *black* (or good and evil). Professor David Aune suggests four major ways to describe the purpose of magic in the Greco-Roman world: (1) protective or apotropaic magic (particularly against dreaded illnesses), (2) aggressive and malevolent magic, (3) love magic and magic aimed at the acquisition of power over others, and (4) magical divination or revelation.[7] We have seen examples of the first three uses in the previous section, and we will discuss the fourth use in more detail below.

Amulets and charms were commonly used for protective magic. It was believed the injurious work of malevolent spirits could be repelled with an effective amulet.

Like the use of a rabbit's foot today, amulets were also used to bring good luck. Two ancient writers relate the humorous account of an Ephesian wrestler who traveled to Olympia, Greece, to compete in the

Olympic games. The wrestler attached an amulet to his ankle that had the Ephesian letters inscribed on it. These were six magical names, probably referring to six powerful supernatural beings. The Ephesian wrestler was readily defeating his opponents and advancing in the event until the referee discovered the ankle bracelet! He then lost three successive matches.[8]

Amulets were sometimes made out of precious stones (thought to contain special magical properties). More often, cheap and easily accessible materials were used, such as papyri, pottery pieces *(ostraca)*, tin strips, linen and seashells. At times, the magical recipe for constructing an amulet called for a special kind of material like hyena parchment. Amulets were usually worn somewhere on the body, for instance, as a ring or a necklace. Virtually thousands of magical amulets have been found all over the Mediterranean world.

Black magic (aggressive and malevolent magic) was frequently performed using inscribed sheets of thin lead. Over 1100 of these "lead curse tablets," or *defixiones,* have been discovered throughout the Mediterranean world. Together with the magical papyri and amulets, these sources constitute our most important witness for understanding the nature of magic in the Greco-Roman world.

A lead curse tablet typically consisted of a magical formula with a curse written on a leaf of lead. Usually the tablet was rolled up and pierced by a nail to symbolize the "fix" on a victim. The tablet would then be deposited in a place where it was thought to have easy contact with the underworld, such as a grave, tomb or well. This procedure would then effect the curse, which would be carried out by supernatural means against the victim. One of the curse tablets discovered in Rome is directed against a competitor in a chariot race:[9]

> I conjure you up, holy beings and holy names; join in aiding this spell, and bind, enchant, thwart, strike, overturn, conspire against, destroy, kill, break Eucherius the charioteer, and all his horses tomorrow in the circus at Rome. May he not leave the barriers well; may he not be quick in the contest; may he not outstrip anyone; may he not make the turns well; may he not win any prizes . . . may he be broken; may he be dragged along by your power, in the morning and afternoon races. Now! Now! Quickly! Quickly!

Spirit Guides

Some people were attracted to magic because of the power it would bring to them through acquiring a spirit guide or assistant *daimōn*. In this type of magic a special formula was used to summon the services of a god (or *daimōn)*. One magical text prescribes a rite in which "a *daimōn* comes as an assistant who will reveal everything to you clearly and will be your companion and will eat and sleep with you."[10] The spirit helper might stay with the person for a long period of time. One formula commands the spirit to "be inseparable from me from this day forth through all the time of my life."

This mighty spirit assistant would help the person in all kinds of ways, as the following text shows:

It is acknowledged that he is a god; he is an aerial spirit which you have seen. If you give him a command, straight-way he performs the task: he sends dreams, he brings women, men without the use of magical material, he kills, he destroys, he stirs up winds from the earth, he carries gold, silver, bronze, and he gives them to you whenever the need arises. And he frees from bonds a person chained in prison, he opens doors, he causes invisibility so that no one can see you at all, he is a bringer of fire, he brings water, wine, bread. . . . He will quickly bring daimons [for a banquet], and for you he will adorn these servants with sashes. These things he does quickly. And as soon as you order him to perform a service, he will do so, and you will see him excelling on other things: He stops ships and again releases them, he stops very many evil daimons.[11]

The text continues by naming numerous other services the spirit would perform and then concludes with the following summary statement and imposition of secrecy:

He will serve you suitably for whatever you have in mind, O blessed initiate of the sacred magic, and will accomplish it for you, this most powerful assistant, who is also the only lord of the air. And the gods will agree to everything, for without him nothing happens. Share this great mystery with no one else, but conceal it, by Helios, since you have been deemed worthy by the lord god.

To use modern terminology, undoubtedly an initiate into this type of magic was "possessed" by the spirit. The person using this kind of magic, however, clearly believed he was receiving a good, helpful spirit and not an evil one. In fact, the recipe asserts that this spirit would drive away the evil *daimones*. Those who practiced magic thus believed they had to be very cautious and discerning about which spirits were evil and which were good.

Divination

There were a number of methods of divining the future in the Greco-Roman period. Some involved the use of lamps, bowls and saucers. Other methods involved the examination of the liver or the observation of strange occurrences in nature (omens), like the birth of a deformed child or the odd behavior of animals. The art of astrology also had a large part in divination.

One aspect of divination, revelatory magic, bears many similarities to the modern New Age movement's practice of channeling.[12] This form of magic involved soliciting the appearance of a divine assistant to impart information regarding the future, or virtually anything else. By using the proper formulas, a supernatural being could be forced to divulge all kinds of secretive information.

One of these spells involved a "serpent faced" god: "Invoke the great name in a time of great stress, in major and pressing crises. If not, you will blame yourself. . . . I call upon you [thirty-one magical names]. . . . Come in, lord, and reveal. The serpent-faced god will come in and answer you. When you dismiss him, make an offering of the skin of a serpent."[13] Here, presumably, the suppliant could gain wisdom and perspective in order to gain control over the crisis situation.

More than one spirit could be summoned simultaneously. The following text seems concerned to call up many powerful evil spirits. The formula reads:

> I call upon you, inhabitants of Chaos and Erebos [the underworld], of the depth, of earth, watchers of heaven, of darkness, masters of things not to be seen, guardians of secrets, leaders of those beneath the earth, administrators of things which are infinite, those who wield power over earth, servants in the chasm, shudderful fighters, fearful ministers, inhabitants of dark Erebos, coercive watchers, rulers of cliffs, grievers of the heart, adverse daimons, iron-hearted ones [seven magical names are given].[14]

These powers are all called to "reveal concerning the matter which I am considering." Someone would use these formulas not merely to satisfy an intense curiosity about what the future held, but also as a means of gaining some measure of control over the future. In magic, fate is something that is not unalterable. In fact, the very purpose of magic is to alter the unfolding of fate.

Revelatory magic offered insight not only into the events of the future, but about anything a person may want to know. It was a means of gaining power, influence and control.

Simon the Magician: Acts 8

In the book of Acts Luke records four separate instances involving the use of magic. In three of these instances Luke directly connects the magic with the work of Satan or his demons.

In Samaria a magician named Simon was bringing great attention to himself because of the amazing things he accomplished with his magic. So awestruck were the people of Samaria that they nicknamed him "The Great Power" (8:10).

Philip's preaching of the gospel proved more compelling, however, and many Samaritans turned their lives to Jesus Christ, eventually even Simon. Luke paints Philip's ministry in terms of what some missiologists would today call "a power encounter." Although Luke does not describe it in terms of a showdown between Philip and Simon, he clearly indicates that Philip's display of divine power is what gave him his hearing: "When the crowds heard Philip and saw the miraculous signs he did, they all paid close attention to what he said" (8:6). Philip's miraculous signs completely overshadowed Simon's. Philip made evil spirits come out of many people and healed numerous paralytics and cripples.

Luke simply tells us about Simon's conversion without going into detail about whether he too had evil spirits commanded out of him. Unfortunately Simon allowed his affection for supernatural powers to take precedence over his devotion to the Lord Jesus and asked to buy the ability to impart the Holy Spirit to others. Detecting his perverse motives, Peter rebuked him in the strongest of terms, telling him to repent of his wickedness and observing that he was "full of bitterness and captive to sin" (8:23).

Some later church tradition claims Simon continued in his quest for divine power and became the originator of what would be known as Gnosticism. The second-century apocryphal book *Acts of Peter* vividly narrates Simon losing in a "power encounter" with the apostle Peter in Rome. After leading many astray with his heretical teaching, Simon allegedly flew in the air over the city of Rome, defying Peter. Peter prayed to the Lord, and Simon was struck down, causing his leg to break in three places.[15]

A Jewish Magician and False Prophet: Acts 13

Luke surprises us by introducing his readers to a Jewish magician who went by the name Bar-Jesus (son of Jesus), or Elymas (13:4-12). Actually, we will later find (chapter four) that there was widespread Jewish involvement in magic, witchcraft and sorcery. The apostle Paul encountered this magician on the island of Cyprus at the outset of his first missionary outreach. Interestingly, this sorcerer was formally attached to a major political figure on the island, the proconsul Sergius Paulus.

Luke does not elaborate on the extent of the influence Elymas wielded with Sergius Paulus. Since political officials frequently consulted astrologers and diviners for guidance, we are safe to speculate that Elymas's influence extended to the proconsul's governance and to the political and economic structures he was responsible for. Most important for Paul, however, was the decisive opposition the magician presented to communicate effectively the gospel to Sergius Paulus and perhaps even to the area over which he governed.

Luke presents this sorcerer as the major opposition to Paul's mission. Paul perceived the man to be under the control of Satan himself and pointedly revealed his true character to his face: "Filled with the Holy Spirit, [he] looked straight at Elymas and said, 'You are a child of the devil and an enemy of everything that is right! You are full of all kinds of deceit and trickery. Will you never stop perverting the right ways of the Lord?' " (13:10). Paul then took firm action against the magician. He announced that the hand of the Lord Jesus would be against him and he will be blinded. Immediately Elymas lost his sight. The "power encounter" again proved effective for the success of the gospel; the proconsul put his faith in the Lord Jesus Christ.

The Spirit of Divination: Acts 16

While Paul was in Philippi, a slave girl with a "spirit of divination" troubled Paul greatly by following him and his companions around day after day shouting, "These men are servants of the Most High God, who are telling you the way to be saved." This spirit of divination was literally a "Python spirit" (Greek=*pythōn*), according to Luke. By this spirit, the girl was able to predict the future. Meanwhile, some profit-seeking individuals, who later created great problems for Paul

(16:16-21), exploited her and her supernatural ability.

The Python spirit was associated with the oracle at Delphi in Greece (about eighty miles northwest of Athens), where the female prophetess was called a Python. In classical mythology the Python was a serpent that guarded the Delphic oracle and was slain by the god Apollo. Throughout antiquity people came from all over the Near East to consult the oracle at Delphi for advice. It was widely believed to be the center of the earth. An opening in the ground at the site emitted a gas that the Delphic prophetess would breathe in order to receive her prophetic insight. She would then pass on the information to the person in verse form. The grateful traveler would then depart, leaving votive offerings and expensive gifts.

Many people also believed the Pythian prophetess had a god living within her belly. This belief led to her being called "a belly talker," since she was observed talking in a deep second voice while making her predictions. In fact, some ancient literature attributes this second voice to a *daimōn*.

Because Paul clearly believed a demon controlled this girl, he commanded the spirit within her: "In the name of Jesus Christ I command you to come out of her!" Without any argument or hesitation, the spirit departed. Luke's attention then shifts to the irate reaction of the girl's owners, and this brief account is all that we know about her in Scripture.

The Burning of the Magical Books in Ephesus: Acts 19

Luke also gives us an incredible account about a situation involving magic during Paul's ministry at Ephesus (Acts 19:13-20). It reinforces the impression that Ephesus was a center of magical practices during the first century. Luke tells us about some itinerant Jewish exorcists, who attempted to use the name of Jesus as part of their exorcism on a man troubled with an evil spirit. Tragically unsuccessful, they were physically assaulted by the demon-controlled man so that "they fled out of that house naked and wounded." As a result, numerous people brought out their books of magical formulas and incantations and burned them. The combined value of the books was estimated by Luke to be worth as much as 50,000 days' wages.

This account is very important for understanding the social and religious situation of the early Christian churches. Luke here gives the distinct impression that those who were burning their magical texts were already Christians. He observes, "Many of those who believed now came and openly confessed their evil deeds. A number who had practiced sorcery brought their scrolls together and burned them publicly" (19:18-19a). It underlines the temptation faced by early believers to return to their former practices, in particular, magic.

Summary
Luke is concerned to show that the gospel of the Lord Jesus and the power of God are indeed mightier than any opposition. Luke also clearly ties magical practices and divination to the work of Satan and his powers.[16] In all of these instances the work of the devil through these people hindered the progress of the gospel. The power of God working through his messengers needed to confront and overcome Satanic opposition.

Each of these accounts in the book of Acts also raises issues that are relevant to understanding better what the apostle Paul has to say about principalities and powers. It helps us clarify the felt needs of the readers Paul addressed in his letters. They would naturally be filled with questions as they sought to make sense of Christianity in light of the religious and magical environment in which they lived. They would ask questions such as: How should converts from a background in the occult and spiritism live in light of their newfound faith in the Lord Jesus? What should they believe about the powers they once thought served them and the powers they feared? Were some of them still to be considered good and others evil? Where does Christ stand in relation to these spirit beings and supernatural powers? Can one still be devoted to Christ and wear an amulet for protection? How should the church respond to non-Christians involved in spiritism?

Knowing the questions that would undoubtedly have been on the minds of new believers in the first century will help the New Testament come alive when we consider the things Paul has to say about principalities and powers.

2
Greco-Roman and Oriental Religions

*T*ODAY WHEN TOURISTS WALK THROUGH THE REMAINS OF THE ANCIENT
acropolis of Athens, a feeling of awe overwhelms the senses
as they experience the grandeur and beauty of the Parthenon
and the adjacent structures—the Temple of Athena Nike, the theater
of Dionysus, the nearby Olympeion and the many other magnificent
edifices. Nearly two millenniums ago, when Paul strolled the Athenian
streets for the first time, surely an aesthetic appreciation for this center of Greek civilization gripped him as well. Luke, however, reveals
that Paul was greatly distressed. Why? Because "the city was full of
idols" (Acts 17:16).

Athens was certainly not the only city "full of idols." Every city,
including Tarsus, the city of Paul's childhood, contained temples and
altars dedicated to a wide assortment of deities. Although Paul wrote
letters to people living in Asia, Greece and Italy, many of the same
gods were worshiped in each place. More importantly, the pre-Christian religious experiences of those people converted from paganism
were quite similar in many fundamental respects.

Pagans believed their gods were alive and could help them in practical ways for their earthly needs and, in many instances, bring them
a blissful afterlife. The early Christians, including Paul, saw these gods
as alive too, but in a different sense. They believed demons, the
powers of Satan, inspired and perpetuated these pagan gods. These
idols greatly distressed Paul because they represented a supernaturally

inspired opposition to the gospel which Paul came to proclaim.

The Melting Pot

Over three centuries before the time of Christ, a Greek named Alexander the Great won a series of unprecedented military victories and expanded his reign eastward to include Asia Minor, Syria, Palestine, Egypt, North Africa, the Middle East and parts of India. He effectively inaugurated a world community that would forever alter the course of history. In fact, historians commonly refer to the next three centuries following his reign as the Hellenistic age.

Not only did Greek become the universal language, but Greek culture was also spread throughout these countries. The influence worked both ways, however, especially with regard to religion. Gods and goddesses worshiped in the Orient were transplanted into Greek and Roman lands. The spiritual and religious ideas from the East proved exceedingly attractive to the West.[1] By the New Testament era an incredible mixture of deities were worshiped in the cities of the Mediterranean world.

Corinth is a good example.[2] There is literary and archeological evidence for the worship of many of the traditional Greek deities—Apollo, Athena, Aphrodite, Dionysus, Asclepius, Demeter, Kore, Poseidon and Zeus—dating to the time of Paul's ministry in that city. In addition, there is evidence that two originally Egyptian deities, Isis and Sarapis, had become quite popular among the Corinthians. The Asia Minor goddess known as the Great Mother received veneration in a sanctuary dedicated to her at Corinth. There was even a Jewish contingent who had erected a synagogue in the city during Paul's life. In Corinth the Roman gods were also worshiped insofar as they were identified with many of the Greek gods. They would have been known by either their Roman or Greek names, such as the Roman god Jupiter and the Greek god Zeus.

During Paul's ministry, syncretism was reaching new heights. Hellenistic Greeks were not compelled to render exclusive allegiance to their ancestral gods. They could now also worship Persian, Syrian, Egyptian or Asian gods. Nor did they feel obligated to worship only one god. In fact, quite the contrary was the case. Numerous gods could be worshiped, although it should be noted that there was an increasing tendency toward a belief in one supreme god, with the rest seen as less powerful gods, or *daimones.*

The Rise of Personal Spiritual Concern

Although the traditional Greek and Roman gods were still being worshiped, they were now viewed differently than during the classical age. Most scholars agree the old cults were fundamentally transformed during the Hellenistic age. This change was due, in part, to their spread throughout the Hellenistic world. The old gods were often reinterpreted in their new settings, which ultimately influenced how they were understood in their original settings. A traditional Greek god often was assimilated with a local deity. When the first Greeks settled in Ephesus, for instance, they apparently renamed a local female fertility goddess, calling her Artemis (or Diana, her Roman name). While these two deities may have shared the common motifs of being goddesses over childbirth, wildlife and hunting, their cultic images bear virtually no resemblance. The Greek Artemis is typically portrayed as a beautiful female figure in flowing robes, whereas the Ephesian Artemis is depicted in richly ornamented vestments standing in a rigid upright position.[3]

While the mythology of Homer still provided a basic framework for understanding the nature of some of the traditional Greek deities, they were increasingly perceived as less remote and more interested in the concerns of the common people. Jonathan Z. Smith explains the change of perception in this way:

Rather than a god who dwelt in his temple, the diasporic traditions evolved complicated techniques for achieving visions, epiphanies (manifestations of a god), or heavenly journeys to a transcendent god. This led to a change from concern for a religion of national prosperity to one for individual salvation, from focus on a particular ethnic group to concern for every man.[4]

Scholars frequently describe the Hellenistic period in terms of a rise in "personal religion." Many accounts and testimonies abound regarding the importance of gods to individuals in their respective conditions. Conversely this period was also characterized as an age of "anxiety" because people seemed more desirous of personal communion with a deity, securing life after death, and averting the influence of fate and malevolent spirits.

During the Hellenistic period, relationship and union with a deity would most commonly occur through a ritual act described by ancient writers as initiation into the mystery of the deity. Although not all of the gods and goddesses had mysteries, the popularity of these rites grew throughout the Hellenistic age and continued to increase in Roman times. A number of the cults probably practiced these mystery initiation rites in all the cities in which Paul preached and planted churches.

Actually, what we know about the form and content of these mysteries is rather sketchy. Initiates into the mysteries were sworn to secrecy with strict penalties for violating the trust. There was no written liturgy. The mysteries were performed with an emphasis on visual symbols and ritual enactment. The priests and priestesses might even lead initiates into a visionary descent into the underworld or even a visionary ascent into heaven. Two examples of well-known mystery religions will give a clearer picture of the meaning of these rites.

The Classical Mystery: The Rape of Kore by Hades

Fourteen miles west of Athens on the road to Corinth, the city of Eleusis was situated in a fertile agricultural area. For hundreds of years before the time of Christ, mystery rites were performed annually in the city celebrating the reunion of a mother goddess with her daughter, who had been abducted for three months by Hades, god of the underworld. According to the informing myth, Demeter, the distraught mother, wandered for days and ended the search for her daughter, Kore (also known as Persephone), in the city of Eleusis. While Demeter was at Eleusis, the supreme god Zeus finally intervened and promised to reunite Kore with her mother for eight months of every year. It turns out that Zeus had also consented for Hades (the Roman god Pluto) to take Kore as his wife. This compromise was struck between the mother and the daughter's prospective husband.[5]

In Eleusis mystery rites were held every year, involving a ritual enactment of many parts of this mythical drama. The "Lesser Mysteries," held in honor of Kore, were conducted in the early spring; the "Greater Mysteries," in honor of Demeter, were performed at the beginning of autumn. The mystery rites symbolized a happy afterlife in the other world, but they were also closely connected with raising a good corn crop in the area each year. The following two themes are very important in this respect.

First, after another deity informed Demeter (also known as the "corn maiden") of the abduction of her daughter, Demeter caused a severe blight on the earth, which effectively twisted the arm of Zeus to intervene. This blight, induced by divine cosmic disharmony, devastated agricultural production. Part of the "Greater Mysteries" celebrate the cosmic harmony that ultimately occurred among the heavens (Zeus), the earth (Demeter) and the underworld (Hades). This harmony was essential to insure continued agricultural stability.

Second, the local interpretation of Kore's annual journey back and forth from the underworld was thought to be related to the seed corn used in the local agriculture. Just as Kore spent four months of the year with Hades and eight months of the year with Demeter, the seed corn at Eleusis was preserved in underground silos for four months of the year and was then sown, cultivated and harvested during the rest of the year. The activities of these gods was believed to be closely intertwined with the local agricultural economy. It was therefore important to please the gods through the annual performance of these mystery rites.

It is difficult to know precisely the deeper spiritual significance given to the mystery rites at Eleusis during the time of Paul. These rites were variously interpreted according to the religious needs of every age. Although Hades was not a symbol of evil to the Greeks, he is often represented as "grim, unpitying, [and] a severe punisher of wrongdoers."[6] Possibly the mystery rites symbolized protection from the harmful influences of Hades. The desire for protection is probably why the dramatic enactment of descent to the underworld is important in connection with the Plutonion, an opening to the underworld, located next to the temple at Eleusis. It is also likely that at the height of the mystery initiation, the new devotees were the awed recipients of an epiphany of the goddess Demeter herself, who would bring them happiness and the hope of a pleasant afterlife in the underworld. Paul and all of his readers in Greece, no doubt, would have been quite familiar with this famous mystery religion.

Taurobolium: Initiation into Cybele

Across the Aegean Sea in Asia Minor where numerous Christian churches were coming into existence, a popular oriental cult observed annual mysteries in honor of the mother-goddess Cybele (pronounced *ku-be'-le*). This Asian female deity, also known as the "Great Mother" and "Mother of the Gods," came to be worshiped in Greece and even Rome before the beginning of the New Testament period.

The best-known part of her mystery rite is an event called the *taurobolium.* In this rite the initiate descends into an underground pit, which is partially covered with a series of wooden lattices. Walking out onto the latticework, the priests of Cybele would slaughter a young bull and allow its blood to pour through the openings of the wood, drenching the initiate in the pit below. The Latin Christian writer Prudentius vividly describes the rite:

> Through the thousand crevices in the wood, the bloody dew runs down into the pit. The neophyte [initiate] receives the falling drops on his head, clothes and body. He leans backward to have his cheeks, his ears, his lips and his nostrils wetted; he pours the liquid over his eyes, and does not even spare his palate, for he moistens his tongue with blood and drinks it eagerly.[7]

For the devotees of Cybele this gruesome rite was filled with deep spiritual significance. The bloody "baptism" was thought to purify the initiates from their faults. Franz Cumont contends that there was even a materialistic concept of a transfer of strength to the initiate. He comments: "by moistening his body with the blood of the slaughtered steer, the neophyte believed that he was transfusing the strength of the formidable beast into his own limbs."[8] As with other mysteries, the initiation probably also signified some mystical union with the deity.

The initiate could now live in greater security and peace. The taurobolium satisfied a spiritual yearning and brought the person closer to the deity. The new access to this deity's cosmic power, symbolized by the blood of the bull, provided benefits, such as coping with malevolent hostile influences and assuring of immortality.

Asclepius: God of Healing

The best way to understand other religions during the time of the New Testament is to look carefully at a few. I have chosen three deities who were popular for different reasons during the time of Paul. Without a doubt many of Paul's converts in Ephesus, Philippi, Thessalonica, Corinth and elsewhere were devoted to these gods before turning to the gospel. The portraits of these three deities will give us some insight into the pre-Christian background of a large segment of Paul's readership.

Often praised as a "savior," the god Asclepius was one of the most popular deities among the masses during the New Testament era.[9] Asclepius was honored throughout the Mediterranean world for his power to heal the sick and afflicted. His symbol was the staff with a snake coiled around it, similar to that of physicians today. He was perceived as a benevolent god, concerned with people's needs. He identified with the feelings of the afflicted because he was believed to be a god-man. Many, in fact, believed Asclepius was half-human and half-divine. Because of these and other similarities to Christ, the cult of Asclepius proved to be a formidable opponent to Christianity.

Pergamum and Epidaurus were two major centers of the worship of Asclepius and were near Ephesus and Corinth, strategic centers of Paul's missionary activities. While Paul never mentioned Asclepius (or any pagan deity) in his letters, he would undoubtedly have had a substantial number of converts who had some contact with the cult of Asclepius.

From all over the Hellenistic world, the sick and ailing flocked to Asclepian centers to seek healing from their diseases. Many reportedly received the divine healing intervention of Asclepius during the rite of "incubation," sleeping in the precincts of the temple in order to receive a visionary epiphany from the god. When Asclepius appeared to the sick person, his healing powers were imparted and the person was healed. This appearance and the apparent healing constituted the essence of initiation into the divine mystery of Asclepius. Before sleeping in the temple, the afflicted individual needed to perform certain purification rites and offer sacrifices to Asclepius. After experiencing the healing powers of this god, it was then important to offer appropriate and acceptable thanksgiving. This rite would often take the form of a thank-offering, which the initiate commonly consumed while the god was in his temple. One writer has observed: "In the Asclepius cult the ancient concept of the sacrifice as a communion between god and man was upheld tenaciously."[10] This description illustrates a distinctive trait of the New Testament era in which the concept of a close personal relationship with a deity was common.

The cured were also encouraged to publicize to others what Asclepius had accomplished for them. We consequently have a number of accounts of people rendering praise to Asclepius for healing them of their illnesses. One papyrus text appears to be the introduction to a much longer document in which a man praises Asclepius because he had been healed of a terrible internal disorder during the incubation rite. Just before the text breaks off, the writer states his intention: "I now purpose to recount his miraculous manifestations, the greatness of his power, the gifts of his benefits. The history is this . . ."[11]

Many of the early Christians did not dispute the evidence for supernatural events happening in connection with the cult of Asclepius. Rather, they attributed the source of the healing powers to Satan and his demons and pointed to its grave dangers. Among the church fathers, Eusebius regarded Asclepius as an evil spirit "who does not cure souls but destroys them" while Lactantius termed Asclepius an "archdemon."[12]

Hekate: Goddess of Witchcraft and Sorcery

The goddess Hekate (sometimes spelled *Hecate*) has much significance for our investigation into the powers of darkness. More than any other Hellenistic deity, Hekate was popularly known for her close connection with evil spirits, strange apparitions and things of danger. Long before the New Testament period, she was widely regarded as the mistress of evil spirits (or demons).[13] Alois Kehl remarks, "In the common belief of Greco-Roman civilization, Hekate appeared above all as the ruler of darkness, of terror, of the dead, of demons, and of magic."[14] Because she was believed to be the ruler of the demons, she was frequently invoked in sorcery and magic; because she controlled the evil spirits, she gave magic its effective power.[15] Because Hekate dispatched demons to carry out the magician's wishes, her name appears repeatedly throughout the magical texts.

She was widely believed to be an underworld goddess; that is, she wielded control over the place of the dead or the disembodied souls. Her power over the various spirits of the underworld was represented by her title "key bearer," meaning she possessed the keys to the fortress of Hades.[16] Because she controlled the passageway to the underworld, she could enable people to communicate with the dead. Her custodianship of Hades also enabled her to control the apparitions or souls who ascend to do the magician's bidding.[17]

Her power was not only limited to the underworld. As with so many other deities of the period, she was viewed as having cosmic power. Her rule extended over heaven, earth and sea. Some texts point to her connection with the lunar element, in which she becomes associated with the moon-goddess, Selene. A few ancient writers even emphasize her role as a cosmic soul.[18]

People worshiped her and made offerings to her for protection from evil. She was called the "goddess of the crossroads." In popular superstition, the intersection of two roads was viewed as haunted. A statue of Hekate was commonly erected at crossroads. Her function as an averter of evil influences reflects her popular title, "protector of the gate."

While Hekate was worshiped throughout the Roman Empire, she was especially at home in Asia Minor, where she is thought to have originated. Her primary cult center was at Lagina, not far from Ephesus. Hekate is closely connected with the Ephesian Artemis, so much so that distinctions between the two female goddesses become blurred in many respects.

During his travels throughout the empire, the apostle Paul probably encountered her image along Roman roads countless times. His converts would have found it difficult to completely forsake honoring her since she was perceived to be a primary source of protection from evil spirits in daily life. Her promise of protection from the underworld would also have posed a significant challenge to the Christian gospel's promise of life after death.

Dionysus: God of Sensual Pleasure

In contemporary Western society Dionysus might be looked at as the ultimate "party animal."[19] Most scholars refer to the three-to-five-day observance of his mysteries as "ecstatic rites": loud, frenzied, drunken celebration. One ancient observer summed up the revelry in this way: "To consider nothing wrong . . . was the highest form of religious devotion among them."[20] In another sense there was a serious spiritual side to the mystery rites of Dionysus; the mystery of Dionysus held out the promise of a blissful life in the other world after death.

The Dionysian mysteries (also called the Bacchanalia) were very popular at the time Christianity began to spread. Celebrated throughout Greece, Asia Minor, Egypt and even Italy, they were widespread. The revelry especially appealed to the lower classes, but those from the higher social classes were also attracted. The celebration of the mysteries of Dionysus (or Bacchus, his Roman name) provided an opportunity for all to transcend the drabness and monotony of day-to-day life.

In 186 B.C. the Roman government condemned this "everything goes" religion, which, however, did not abate its ongoing popularity. In fact, prior to the time of Christ, some high-level Romans favored this cult. Writing close to the time of Christ's birth, the Roman historian Livy provides us with an incredible description of the nature of the Bacchanalia:

There were initiations which at first were imparted only to a few; but they soon began to be widespread among men and women. The pleasures of drinking and feasting were added to the religious rites, to attract a larger number of followers. When wine had inflamed their feelings, and night and the mingling of the sexes and of different ages had extinguished all power of moral judgment, all sorts of corruption began to be practiced, since each person had ready to hand the chance of gratifying the particular desire to which he was naturally inclined. The corruption was not confined to one kind of evil, the promiscuous violation of free men and of women; the cult was also a source of supply of false witnesses, forged documents and wills, and perjured evidence, dealing also in poisons and in wholesale murders among the devotees, and sometimes ensuring that not even the bodies were found for burial. Many such outrages were committed by craft, and even more by violence; and the violence was concealed because no cries for help could be heard against the shriekings, the banging of drums and the clashing of cymbals in the scene of debauchery and bloodshed.[21]

From the official testimony to the Roman proconsul, which resulted in the condemnation of the cult in 186 B.C., comes this exposé:

From the time when the rites were held promiscuously, with men and women mixed together, and when the license offered by darkness had been added, no sort of crime, no kind of immorality, was left unattempted. There were more obscenities practiced between men than between men and women. Anyone refusing to submit to outrage or reluctant to commit crimes was slaughtered as a sacrificial victim. To regard nothing as forbidden was among these people the summit of religious achievement. Men, apparently out of their wits, would utter prophecies with frenzied bodily convulsions: matrons, attired as Bacchantes, with their hair disheveled and carrying blazing torches, would run down to the Tiber.[22]

Drunkenness stamped the revelry of the Bacchants (those celebrating the Dionysian mysteries). During the Roman period, wine was a key symbol of Dionysus, who was often represented with clusters of grapes and known as the god of wine and intoxication. No doubt this contributed significantly to the wild, uncontrolled frenzy of the celebrations.

Sex and sensual pleasures also played a vital role in the Bacchanalia. Another important symbol of the cult was a wicker basket laden with fruit from which a male phallus arose. A representation of the phallus was carried at the front of all the processions of those celebrating the Dionysian rites. The culminating point of the mystery initiation may have been the revelation of the phallus. It was likely a symbol of life-giving power; and as such, it may have insured the hope of a joyous and blissful afterlife.[23] It is also possible that the phallus simply symbolized the mystery and joy of sexuality.[24]

After the celebration of the mysteries, a time of feasting, dancing and revelry occurred. Scattered ancient documents report the sacrifice of live animals, taking place while the Bacchants are wildly eating the raw, bloody parts of the animal. The reports from Livy cited earlier give the impression of murder and possible human sacrifices.

During the Roman period, people's increasing concern with the afterlife made the cult of Dionysus attractive. Initiation into the mystery of Dionysus could help the person avoid the dreaded punishing demons *(poinai)* after death. These punishing entities are often depicted as ugly winged female demons who bring a chill of horror. The initiates did not anticipate a resurrection after death, but a blissful life in another world filled with continuing sensual pleasure (anticipated in the mystery celebrations).

Dozens of other gods and goddesses could be portrayed. During the New Testament period, Isis, Mithras and others were extremely important. My purpose, however, is not to provide a thorough overview of Hellenistic religions, but merely to give a brief glimpse at the practices and beliefs surrounding three deities who rivaled the Lord Jesus Christ for adherents. The church fathers strongly believed Satan himself animated those gods and goddesses with his powers of darkness. Their demonic interpretation of these religions originated, in part, with the apostle Paul.

Gods and Goddesses in the Book of Acts

While the Pauline epistles have little explicit information about Paul's contact with the worship of pagan gods, Luke records some specific instances in the book of Acts.[25] The first encounter that Luke chooses to record occurs in south Galatia in the city of Lystra (Acts 14:8-20). After Paul healed a crippled man, the crowd concluded that Paul and Barnabas were an incarnation of Hermes and Zeus. It is interesting that Barnabas is equated with Zeus, the highest god, while Paul is associated with Hermes. Hermes was regarded as a messenger of the greater gods, especially Zeus. Paul's dominant role in the situation probably garnered him this identification as the herald of Zeus. Not receiving the response from the crowd they anticipated, Paul and Barnabas immediately renounced their association with these pagan deities. They did not denounce the gods as demons, but rather as "worthless things," a common Jewish way of referring to pagan gods. Paul pointed them to "the living God," who is the creator and who exercises his gracious providence for their well-being.

In Athens Paul found a point of entry to communicate effectively to his audience based on an altar inscription, which read: "to an unknown god" (Acts 17:16-34). By calling attention to this inscription, he affirmed their keen spiritual interest, but redirected their focus to the God he considered supreme—the God who is the Creator, who is providentially sovereign, who is not a carved image of human design, who is the judge of the world—the God who raised the Lord Jesus Christ from the dead. In this evangelistic context, Paul did not deem it appropriate to associate the Athenian gods with Satan and his demons, perhaps partly because such an indictment would assume a familiarity with Jewish demonology that these Athenians would not have understood. Furthermore, he may not have considered it evangelistically wise to indict their gods as demonic counterfeits. We know from his correspondence with established churches (especially Corinth), however, that he would subsequently teach Christians about the connection between pagan religion and the demonic.

One of the most dramatic encounters Paul had with worshipers of a pagan deity occurred at Ephesus, the key port city of western Asia Minor (Acts 19:23-41). Here Paul incurred the wrath of a great mob incited by the members of a trade guild who made and sold silver shrines of the patron deity of the city, Artemis of Ephesus. Because of a large number of conversions to Christianity, these tradesmen perceived Paul to be a considerable threat, not only to their business, but also to the worship of their revered goddess. The tradesmen successfully fomented a mob scene at the beautiful theater in Ephesus that resulted in an uproar of praise to Artemis lasting two hours. Everyone shouted in unison: "Great is Artemis of the Ephesians." In spite of the mob's fury, Paul wanted to address the crowd, but some insistent fellow believers prevented him from doing so. Such was the danger now present for Paul that he immediately left the city to continue his ministry elsewhere. Significantly, in describing Paul's nearly three-year ministry at Ephesus, Luke chooses to write mainly about Paul's conflict with the followers of this pagan deity. As we noted in chapter one, it is also important to recall the connections of this goddess with magical practices (manipulation of spirits).

Luke records one other incident involving pagan gods. In this instance people again had mistaken Paul as a god. The situation occurred on the island of Malta after he was bit by a poisonous snake and neither took ill nor died (Acts 28:1-6). When Paul was first bit, however, the people immediately assumed the goddess Dike (Justice) was punishing Paul for murder. Luke then says, "[the people] changed their minds and said he was a god" (Acts 28:6), after seeing that the venom had no effect on Paul. Luke's account is so abbreviated at this point that he does not tell us how Paul responded to their claims. Presumably, Paul responded in a way similar to the Lystra situation by denying their wrongly directed adulation and pointing to the one true God.

Finally, Luke mentions by name two other pagan gods, Castor and Pollux, also known as "the Twin Gods" (Acts 28:11). They were the figureheads on an Alexandrian (Egypt) cargo vessel which Paul boarded. No indication is given of Paul's response, but Luke is interested in mentioning this fact. These gods were popular with navigators in the ancient world, perhaps because their constellation, Gemini, was regarded as a sign of good fortune in a storm.[26] This reference serves as one more reminder of the multiplicity of deities in the New Testament world and their involvement in the everyday life of people of that time.

The book of Acts is largely taken up with the geographical spread of the gospel from Palestine and across the Mediterranean lands to Rome. Luke is concerned with recording the opposition that the pagan cults posed to the spread of the gospel, but only superficially. He does not embark on detailed descriptions of any of the pagan cults. Neither does he seem concerned with describing the difficulty that pagan converts faced when reconciling their new allegiance to the risen Christ with their former religious practices. Paul was more reflective on this issue because of his concern to strengthen his congregations with sound teaching that is exceptionally relevant to people who had formerly worshiped these various gods and goddesses. Paul clearly believed these deities and their respective systems of cultic worship are closely associated with demons.

3
Astrology

*H*OROSCOPES APPEAR IN OUR NEWSPAPERS EVERY DAY. ALTHOUGH MANY people have been reading them more for their entertainment value than as a basis for decision making, motivations are changing. Western culture is showing an increasing fascination with the stars and how their influence is felt in day-to-day situations.

In the first century virtually no one was skeptical about the major tenets of astrology. From the highest social classes (including the Caesars) to the lowest classes, everyone believed the motions and positions of the heavenly bodies directly corresponded to the course of events on earth.

Astrological belief and practice varied from a quasi-scientific approach to an "animistic" perspective on the stars; that is, the heavenly bodies either represent or actually are spirits, gods and supernatural powers. In the Greco-Roman world the bulk of ordinary people believed the latter.[1] This fact is important to know in order to understand the background of Paul's readers. The terms that Paul used for the principalities and powers and what he had to say about them was especially relevant to people who believed the luminaries populating the heavens were gods and spirits.

Cosmic Sympathy: A System of Correspondences
Astrology was an accepted profession in antiquity. Learned astrologers were called "mathematicians" *(mathematikoi)* by the Greeks. These professionals used their skill in charting the daily positions of the sun, moon, planets and stars. They recorded the data in complex tables

(ephemerides), which plotted the relative positions of the heavenly bodies. Based upon this information, they could extrapolate the future relative position of the stars for a given point in time. People believed a skilled astrologist could use these charts to predict future events on earth with the same precision that the next eclipse could be forecasted.

Astrology distinguished itself from astronomy by assuming there is an inextricable relationship between movements in the heavens and the unfolding of life on earth. Astrology was based on a world view that saw the universe as an integrated whole: what affects one part affects the other. This "cosmic sympathy" enabled the astrologer to give inquirers fairly detailed insight into what they could expect in the future. The astrologer was essential for his or her role in interpreting the stellar phenomenon and relating it to the concerns and situations of people.

Ironically the various ancient (and modern!) systems of astrology were actually based on two faulty assumptions about the universe. First, astrology presupposed that the earth was the center of the universe and that all of the celestial bodies revolved around this one motionless constant suspended in space (a geocentric universe). Second, the ancients based their division of the heavens on an errant spherical understanding of the universe in which the planets and stars all seemed to move on one plane. This belief enabled them to divide the heavens into twelve, 30-degree houses, which became the basis for the zodiac. Each house of the zodiac was further divided into three decans for a total of thirty-six, with each constituting a span of 10 degrees. In popular belief both the zodiac and the decans were deified and thus regarded as quite powerful over the affairs of life.

The zodiac, together with all of the foundational astrological beliefs, is quite ancient, dating back centuries before the time of Christ. In ancient Babylon astrology flourished, playing a significant role in all succeeding civilizations and generations. In its Chaldean (Babylonian priestly) roots astrology was closely attached to religious beliefs. In fact, the figures of the zodiac were linked to Babylonian deities. By the time of the New Testament era astrology held an integral, unquestioned part of the peoples' world view throughout the Roman Empire.

The Relentless Grind of Fate
Among many of the well-educated people of Paul's time, the philo-

sophical and religious outlook of Stoicism was popular. In fact, after Zeno founded Stoicism in Athens early in the third century B.C., the great Roman philosopher Seneca expounded it during Paul's lifetime. The Stoics believed a single divine principle permeated all of life. This divine principle was often identified with Zeus, the one divinely powerful spirit who governed the mutual relationships of all of life in a way that results in cosmic sympathy, one part affecting the other. For the Stoics, the movement of the stars directly affected the fate of people on earth.

The Stoic writer Manilius, also a contemporary of Paul, had an unswerving belief in astrological fate. In his writing he lauds the Egyptians for passing on what they had learned about interpreting the movements of the stars. He writes:

> They [the Egyptian priests] were the first to see, through their art, how fate depends on the wandering stars. Over the course of many centuries they assigned with persistent care to each period of time the events connected with it: the day on which someone is born, the kind of life he shall lead, the influence of every hour on the laws of destiny, and the enormous differences made by small motions. . . . From long observation it was discovered that the stars control the whole world by mysterious laws, that the world itself moves by an eternal principle, and that we can, by reliable signs, recognize the ups and downs of fate.[2]

While Stoics were convinced some of the details of fate could be known ahead of time, adherents to this mode of thought were equally convinced it was unalterable. Fate must run its course. Each person should therefore accept what happens and view it as part of the mysterious outworking of fate. The secret of happiness in this life is to quit worrying about the future. Manilius advises, "Set your minds free, mortal men, let your cares go and deliver your lives from all this pointless fuss. Fate rules the world; everything is bound by certain laws; eternities are sealed by predetermined events. . . . No one can catch Fortune by praying against her will or escape her if she comes close to him. Everyone must bear his appointed lot."[3]

Some astrologers assumed a dual role for themselves in dealing with people, something like an astrologer-psychotherapist. Knowing that most people were either unwilling or unable to accept their allotted fate, Stoic astrologer Vettius Valens felt responsible to tell his clients the truth about the future and help them face up to it.[4]

The Quest to Alter Fate

In popular belief during the time of Paul, astrology was closer to religion than to science, although people then would not have made such a distinction. Astrology was closer to religion in the sense that people believed the heavenly bodies were deities or disembodied spirits. The known planets were named after deities. In fact, we still refer to the planets by their Roman names: Venus (Aphrodite in Greek), Mars (Ares), Mercury (Hermes) and so on. The spirits of heroes who had died on earth were also believed to continue existing in an etherform, populating the heavens and constituting what we know today as the Milky Way. Because the planets and stars were seen as deities, they were capable of being prayed to, invoked, propitiated and even manipulated. In contrast to the Stoics who resigned themselves to the decrees of fate, the masses felt that fate could conceivably be altered. Franz Cumont provides us with a clear statement of this common belief:

> [The masses] looked at astrology far more from a religious than from a logical standpoint. The planets and constellations were not only cosmic forces, whose favorable or inauspicious action grew weaker or stronger according to the turnings of a course established for eternity; they were deities who saw and heard, who were glad or sad, who had a voice and sex, who were prolific or sterile, gentle or savage, obsequious or arrogant. Their anger could therefore be soothed and their favor obtained through rites and offerings; even the adverse stars were not unrelenting and could be persuaded through sacrifices and supplications.[5]

Astrology thus became closely connected with the other forms of popular devotion to the gods—the mystery cults and magic. The presence of the zodiacal images on large numbers of statues and monuments of pagan worship confirm this association with the mystery religions. A beautiful marble cult statue of the Ephesian Artemis dating back to the second century A.D., for example, depicts the female goddess wearing the signs of the zodiac as a necklace. It is likely that this artistic rendering was a method of portraying Artemis as having power and authority over those astral signs. The goddess Artemis might therefore benevolently exercise her control over those forces for the good of her devotees.

Magic could be used with great success by manipulating and invoking the assistance of the astral spirits. Magic thus was not only a mechanism for altering fate, but also a means of tapping into the power of the astral spirits to carry out the varied demands of the conjurer. Some papyri are full of examples of this kind of magic.[6] One text bases the effectiveness of all conjurations on the position of the moon in the various houses of the zodiac:

> Orbit of the moon: Moon in Virgo: anything is rendered obtainable. In Libra: necromancy. In Scorpio: anything inflicting evil. In Sagittarius: an invocation or incantations to the sun and moon. In Capricorn: say whatever you wish for best results. In Aquarius: for a love charm. Pisces: for foreknowledge. In Aries: fire divination or love charm. In Taurus: incantation to a lamp. Gemini: spell for winning favor. In Cancer: phylacteries. Leo: rings or binding spells.[7]

Sometimes a magical recipe might prescribe an offering directly to a star, as for instance, to "the star of Aphrodite" (Venus).[8] A heavenly sign might indicate the completion of a task by a conjured deity. A love spell performed by the goddess Kythere (perhaps Venus/Aphrodite), for example, instructs the suppliant to watch the star of the goddess: "If you see the star shining steadily, it is a sign that she [the victim] has been smitten, and if it is lengthened like the flame of a lamp, she has already come."[9]

Certain groupings of stars, or constellations, were often identified with a figure, whom they were thought to resemble. This association explains the origin of the zodiac with its twelve signs, such as the crab, lion, scales and archer. In popular belief they were identified as gods and could also be invoked for magical purposes. A constellation that was not part of the zodiac, but was nevertheless well known in popular belief, was the constellation of the bear (Arktos). The bear was conjured frequently in the magical papyri. The following magical recipe illustrates one formula in which the bear could be called upon to accomplish anything the person might request:

> Bear, Bear, you who rule the heaven, the stars, and the whole world; you who make the axis turn and control the whole cosmic system by force and compulsion; I appeal to you, imploring and supplicating that you may do the [space for request] thing, because I call upon you with your holy names at which your deity rejoices, names which you are not able to ignore.[10]

During the time of the New Testament, some people resigned themselves to the unfolding of fate; others tried to alter fate through the practice of magic or by worshiping a cosmic deity. Whether through surrendering to fate or by trying to change it, people gave full credence to the tenets of astrology.

Concern about fate and the influence of the stars was probably a continuing issue for Paul's converts. In Ephesians 1, however, Paul's eloquent and artistic testimony to God's electing and predestining activity would have provided soothing comfort to those new Christians on the west coast of Asia Minor.

The Elementary Spirits of This World

An intriguing aspect of Paul's vocabulary for the principalities and powers is that both pagans and Jews used the same expressions for astral spirits. The word "powers" *(dynameis)* itself can be found in astrological contexts for star spirits. The expression "world rulers" *(kosmokratores)* of Ephesians 6:12 is also used of astral deities.[11]

Paul used one other expression for evil spirits associated with the stars: *stoicheia*. This term appears four times in two of Paul's letters, both of which were sent to churches in Asia Minor (Col 2:8, 20; Gal 4:3, 9). Scholars actually have been divided in trying to determine whether Paul was using this term with reference to spirit beings. This debate is evident in the variant translations:

As Personal Beings
RSV/NEB: "the elemental spirits of the universe"
TEV: "the ruling spirits of the universe"

As Nonpersonal Entities
NIV: "basic principles of this world"
NASB: "elementary principles of the world"

In these two letters the interpretation of *stoicheia* is difficult because the term has a range of meanings and because scholars have felt that more than one of these meanings could appropriately fit each of the contexts. Those who take a nonangelic interpretation of *stoicheia* point to its most basic meaning as "elements," such as the letters of the alphabet (which constitute the foundation of language), or the basic "elements" of the universe, such as earth, air, fire and water. They contend that the phrase could then be interpreted as the basic principles common to all religion, or as the Pauline concepts of "law" and "flesh," or even as the actual physical elements.

The interpretation of *stoicheia* as personal spiritual entities is the most compelling view. Consequently this interpretation has commanded the consent of the majority of commentators in the history of the interpretation of the passages.[12] This view is based partly on the widespread usage of *stoicheia* for astral spirits in the second and third centuries A.D. (and probably before). The word was used, for instance, in the Greek magical papyri in connection with the Zodiac: "I conjure you by the 12 stoicheia of heaven and the 24 stoicheia of the world in order that you would lead me to Heracles."[13]

It is important to realize that not only pagans used this word to refer to spirits, but Jews also used this word in that sense. The Jewish *Testament of Solomon*, written during the Roman Imperial period, includes five references to *stoicheia* as spirit beings. In the following passage the *stoicheia* are linked with the *kosmokratores* (cf. Eph 6:12):

> I commanded another demon to appear before me. There came seven spirits bound up together hand and foot, fair of form and graceful. When I, Solomon, saw them, I was amazed and asked them, "Who are you?" They replied, "We are heavenly bodies *[stoicheia]*, rulers of this world *[kosmokratores]* of darkness. The first said, "I am Deception." The second said, "I am Strife." The third said, "I am Fate." The fourth said, "I am Distress." The fifth said, "I am Error." The sixth said, "I am Power." The seventh said, "I am The Worst. Our stars in heaven look small, but we are named like gods. We change our position together and we live together, sometimes in Lydia, sometimes in Olympus, sometimes on the great mountain." (*Testament of Solomon* 8:1-4)[14]

These terms further reflect the wide array of vocabulary in reference to spirit beings, shared by Jews and Gentiles alike. Paul drew from this reservoir of terminology with which his readers would be readily familiar. He showed no interest, however, in discussing what he believed to be true about the starry host. Rather, he lumped all manner of spirits together, affirmed Christ's superiority, and encouraged believers to be prepared for their hostile intentions and attacks by reminding his readers of their past ability to enslave.

4
Judaism

*T*HE APOSTLE PAUL WAS A JEW. HIS LINEAGE WAS ROOTED IN THE TRIBE of Benjamin; he was circumcised as a Jew, trained by the rabbis, and became a zealous Pharisee, a "Hebrew of Hebrews." After Paul encountered the risen Christ, Jewish Christians nurtured him. Although he was commissioned to be the apostle to the Gentiles, he still proclaimed Christ to the Jews throughout Asia and Greece, following his guiding principle, "to the Jew first and also to the Greek." He planted a number of churches, all having a strong, if not dominant, Jewish contingent.

We should therefore learn to appreciate what first-century Judaism believed about evil spirits if we want to understand what Paul believed about the powers of darkness and if we want to see how he applied his theology of the powers to the early Christian congregations. To what extent did a belief in the influence of evil spirits factor into the world view of the Jews of Paul's day? An answer to this question will help us paint a sharper portrait of Paul's views in terms of the continuity and contrast to his religious upbringing and the beliefs of the Jews to whom he writes. Since Paul accepted the Old Testament as an authoritative informing source for his theology, it is best to begin there.

It is often thought there is virtually no demonology in the Old Testament, and it is only when we turn to the New Testament that we find any substantial teaching on this theme. While the issue of the demonic is more to the forefront in the New Testament, demonology is not absent from the Old Testament. The Old Testament writers assume the existence of a major figurehead of evil and a plethora of evil spirits. The authors spend no time reflecting on the nature of this realm. Satan, demons or evil spirits suddenly make an appearance from time to time in the text as hostile opponents to the people of God, with the writers giving very little description of their identity or how they operate. The Old Testament authors apparently felt little need to explain what these beings were; rather, writers and readers apparently shared a common awareness of the distinctive traits of this realm.

Demons and False Gods

The nations around Israel worshiped a multiplicity of gods and goddesses. In every century and in every geographical region, including Palestine, the Jews lived in a polytheistic environment. Among the hundreds of deities they were exposed to were the Assyrian gods Anu and Ishtar; the Canaanite deities El, Baal, Dagan, Anat and Ashtoreth; the Egyptian deities Re, Atan, Amon, Thoth, Isis and Osiris. Later in their history they were introduced to the numerous Persian, Greek and Roman gods.

Biblical writers attributed no real, independent existence to these deities. Instead they called them idols, a way of referring to the images of these gods and goddesses as the focus of worship. The term *idol,* meaning copy or image, emphasized the unreality of all the pagan gods, and was clearly a slur on non-Jewish religions. The Jews claimed to worship the one true, real God. All the rest were phonies.

These idols, however, were not mere harmless stone images a covenant person could be indifferent to. There was a real spiritual dimension to the pagan cults and the worship of idols. Biblical writers complete the picture of Yahweh's attitude toward false gods by portraying the pagan cults as the work of demons. In Deuteronomy 32:16-17, Israel's abandonment of God for idols in the wilderness is explicitly described:

> They made him jealous with their foreign gods and angered him with their detestable idols. They sacrificed *to demons,* which are not God—gods they had not known, gods that recently appeared, gods your fathers did not fear. (italics mine)

The Psalms express the same thought. One psalm describes Israel's entry into Canaan, deploring the fact that God's people had adopted many of the local customs and had worshiped the local idols. They also "sacrificed their sons and their daughters to demons," which the psalmist sets parallel with the statement that they "sacrificed to the idols of Canaan" (Ps 106:37-38). In Psalm 96:5, where the Hebrew text reads, "for all the gods of the nations are idols," the Septuagint text (the Greek translation) reads, "for all the gods of the nations are demons." The Septuagint reflects the Jewish conviction that pagan religions had a close affiliation with the demonic realm. This belief also became the conviction of the apostle Paul (1 Cor 10:19-21).

The Night Hag and Other Evil Spirits

The Old Testament also ascribes names to some evil spirits. Lilith (translated "Night Hag" by the RSV) is a demon who will inhabit Edom after it experiences God's desolating judgment (Is 34:14).[1] Although this is the only time Lilith is mentioned in the Old Testament, she was a well-known evil spirit in Mesopotamia. She also figured prominently in later noncanonical Jewish texts, as, for example, in a Jewish targum, which records the following prayer: "May the Lord bless you in all your deeds and protect you from the demons of the night [Lilith] and from anything that frightens and from demons of evening and morning, from evil spirits and phantoms."[2] Lilith also makes her appearance on some of the Aramaic incantation bowls. One bowl reads, "Bound is the bewitching Lilith who haunts the house of Zakoy."[3]

In Isaiah 34:14, the spooky and terrifying place of desolation is portrayed as being inhabited by wild animals and other demonic spirits. This passage speaks of Edom becoming a den for jackals and an enclosure for hyenas. It then goes on to say "demons" *(daimonia)*, "phantoms" and "goat spirits," as well as Lilith, will haunt this place.[4]

In a similar way the Isaianic prophecy of the desolation of Babylon predicts that it will become a haunt for "goat spirits" and other sorts of demons (Is 13:21). As in Isaiah 34:14, the Greek Old Testament uses the word *daimonia* ("demons") to translate some of the Hebrew words here for wild animals. There was a strong connection between wild animals and evil spirits throughout antiquity. The "goat demon" was thought to be in the form of a shaggy he-goat.[5]

In the Old Testament Levitical law the goat demons also appear. Israel was prohibited from offering sacrifices to goat idols. The law states: "They must no longer offer any of their sacrifices to the goat idols to whom they prostitute themselves" (Lev 17:7a). Rehoboam violated this statute when he set up "high places" and "appointed his own priests for the high places and for the goat and calf idols he had made" (2 Chron 11:15). In both of these instances demonic involvement in pagan cults is reaffirmed.

Witches, Mediums and Spiritists

Occultic practices were common among the neighbors of Israel, and they proved to be a great temptation to God's people.[6] Consequently we find numerous commands and admonitions throughout the Old Testament, warning Israel to stay away from every form of magical practice. The Torah specifically says, "Do not practice divination or sorcery" (Lev 19:26). In the Torah the most comprehensive list of occultic prohibitions is given:

> Let no one be found among you who sacrifices his son or daughter in the fire, who practices divination or sorcery, interprets omens, engages in witchcraft, or casts spells, or who is a medium or spiritist or who consults the dead. Anyone who does these things is detestable to the LORD, and because of these detestable practices the LORD your God will drive out those nations before you. (Deut 18:10-12)

Throughout the Old Testament these kinds of occultic practices are often catalogued, either in a list of prohibitions or in a historical narrative where the sins of a key figure are mentioned.

Manasseh, one of the kings of Judah, was guilty in the eyes of the chronicler for breaking the occult prohibitions of the Torah. He worshiped the Canaanite gods, practiced astrology or a form of astral religion ("bowed down to all the starry host and worshiped them"), "sacrificed his sons in the fire in the Valley of Ben Hinnom, practiced sorcery, divination and witchcraft, and consulted mediums and spiritists" (2 Chron 33:1-6). The chronicler concludes, "He did much evil in the eyes of the LORD provoking him to anger."

Likewise, Hoshea, the last king of the northern kingdom, led Israel away from God to pursue the worship of foreign gods and engage in occultic practices, including astrology. The text says they set up sacred stones and Asherah poles, they worshiped idols, they imitated the nations around them, they bowed down to all the starry hosts, they worshiped Baal, they sacrificed their sons and their daughters in the fire, and they practiced divination and sorcery. The biblical writer interprets their action as selling "themselves to do evil in the eyes of the LORD, provoking him to anger." As a result, the Lord was "very angry with Israel," removing them from his presence (2 Kings 17:7-23).

In the Old Testament none of these occult practices are ever described in any detail. Instead, they are usually mentioned in a list and condemned. There was a clear assumption on the part of the various Old Testament writers that the readers would know precisely what was being referred to.

In Old Testament history burning children in a fire as part of pagan worship was something that occurred on more than one occasion (see Jer 7:31; 19:5; 32:35; Mic 6:7). Outside of the Old Testament, however, there is little information that describes the practice of child sacrifice.

As we have seen from the accounts about Manasseh and Hoshea, astrology was widely practiced during their times. Biblical writers describe it as "bowing down to the starry hosts." We would be remiss to think they viewed the stars merely as material objects. Throughout the history of the ancient Near East, the stars were deified and thought to represent various gods and goddesses. In fact, the book of Amos actually names two Assyrian astral deities that Israel worshiped: "Sakkuth your king and Kaiwan your star god" (Amos 5:26). Jeremiah mentions the worship of Ishtar, the "Queen of Heaven" (Jer 7:18; 44:17-19). Then, as well as in the later Greco-Roman forms of astrology, the stars were believed to control the unfolding of history. The law expressly prohibited Israel from worshiping the stars (Deut 4:19), in spite of the fact that this was the common practice of all the other nations around Israel.

In the ancient Near East many forms of divination were practiced. One of the most popular forms was liver inspection (hepatoscopy). Perhaps, because the liver was the seat of the blood, and thus the center of life, it was especially important in popular belief as an object that could help determine the future. Another well-known form of divination was necromancy, the conjuring of the dead, of which King Saul was culpable when he visited the witch at Endor (1 Sam 28:3-25). Since divination was closely associated with magic in all its forms, biblical writers roundly condemned it (see Lev 19:26, 31).[7]

Magic, witchcraft and sorcery have played a part in every society in the history of religion. The main features are always the same. Of special significance for our topic is the fact that these practices were based on a firm belief in the realm of good and evil spirits. Those who practiced magic believed the supernatural beings could be manipulated to bring positive benefit or harm. For the covenant people of God these practices were regarded as evil and detestable to the Lord.

Situations Involving Evil Spirits

In the Old Testament the activity of evil spirits is described a few times, and usually with the author carefully subordinating them to God's sovereign control. During the time of the Judges, Abimelech sought to rule over a segment of the northern kingdom, which included the city of Shechem (Judg 9). After soliciting and receiving the support of the citizens of Shechem, he quickly eliminated all his competition for the throne by murdering his seventy brothers (except for one, Jotham). Because of his treacherous bloodshed, "God sent an evil spirit between Abimelech and the citizens of Shechem" after he had ruled over Israel for three years (Judg 9:23a).[8] This conflict resulted in a time of great civil strife, war and death.

Because an evil spirit tormented King Saul, his advisors counseled him to find someone who could play the harp, believing music would bring him relief (1 Sam 16:14-23). Saul's attendants discovered the talents of a young man named David, who was then summoned into the king's service. Whenever this malignant spirit afflicted Saul, David would play the harp, and Saul would be relieved. The text says, "He would feel better, and the evil spirit would leave him" (1 Sam 16:23b). It was this same evil spirit who twice prompted Saul to attempt to kill David (1 Sam 18:10-11; 19:9-10).

One other account presents a situation in which an evil spirit inspired 400 prophets to give false advice to Ahab, king of Israel, when he inquired whether he should go to war to reclaim a foreign-occupied city (1 Kings 22:1-40). The text depicts a heavenly session with the Lord in which evil spirits were permitted to suggest to him ways of luring Ahab into attacking the city. Finally one of the wicked spirits suggests that it would go out and be "a lying spirit in the mouths of all his prophets" (1 Kings 22:21-22). Receiving Yahweh's approval, the spirit was successful in its deceitful activity despite the Lord's prophet disclosing to the king all the details of the heavenly plan as they had been revealed to him. Contrary to the advice of the Lord's prophet, Ahab attacked the city, and in the ensuing battle he was killed. Some commentators on this text have much difficulty on deciding what to make of this "spiritual interpretation" of the events. It must be seen, however, in conjunction with the account of Satan asking Yahweh for permission to afflict Job (Job 1:6-12). All three of these scenarios not only stress God's ultimate control over the realm of evil spirits, but also make the point that God even permits these forces to carry out their evil deeds as a means of accomplishing his own divine purposes.

The Serpent of Old

The Apocalypse of John brings its readers hope by predicting a future overthrow of "the serpent of old," also known as Satan or the devil (Rev 20:2). This allusion is to the Genesis account of creation and the serpent's temptation of Adam and Eve in the garden (Gen 3:1-15). Paul also spoke of this event in his second letter to the Corinthians, in which he compared the serpent's effective cunning with the deceitful work of Satan on the Corinthians (2 Cor 11:3, 14-15). Although some scholars hesitate to identify the serpent in Genesis 3 with Satan, this was the unanimous early Christian (and Jewish) interpretation.

The scene in the garden is the classic portrayal of Satan's character as the tempter—a motif found throughout the New Testament, especially in Paul's treatment of the powers of darkness. This narrative does not reveal the devil as a spirit or angel, but his supernatural character comes to light for the reader when he animates a snake causing it to talk. The snake represented an "archetypal unclean animal" in the law of God (see Lev 11 and Deut 14).[9]

This passage marks the beginning of salvation history. It establishes the need for the redemption of humanity because of the Fall. It points to the devil's activity in promoting sin and rebellion against God and consequently to the need for this evil being to be dealt a crushing blow for God's purposes to be brought to completion (Gen 3:15).

The Old Testament never explicitly addresses the origin of Satan or how or when he turned against God. It is possible that couched in the prophecies against the king of Tyre (Ezek 28) and the king of Babylon (Is 14) are insights into the original state and fall of Satan.[10] This connection was certainly how early Jewish interpreters understood these passages. These texts, however, may also point to the heavenly angelic figures associated with those nations, as was the case with the angelic "prince of Persia" in Daniel 10:13.

Satan is mentioned only at three other places in the Old Testament (Job 1—2; Zech 3:1-2; 1 Chron 21:1). In all of these passages he appears as a supernatural enemy of both God and humanity. In Job Satan appears as an accuser and an afflicter. He challenges the genuineness of Job's righteousness and commitment to God, claiming that Job fears God because God had so richly blessed him (Job 1:6-11). God sovereignly permits Satan to afflict Job. Satan then strips Job of his wealth, makes him dreadfully ill, kills all of his children and turns his wife against him. Yet Job responded to these overwhelming trials with integrity and did not sin or turn from God. This passage shows what great power the Lord God permits Satan to exercise on earth and even over his people. Not only does he function as an accuser, but God also gives him the authorization to control such things as sickness, robbery and even natural disasters that cause death.[11]

The writer of 1 Chronicles reaffirms Satan's activity as a tempter: "Satan rose up against Israel and incited David to take a census of Israel" (1 Chron 21:1). In this passage Satan is also portrayed as Israel's adversary—a role that corresponds to the meaning of the word "devil" (*diabolos*), which the Greek translators of the Old Testament chose to translate the term "Satan."

Finally in the vision of Zechariah Satan accuses the high priest Jonathan for his past sins in an apparent attempt to disqualify him from his office (Zech 3:1-2). Satan's activity of bringing accusation is more in line with the extended usage of the Hebrew term *satan*. In the Old Testament the word is used elsewhere with the simple meaning of "accuser" or "adversary." The writer of 1 Samuel records, for instance, that the Philistines were opposed to David fighting with them, "lest in the battle he become an adversary *[satan]* to us" (1 Sam 29:4 RSV).

Satan is thus an accuser and a powerful adversary against God's people. He performs his hostile functions against them by luring them into rebelling against the express will of God and by causing even physical destruction, pain and grief. In spite of Satan's powerful malignant activity, God's people are called to maintain their pure devotion to the Lord.

Angelic Powers over the Nations

The Old Testament gives yet another insight into the unseen realm of spirits and angels by speaking of supernatural beings that are closely attached to all the nations. The idea first appears in Deuteronomy 32:8-9: "When the Most High gave to the nations their inheritance, when he separated the sons of men, he fixed the bounds of the peoples according to the number of the sons of God. For the LORD's portion is his people, Jacob his allotted heritage" (RSV). The Greek version of the Old Testament interprets "the sons of God" as angels and thus translates the key phrase "he fixed the bounds of the peoples according to the number of the angels of God."[12] This passage is best explained as teaching that "all the nations of the earth are given over into the control of angelic powers."[13]

Although the Old Testament as a whole has little to say about this idea, the book of Daniel does present us with the clearest picture of this Jewish belief. The book gives the details of a vision that God granted to the prophet Daniel—a vision in which he learns about the activities of the angels set over the nations of Persia, Greece and even Israel. In fact, an angel mediated the vision to Daniel. The one who appeared to Daniel is described as a man dressed in linen with a dazzling appearance. The first part of the vision is taken up with descriptions of angelic war and conflict. Yet this heavenly conflict was closely tied to the fate of nations and peoples. Received during the third year of Cyrus, king of Persia, the vision describes the position of Israel in relation to the Persian and Greek empires. The angel said:

The *prince* of the kingdom of Persia withstood me twenty-one days; but Michael, one of the *chief princes,* came to help me, so I left him there with the *prince* of the kingdom of Persia and came to make you understand what is to befall your people in the latter days. . . . But now I will return to fight against the *prince* of Persia; and when I am through with him, lo, the *prince* of Greece will come. . . . There is none who contends by my side against these except Michael, your *prince.* (Dan 10:13-14, 20-21 RSV, italics mine)

The many references to *princes* are to angelic powers. The title of authority probably indicates that these various angelic princes are leading hosts of other angelic powers into battle.

The word *prince* in this passage is translated from the word *archōn* in one of the Greek versions of the book of Daniel.[14] *Archōn* is a word that all four of the Gospel writers and Paul later used either for Satan or for evil spirit powers.

There appears to be a direct correspondence between the outcome of the angelic battles and the fortunes of the corresponding nations. This vision was not intended to lead Daniel into a fatalistic resignation of life. Daniel himself could wield influence over the unseen angelic powers. The angel who visited Daniel came in response to his piety and prayer. The angelic messenger told Daniel: "Since the first day that you set your mind to gain understanding and to humble yourself before your God, your words were heard, and I have come in response to them" (Dan 10:12).

The vision functions not only as a means of giving Daniel information about future events and therefore hope, but also as a stimulus to continued godliness and prayer. God directs his angels as a result of the prayer of his people.

Michael is the only angel whose name is revealed in this passage. He is described as Israel's prince (10:21), the one who protects Israel (12:1).

While the book of Daniel does not describe precisely how the angels exert their control over nations, later Jewish tradition is more explicit. The ruling angels over nations, other than Israel, function as deceiving angels. One Jewish text teaches, "[there are] many nations and many people, and they all belong to him [God], but over all of them he caused spirits to rule so that they might lead them astray from following him" (Jubilees 15:31).

Increasing Jewish Interest in the Spirit Realm

During the two centuries leading up to the time of Jesus, a sharp increase of interest in the realm of angels, spirits and demons is observable in Jewish literature. This preoccupation with the spirit world can be traced in virtually all facets of its literature—the Old Testament Apocryphal writings (especially Tobit), the Qumran literature, the pseudepigraphal testamentary literature and particularly in the Jewish apocalyptic writings.

Going far beyond what was revealed in the Old Testament, the Jews of this period gave details of the numbers of angels, their names and their hierarchies. Where the Old Testament was silent about the rebellion of the evil angels, Jewish writings of the second temple period provided a full account. There is also much discussion on the nature of angelic influence over the destiny of nations as well as over the daily life of the individual.

Much of this burgeoning curiosity about the spirit realm can be attributed to a growing tendency to distance God from direct involvement in daily life. His perceived transcendence led many Jews to begin postulating the intermediary role of angels. God was still in control and would bring history to a climax with the destruction of evil, but he had entrusted the administration of the world to angels, and many had gone astray. For the Jews of this period, this belief gave perspective to the problem of their suffering.[15] The illegitimate rule of Palestine by Roman usurpers could now be explained from a demonological perspective; the kingdom of Satan had gained a temporary victory.

The Qumran community, which produced the Dead Sea Scrolls, explained the prevailing political situation in those terms. The community published a document, now known as the *War Scroll* (1QM), which describes an impending battle between the "children of light" and the "children of darkness." On one level "the sons of darkness" are defined as the Romans *(Kittim)*, but on another spiritual level they are identified with Satan and the evil angelic forces of his kingdom (1QM 13.4-5). When the battle occurs, it would be decided by the direct intervention of God, who would raise his hand "in an everlasting blow against Satan and all the hosts of his kingdom" (1 QM 18.1). The scroll sees the battle taking place on two dimensions, with men fighting men and angels fighting angels. There is, however, a crossover in which the good angels are portrayed as helping God's people and Satan's hosts as helping the Roman soldiers.[16]

Other segments of Jewish literature show greater interest in exposing the influence of evil spirits on the daily life of the individual. Reflecting popular belief, the Testaments of the Twelve Patriarchs give a demonic root to much moral evil—people often succumb to the influence of evil spirits of deceit.

This literature is extremely important when we approach the New Testament since it gives us a glimpse into the Judaism of Jesus' day and the time of Paul's ministry. It helps us see the teaching of Jesus and Paul on Satan's kingdom with a new freshness and vitality. Jewish demonology is also important for us because of the significant formative influence it had on the development of early-Christian angelology and demonology as seen by many of the church fathers.

The Angelic Fall

In the Jewish literature of this period one of the most prominent themes was the belief that demons came into the world as a result of unnatural sexual relations between angels and human beings. This belief is based on an interpretation of Genesis 6:1-2 and 4, which says:

When men began to increase in number on the earth and daughters were born to them, the sons of God saw that the daughters of men were beautiful, and they married any of them they chose. . . . The Nephilim were on the earth in those days—and also afterward—when the sons of God went to the daughters of men and had children by them.

Many Jewish writers interpreted the reference to "sons of God" as angels (called "Watchers"), who rebelled against God. The disastrous consequence of this unnatural union resulted in the birth of the Nephilim, the source of demons and evil spirits. The Jewish apocalyptic book of *1 Enoch* spends thirty-one chapters elaborating on this fall (*1 Enoch* 6—36). According to this account, after the physical beauty of women on earth erotically tantalized some 200 angels, led by a certain Semyaz, the angels made a joint decision to violate their divinely given boundaries by engaging in sexual activity with the women. While they were occupying the earth, they taught people many evil arts, including alchemy, astrology, incantations and warfare. The women, made pregnant by these supernatural beings, gave birth to freakish giants. These giants committed numerous atrocities, yet their deaths did not prove to be the end of rampant evil—demons came from them:

But now the giants who are born from the union of the spirits and the flesh shall be called evil spirits upon the earth, because their dwelling shall be upon the earth and inside the earth. Evil spirits have come out of their bodies. . . . The spirits of the giants oppress each other; they will corrupt, fall, be excited, and fall upon the earth, and cause sorrow. They eat no food, nor become thirsty, nor find obstacles. And these spirits shall rise up against the children of the people and against the women, because they have proceeded forth from them. (*1 Enoch* 15:8-12)

It was believed these evil spirits, which issued from the giants, would continue to corrupt humanity until the end of the age when God would put an end to their hostility and judge them. In Jewish literature this rebellion is referred to many times as responsible for the presence of demons. Meanwhile, the good angels, Raphael and Michael, have bound those angels who were guilty of this crime against women under the earth, where they will remain until the judgment (*1 Enoch* 10:1-14; cf. Jude 6; 1 Pet 3:19-20; 2 Pet 2:4).

We may wonder about the time before this rebellion, especially in view of the Genesis account of the serpent's temptation of Eve. Was there some prior angelic rebellion in Jewish belief? It is clear that the same Jewish literature speaks of the existence and malignant workings of evil angels prior to the Fall.[17] There is virtually no discussion, however, about how or when Satan and his angelic cohorts came on the scene. This literature refers to a major figurehead of evil called "Satan," the leader of a group of angels also referred to as "Satans." These Satans accuse people and lead them astray. Interestingly, according to *1 Enoch*, it was one of these Satanic messengers, named Gader'el, who misled Eve in the garden (*1 Enoch* 69:6). The Jews must have assumed true some kind of pre-Adam fall in order to explain the evil character and function of this Satan and his hostile messengers (see *1 Enoch* 40:7; 53:3; 54:6).

Classes and Names

Asmodaeus, Semyaza, Azazel, Mastema, Beliar, Satan, Sammael and Satanail are just a few of the names used to refer to the evil angelic powers current in Judaism by the time of Paul. While there is a certain amount of diversity regarding the specific functions of each of these powers, there is a fairly common belief in Satan as the chief. These powers of evil are represented as each having a significant measure of authority within the structured hierarchy. For example, Semyaza is identified as the chief of those angels who cohabited with women. Of the 200 angels who came to earth with him, they were divided into groups of ten, with a prince, such as Arakeb, Rame'el and Tam'el, set over each.

A similar concern to name the evil angels and classify them according to their function was typical of much of this Jewish literature. Equally prominent is the arrangement and naming of the good angels surrounding the throne of God.

In the years following the New Testament era this fascination with the spirit realm did not diminish. There are frequent references to evil angels and spirits in the rabbinic literature. Far more evil spirits are identified and described. In fact, one scholar has counted 123 different demons identified by name in the rabbinic literature![18]

The Influence of the Powers on Individuals

Inimical to the purposes of God, the evil powers were believed to exert their supernatural influence to lead people astray from the revealed will of God. They lead people into all kinds of moral impurity. This is one of the reasons that the Qumran community could refer to this evil dominion as "the company of Darkness." Note how the Qumran *War Scroll* describes this activity of Satan and his powers:

Satan, the Angel of Malevolence, Thou hast created for the Pit; his [rule] is in Darkness and his purpose is to bring about wickedness and iniquity. All the spirits of his company, the Angels of Destruction, walk according to the precepts of Darkness; towards them is their [inclination]. (1QM 13.11-12)

The *Testaments of the Twelve Patriarchs* elaborate extensively on this activity of the powers of darkness and are important for giving us an understanding of Jewish belief. The *Testaments*, dating roughly back to the first or second century B.C.,[19] purportedly record the final utterances of each of Jacob's twelve sons. The *Testaments* are largely concerned with ethical issues and attempt to promote virtuous conduct among the Jewish readership. The *Testaments* paint a picture of common Jewish thinking about the way evil spirits influence people in their daily lives. For this reason, they are especially valuable for understanding Paul's discussion of evil spirits.

According to the *Testaments*, every individual must personally struggle against evil spirits of deceit, who are ruled by the devil, or Beliar. They exploit human drives and frailties to promote their evil ends.

Sexual promiscuity, in particular, is pinpointed as one of the areas of sinful activity instigated by evil spirits. In the *Testament of Reuben*, sexual sin is called "the plague of Beliar" and is inspired by a "spirit of promiscuity (porneia) that resides in the nature and the senses" (*Testament of Reuben* 6:3; 3:3). The *Testament* does not give the devil and his powers full responsibility for human lapses into sexual trysts; the involvement of the human mind and senses is given an equal role. In reflecting on Reuben's incestuous sin with his father's mistress, Bilhah (cf. Gen 35:22), the *Testament* places more emphasis on Reuben's own lust and mental titillation: "For if I had not seen Bilhah bathing in a sheltered place, I would not have fallen into this great lawless act. For so absorbed were my senses by her naked femininity that I was not able to sleep until I had performed this revolting act" (3:11-12). Based on his regrettable experience, Reuben's advice to his offspring focuses on disciplining their minds: "Do not devote your attention to the beauty of women, my children, nor occupy your minds with their activities. But live in integrity of heart in the fear of the

LORD . . . until the LORD gives you the mate whom he wills, so that you do not suffer as I did" (4:1). Nevertheless, in continuing to reflect on what he had learned from the event, he points to the devil's involvement: "For promiscuity has destroyed many. Whether a man is old, well born, rich, or poor, he brings on himself disgrace among mankind and provides Beliar with an opportunity to cause him to stumble" (4:7).

The evil spirits of error also take advantage of the debase human tendency toward jealousy. The *Testament of Simeon* reflects on Simeon's role in the betrayal of Joseph by his brothers (Gen 37:12-36). Simeon relates how a powerful evil spirit exploited his jealousy toward Joseph:

> In the time of my youth I was jealous of Joseph, because my father loved him more than all the rest of us. I determined inwardly to destroy him, because the Prince *(archōn)* of Error blinded my mind so that I did not consider him as a brother nor did I spare Jacob, my father. (*Testament of Simeon* 2:6-7)

Simeon thus advises his children to "beware of the spirit of deceit and envy" (3:1). If the influence of such a spirit is detected, one must turn to the Lord. Simeon counsels, "If anyone flees to the Lord for refuge, the evil spirit will quickly depart from him, and his mind will be eased" (3:5). Simeon holds Joseph up as a positive example. Joseph was able to love his brothers, in spite of their treachery toward him, because he possessed the Spirit of God" (4:4).

These two examples help us gain insight into what Jews in the first century believed to be true regarding the role of evil spirits in the affairs of daily life, especially with respect to personal morality. Some of the thoughts on evil spirits contained in these Testaments are also reflected in the apostle Paul's writings.

The Influence of the Powers on Society: Pagan Religion

Jewish writers ascribed the rise of all non-Jewish religions to the inspiration of evil powers. In discussing the influence of the powers on the rise of civilization after the flood, the book of Jubilees, a second-century B.C. writing, refers to the beginnings of idolatry. The inhabitants of Ur of the Chaldees "made for themselves molten images, and everyone worshiped the icon which they made for themselves as a molten image. And they began making graven images and polluted likenesses. And cruel spirits assisted them and led them astray so that they might commit sin and pollution. And the prince, Mastema, acted forcefully to do all of this" (*Jubilees* 11:4-5). Likewise, the apocalyptic book of 1 Enoch speaks of the demonic root of idolatry: "The spirits of the angels . . . have defiled the people and will lead them into error so that they will offer sacrifices to the demons as unto gods, until the great day of judgment in which they shall be judged till they are finished" (*1 Enoch* 19:1).

Although the Old Testament is not as explicit about the involvement of the evil powers in the origins of idolatry, it does affirm that sacrificing to idols is tantamount to sacrificing to demons (Deut 32:16-17). Such a sentiment is also known in the New Testament (Rev 9:20). Most important is the fact that this perspective about demonic involvement in pagan religion characterized the apostle Paul's belief, which he in turn passed on to the Corinthian church (1 Cor 10:19-21).

Many streams of Judaism also believed occultic practices were the work of the devil and his powers. According to *1 Enoch*, the fallen angels taught people magic, incantations, alchemy and astrology (*1 Enoch* 7—8; see also *Jubilees* 11:1-8).

The Influence of the Powers on Society: Warfare and the State

Even civil unrest among the nations and their hostility toward Israel is attributed to the devious work of the evil powers. The book of Jubilees ascribes a murderous tendency in people to the influence of the forces of Mastema, an evil angel corresponding to Satan: "And [Mastema] sent out other spirits to those who were set under his hand to practice all error and sin and all transgression, to destroy, to cause to perish and to pour out blood upon the earth" (11:5). All the weaponry of warfare was also inspired by fallen angels: "And Azaz'el taught the people the art of making swords and knives, and shields, and breastplates" (*1 Enoch* 8:1).

Egypt's hostility to Israel, and especially to Moses, is interpreted by the book of Jubilees as stemming from the supernatural opposition of the evil Mastema. It was actually Mastema who used the Egyptian Pharaoh in an attempt to kill Moses; it was also Mastema who enabled the Egyptian magicians to perform the great wonders in opposition to Moses; furthermore, it was Mastema who exerted his evil-inspiring influence on the Egyptians to pursue Israel into the sea (*Jubilees* 48).

As we have already seen, the Jewish community, which produced the Dead Sea Scrolls, gives a similar prominence to the demonic in their understanding of society. According to the Qumran *War Scroll* (1QM), it is Satan and his powers who are behind the Roman usurpers: "All those [who are ready] for battle shall march out and shall pitch their camp before the king of the Kittim [Romans] and before all the host of Satan gathered about him for the Day [of Revenge] by the Sword of God" (1QM 15.2-3).

The demonic, therefore, had a major role in a popular Jewish understanding of society during the time leading up to the New Testament period. Any early Jewish theory of social justice would have given a prominent place to the spiritual and supernatural dimension of life. In the eyes of the writer of the book of Jubilees, justice and freedom from oppression would have been impossible to obtain for Israel without addressing the powerful demonic hostility of Mastema. The people of Israel were freed from their formidable conditions because Yahweh worked through his servant Moses to redeem them as part of his larger plan for his people. The Qumran community was anticipating the direct intervention of "the mighty hand of God" to deal an everlasting blow to "Satan and all the host of his kingdom."

Jewish Magic

Perhaps nothing reflects Jewish popular belief in demons, spirits and the powers of evil more clearly than the widespread information illustrating Jewish involvement in magic. Contrary to Old Testament and official Jewish restrictions against the use of magic, many Jews throughout the Mediterranean world adopted and even further developed these occult practices of their pagan neighbors. In fact, Jewish magic gained a notoriety of its own in antiquity. Its importance for illuminating folk belief is rightly stressed by P. S. Alexander:

> [Jewish] incantations and books of magic . . . open up areas of popular religion which are often inadequately represented in the official literary texts, and which are in consequence frequently ignored by historians. As an indicator of the spiritual atmosphere in which large sections of the populace lived—rich and poor, educated and ignorant—their importance can hardly be overestimated.[20]

The New Testament itself helps to confirm this Jewish interest in magic by specifically naming two Jewish magicians—Simon (Acts 8:9) and Bar-Jesus, or Elymas (Acts 13:6-12). Luke also writes about certain itinerant Jewish exorcists, who had added the name of Jesus to their repertoire of magical names (Acts 19:13-20).

Over the past century archeologists have discovered numerous Jewish magical charms and amulets. Many of these have been collected and published with photographic reproductions as part of a beautifully done twelve-volume work by Jewish scholar E. R. Goodenough on Jewish symbols of the Greco-Roman period.[21] Goodenough helped call the scholarly world's attention to Jewish involvement in magic (and perhaps even mystery religions) by his analysis of the material evidence. The magical charms typically have a depiction of some Jewish symbol (such as a menorah or a representation of Solomon) on one side; the other side may contain a series of magical words or names (such as Sabaoth, angel names, names of patriarchs and often names of pagan deities). These amulets were used for many purposes, but most commonly for protection from evil spirits.

There are also a number of Jewish magical documents. In the standard collection of Greek magical papyri edited by Karl Preisendanz, some of the magical texts are distinctively Jewish. Just as significant is the extent to which Judaism influenced the development of the magical tradition as a whole. A number of scholars agree there are few Greek magical texts from late antiquity without some sort of Jewish component.[22] The Jews provided the Greeks with new magical names to invoke, such as *Iao* (a Greek form of Yahweh) and numerous other names thought to be laden with power. Most scholars are not concerned to draw any firm distinction between Jewish and pagan magic. The occult sciences crossed all religious boundaries and borrowed from all religions.

In Jewish magic it is interesting to note the prominence of Solomon. According to the biblical account of Solomon's life, he was granted a measure of wisdom from God unsurpassed by anyone preceding or following him (1 Kings 3:12). Later Judaism understood this gift to include wisdom and expertise in dealing with the spirit realm. The eminent Jewish historian Josephus believed this tradition:

God also enabled him [Solomon] to learn that skill which expels demons, which is a science useful and sanative to men. He composed such incantations also by which distempers are alleviated. And he left behind him the manner of using exorcisms, by which they drive away demons, so that they never return, and this method of cure is of great force unto this day; for I have seen a certain man of my own country whose name was Eleazar, releasing people who were demonic in the presence of Vespasian, and his sons, and his captains, and the whole multitude of his soldiers. (Josephus *Antiquities* 8.2.5)

Josephus then gives a very detailed account of how this Eleazar performed exorcisms using a magical ring and by reciting incantations ostensibly written by Solomon. A number of these Solomonic magical traditions have been preserved in the form of a document known as the Testament of Solomon. Although the Testament postdates the New Testament, many scholars agree it may have been put together in the first century A.D. It is a major source for helping us to understand early Jewish demonology.[23] The Testament functioned as a serious Jewish work on magic and a sort of encyclopedia of demonology. The work centers on Solomon's rebuilding of the temple in Jerusalem, but focuses specifically on the demonic opposition he faced and his ability not only to thwart the evil powers but also to manipulate them into actually aiding the construction of the temple! According to the Testament, the archangel Michael gave Solomon a magical seal ring that he used to interrogate the evil powers. By using it, Solomon was able to find out their names and evil activities, and to force them to divulge how they could be thwarted. The Testament is thus filled with accounts of Solomon's interrogation of the demons and how he manipulated them.

These traditions about Solomon would have had great significance for the Jew, who was fearful of evil spirits, and who sought a means for protection. A number of early Christian writers are familiar with the Solomon tradition and allude to exorcisms taking place using Solomonic formulas. The Testament is significant for our study by giving us yet another glimpse into the belief in demons and the use of magic that flourished throughout the Mediterranean world in popular culture, even in Judaism. The Testament also employs many of the terms used by the apostle Paul when he referred to the powers of darkness. This certainly does not imply that Paul agreed with everything said in this Testament, but it does show that Paul was concerned to give a perspective on these evil powers (that he believed to exist)—a perspective he based on the Christ event.

One final point needs to be made about first-century Judaism. Many of the common Jews were firm believers in astrology. The Testament of Solomon itself testifies to this Jewish interest in astrology (since magic and astrology overlap significantly). In the past fifty years, new archeological data and newly discovered documents have confirmed and further illustrate this interest in astrology. For example, among the Dead Sea Scrolls was an astrological document (a horoscope containing the signs of the zodiac) that likely reflects part of the beliefs of the Qumran community, also illustrating that astrological beliefs even extended to some of the Jewish sages.[24]

This discussion verifies and illustrates the strong Jewish belief in the powers of darkness throughout their history, and which intensified as the birth of Jesus approached. Furthermore, the Judaism of the Roman period shows a prevalent tendency toward overlooking the Old Testament restrictions against practicing magic and astrology. These activities became a common mechanism for overcoming the fearful threat posed by the powers of darkness.

5
The Teaching of Jesus

*T*RAVELING ON A LONG, DUSTY ROAD TO DAMASCUS, SYRIA, PAUL OF TARSUS met a person who forever changed the course of his life— he encountered the resurrected Lord of the Christians whom he was persecuting. Jesus Christ appeared to Paul and called him to proclaim his death and resurrection to the Gentiles. The person and teaching of Jesus was to become the single most influential factor in the thinking and writing of Paul.

Jesus was by no means silent about the realm of evil spirits. In fact, Jesus' conflict with the powers of darkness is a major theme in all of the Gospel accounts of his ministry. After the ruler of demons had tempted him, he went on the attack engaging many of the forces of evil. He also reflected on the meaning of his mission and passion in relationship to the devil and the powers of darkness. Jesus' teaching about evil powers had great influence on the apostle Paul, and therefore, it is very important for us to consider.

Jesus Is Attacked—The Temptation
Satan made his first appearance in all three synoptic Gospels as the supernatural tempter of Jesus (Mt 4:1-11; Mk 1:12-13; Lk 4:1-13). Recognizing Jesus as the Son of God, the devil came and made a bold attempt to divert Jesus from his divinely intended redemptive mission.

The attacks apparently did not take Jesus by surprise nor were they outside the design of God's sovereign leading. Each Gospel tells us it was the Holy Spirit who led Jesus into the wilderness. There, as Jesus fasted for an extremely long period of time, the devil tried to take advantage of his weak physical condition to entice him to behave in a way contrary to God's plan. He tested Jesus' devotion to his Messianic call.

First, the devil tempted Jesus where he was extremely vulnerable—hunger. He wanted Jesus to use his divine powers to satisfy his hunger; he did not want Jesus to wait until after his fast to obtain food through normal means. Jesus repulsed the attack by citing a passage from the Old Testament, which reflected his devotion to life's more important matters: "Man does not live on bread alone" (Deut 8:3). In his experience of hunger, Jesus realized that God was teaching him this important lesson.[1]

Second, the devil tested Jesus on whether or not he was susceptible to pride and had a potential thirst for power—ultimately, testing his loyalty to the Father. Showing Jesus all the kingdoms of the world and their splendor, the devil offered them to Jesus in return for his obeisance and worship. Again and again the nation of Israel had succumbed to this temptation, forsaking God and worshiping foreign gods. Jesus, in contrast, resisted the devil's temptation. He revealed to Satan his intense devotion to God alone by citing a portion from the Law: "Fear the LORD your God, serve him only" (Deut 6:13).

Finally, the tempter tried to compel Jesus to test God's devotion to him, perhaps to silence any lingering doubts, by challenging Jesus to jump from a high elevation and thus force God to rescue him. As part of his strategy, the devil even reminded Jesus of a divine promise that he would never be harmed. Jesus, so in tune with God's written revelation of his will, resisted (now for the last time) by expressing his desire not to put God to the test. Jesus verbalized the content of God's command, recorded in Deuteronomy 6:16: "Do not test the LORD your God."[2] As Richard France observes, "the Son of God can only live in a relationship of trust which needs no test."[3]

Failing both to influence Jesus at this time and thwart God's purpose through him, the devil leaves Jesus. Jesus is victorious over the devil. This is one of the reasons Jesus could later tell his disciples that "the prince of this world . . . has no hold on me, but the world must learn that I love the Father and that I do exactly what my Father has commanded me" (Jn 14:30).

The use of Scripture was the vital part of Jesus' successful resistance of the devil's enticements. In fact, Jesus' only words recorded by the Gospel writers in their recounting of the temptation scenes are Jesus' quotation of the three passages from Deuteronomy. As we will see later, Paul also counseled Christians about the significant role of God's Word ("the sword of the Spirit") in resisting the devil (Eph 6:17). It is important, however, to recognize that Jesus was not using the Scripture in some magical sense, like holding up a crucifix, to ward off the evil one. The Scripture Jesus chose was not only appropriate to the nature of the temptation, but each passage also accurately reflected the Son's devotion to the Father. The texts convey the unity of purpose that the Son shared with the Father.

A second aspect of Jesus' victory in facing supernatural temptation can be attributed to the Spirit's work in his life. Luke emphasizes that when Jesus went out to the desert, he was "full of the Holy Spirit" (Lk 4:1). The temptation scenes also follow Jesus' baptism by John, at which time the Spirit descended on him in a visible form like a dove (Mk 1:9-11; Mt 3:13-17; Lk 3:21-22; Jn 1:29-34). Paul also reaffirms the experience of being filled with the Spirit as prerequisite to resisting the onslaught of evil forces (Eph 5:18; 6:10-20).

The temptation of Jesus by the devil was intensely personal. No other person stood by his side as he experienced the wooing of the evil one in the Judean desert. Were it not for Jesus relating his experience with the devil to his disciples, we would have no knowledge of it. Fortunately Jesus has provided us with an account of his struggle, an account that influenced the apostle Paul's words on spiritual warfare and serves as a relevant model for the church today.

Unlike the people of Israel, who were put to the test in the desert after the exodus and failed, Jesus succeeded. Unlike Adam, who gave in to the devil's enticement in the garden, Jesus resisted. He continued to resist to the point of his death—a death that secured our atonement and reconciliation with the Father.

Jesus on the Attack—Exorcism

Jesus' activity in casting out evil spirits was one of the most remarkable things about him to the people of his day. The Gospel writers devoted substantial portions of their narrative, recounting Jesus' engagement with these spirits. It is thus important to draw out the meaning of this significant activity of Jesus.

As Jesus began his ministry, he described himself as fulfilling the prophecy of Isaiah 61:1-2:

The Spirit of the Lord is on me, because he has anointed me to preach good news to the poor. *He has sent me to proclaim freedom for the prisoners* and recovery of sight for the blind, to release the oppressed, to proclaim the year of the Lord's favor. (Lk 4:18-19, italics mine)

The Father sent Jesus to proclaim a message of liberation—liberation for people enslaved to sin and trapped in the bondage and oppression of Satan's kingdom. Jesus interpreted Isaiah's "prisoners" not as literal criminals in chains serving their just sentence for a crime (as, for example, imprisoned debtors). Jesus came to set free all those imprisoned by sin—prisoners of Satan.

While Luke used the Isaiah passage to set the stage for his entire Gospel,[4] Jesus' conflict with Satan and his evil powers has a major part in all of the Gospels. Many commentators have remarked on the overtones of Jesus' message of liberation for the forgiveness of sins, but surprisingly few have brought out the spiritual dimension of this liberation—freedom from captivity to Satan's kingdom.

Significantly, in Luke's Gospel, immediately after Jesus preached in the synagogue at Nazareth, he released a man from control of a demon in the synagogue of Capernaum (Lk 4:31-37; Mk 1:23-28). This incident is the first time we see Jesus on the attack. He exerted his divine power to free the man from the tyrannizing influence of the evil spirit.

In stark contrast to the elaborate methods of the exorcists of his time, Jesus merely uttered a simple command: "Be quiet and come out of him." Typically, Jewish and Hellenistic exorcistic formulas consisted of invoking numerous deities, using magical names (unintelligible combinations of letters), the use of some kind of magical material (such as a gem or a piece of lead) and often the performance of some rite. Jesus, however, is able to cast out the spirits by his own authority, much to the surprise of the leaders of the Capernaum synagogue and the crowds.

This manifestation of his power often resulted in a popular notoriety that Jesus was quick to suppress. Nevertheless, Jesus healed many from their direct demonic affliction. In addition to the specific accounts of exorcism in the Gospels are a number of summary statements recounting Jesus' frontal assault on Satan's kingdom. Mark, for instance, tells us that at Capernaum, "the whole city had gathered at the door. And he healed many who were ill with various diseases, and cast out many demons" (Mk 1:33-34 NASB). Exorcism was an ongoing part of Jesus' earthly ministry.

Jesus gives a parabolic explanation of the meaning of his exorcisms in all three synoptic Gospels (Mk 3:20-30; Mt 12:22-30; Lk 11:14-23). His statement came in response to an incisive accusation from Jewish authorities from Jerusalem. They accused Jesus of being possessed by Beelzebub (an alias of Satan) and of performing his many exorcisms by the ruler of the demons.

In response Jesus contends, first of all, that it is foolish to think Satan would work against his own purposes by fighting against his own forces. If he does, he is finished! Second, Jesus relates the following parable:

> No one can enter a strong man's house and carry off his posses-
> sions unless he first ties up the strong man. Then he can rob his
> house. (Mk 3:27; see also Mt 12:29; Lk 11:21-22.)

From the context of Jesus' words it is clear "the strong man" is a reference to Satan, and his "house" corresponds to his kingdom. "Possessions" are Satan's greatest value and are not things, but people. Satan holds unbelieving humanity in bondage. Christ has come to engage this "strong man" and plunder his house; that is, to release the captives in Satan's kingdom.

This passage thus becomes a very important testimony to Jesus' mission. It provides additional clarification to the nature of the atonement. Jesus came not only to deal with the problem of sin in the world, but also to deal with God's prime supernatural opponent—Satan himself!

Jesus' many exorcisms clearly demonstrate his power over the evil one. They also provide numerous examples of Jesus' ability to "bind" Satan and "rob his house." In Mark's account of the Gerasene demoniac, a man plagued with perhaps thousands of demons, it is highly significant to note that "no one could bind him" (Mk 5:1-20, esp. v. 3). With only the concise command, "come out of the man, you unclean spirit," Jesus freed this man from horrific demonic influence.

The exorcisms, however, were not adequate by themselves to deal in any decisive way with the devil and his powers; that is, to "tie him up." They can only foreshadow an event of much greater importance. Early Christian tradition uniformly looks to the cross/resurrection event as the point of fundamental significance in Christ's conflict with the powers (Jn 12:31-33; Acts 2:34-35; Eph 1:20-22; Col 2:15; Phil 2:9-11; Heb 2:14; 1 Jn 3:8). It was through this event that Satan and his hosts were dealt the fatal blow that spelled their final doom. The "strong man" was defeated.[5]

Having defeated Satan, Christ is able to plunder his kingdom through the church's evangelistic outreach. The parable of the binding of the strong man probably provided great encouragement to the evangelistic efforts of the early church. Since Satan was in some sense "tied up" at the cross, the church (as Christ's agents) could now "carry off his possessions."

The demons themselves seemed to be aware of the significance of Christ's mission when they said to him, "Have you come to destroy us?" (Mk 1:24). This statement looks beyond their defeat at the cross to forebode their ultimate eschatological destruction at Christ's Second Coming. The strong man was indeed vanquished at the cross, but he is still active and still powerful. He has no authority over Christ and the kingdom of God—this was settled at the cross. Until the kingdom of God comes in its fullness, however, Satan will continue opposing God's people in an attempt to extend his own kingdom. The church needs to watch, pray and proclaim the gospel.

Matthew and Luke make it clear that the exorcisms are in some way a sign of the presence of God's kingdom. Jesus once told his accusers, "But if I drive out demons by the Spirit [*finger* in Luke] of God, then the kingdom of God has come upon you" (Mt 12:28; Lk 11:20). Ethelbert Stauffer explains the meaning in this way, "The Kingdom of God is present where the dominion of the adversary has been overthrown."[6] His explanation certainly does not exhaust the full meaning of God's kingdom, but it does place an appropriate emphasis on the meaning of the kingdom in relationship to the work of Satan. Susan Garrett remarks, "As the Kingdom of Satan diminishes, the Kingdom of God grows proportionately. . . . Every healing, exorcism, or raising from the dead is a loss for Satan and a gain for God."[7]

The World Is Under the Authority of Satan
Satan is called a "strong man" because of his wide-ranging power and authority. He is the ruler *(archōn)* over an entire army of evil spirits (Mk 3:22), and he possesses a measure of authority over all the kingdoms of the world (Mt 4:8-9; Lk 4:6). The Johannine literature has much to say about Satan as a "ruler." The Gospel of John refers to Satan as "the prince *(archōn)* of this world" three times (Jn 12:31; 14:30; 16:11). In his first epistle, John states the idea most forcefully:

"We know that we are children of God, and that the whole world is under the control of the evil one" (1 Jn 5:19).

His world rule does not mean the whole world is involved in the occult or is engaged in grossly immoral conduct. It does mean the world stands apart from God; and therefore, the world has affiliation with the devil. In Jesus' teaching (and subsequently in John's teaching), there are only two masters—God and Satan. Those who have not professed Christ are still a part of Satan's kingdom. John records Jesus' comments to a group of Jewish religious leaders, who had rejected him: "If God were your Father, you would love me, for I came from God and now am here. . . . You belong to your father, the devil, and you want to carry out your father's desire" (Jn 8:42, 44). A similar thought is conveyed in Jesus' parable of the weeds, where the weeds represent "the sons of the evil one" (Mt 13:24-30, 36-43). The weeds, sown by the devil, grow alongside the wheat ("sons of the kingdom") until the end of the age when there is a separation and the grain is harvested and the weeds are burned.

John's Gospel contains no reflection on the meaning of Satan's title, "prince of this world." The term "prince," or *archōn*, was used widely to denote the highest official in a city or a region in the Greco-Roman world. Even in the Greek Old Testament *archōn* was used for a national, local or tribal leader. This common political term was first applied to the hierarchical organization of the supernatural realm in the book of Daniel (10:13, 20-21 and 12:1), where it refers to the chief or leader among the angelic powers. In the synoptic Gospels the devil is described as the "chief ruler" *(archōn)* of the demons (Mt 9:34; 12:24; Mk 3:22; Lk 11:15). In John's Gospel this rulership is extended to the entire world. For John the "world" refers to human society in terms of its organized opposition to God. It appears that while Satan's influence and control is primarily over people, it also extends to human institutions and organizations, the social and political order.

Victory on the Cross
As seen in the parable of the strong man recorded in all three synoptic Gospels, Christ's death and resurrection marked the decisive defeat of Satan. The Gospel of John also looks to the paramount significance of the cross in terms of its implications for Satan. In John's recounting of Jesus' passion prediction, Jesus said, "Now is the time for judgment on this world; now the prince of this world will be

driven out" (Jn 12:31). Later in the same Gospel, Jesus speaks of the Spirit convicting the world concerning judgment, "because the prince of this world now stands condemned" (Jn 16:11). In his epistle John summarizes Jesus' mission, which culminated in the death and resurrection of Christ, by affirming that "the reason the Son of God appeared was to destroy the devil's work" (1 Jn 3:8b).

In speaking of the devil being "driven out" as a result of the cross, John is not representing Jesus as a helpless romantic who cannot recognize existing evil in the world. Neither should the statement be interpreted as Satan's expulsion from heaven (cf. Rev 12:7-9). Rather, Jesus is speaking of a definite loss of authority by Satan over the world.[8] Christians face the unique tension of having conquered Satan by virtue of their identification with Christ's work on the cross (cf. 1 Jn 2:13-14) and needing to continue the war with Satan while they still live in this world during the present evil age. New Testament scholars describe this paradox as an "eschatological tension"—the "now" but "not yet" of our Christian lives. The new age has dawned, the kingdom of God is present, but only partially. Satan continues his hostile activity, but he has no power, authority or control over those who appropriate their new identity in Christ. Thus Jesus exhorts his disciples to "remain in me" as a branch remains in a vine (Jn 15:1-8).

Now that Satan has been "cast out," Christ can build his church. In John 12, Jesus continues by saying, "But I, when I am lifted up from the earth, will draw all men to myself" (Jn 12:32). Jesus now exercises a saving sovereignty over the world, but not a political sovereignty.

The cross also condemns Satan (Jn 16:11). There will be an ultimate future condemnation of Satan, but on the basis of the cross. Raymond Brown comments, "The very fact that Jesus stands justified before the Father means that Satan has been condemned and has lost his power over the world."[9] Jesus' death may have seemed to be a major victory for his enemies, but it had a surprising outcome. Jesus was raised, redemption was procured, and Satan was condemned. Moreover, Jesus is still present after his death in the person of the *Paraclete*, the Holy Spirit (Jn 16:7).

Whereas, in the exorcisms Jesus liberated a few individuals from the power of the devil, by his death and resurrection he liberated the entire race. All who exercise faith in Christ, and "abide" in him, can share in his victory over Satan and the powers of darkness.

The Mission of the Disciples

Jesus procured the redemption of all who believe in him through his death on the cross. He now continues his redemptive mission to the world through the agency of the church.

He prepared the Twelve for this proclamational mission by sending them on a preliminary mission of a limited scope (Mt 10:1-16; Mk 6:7-11; Lk 9:1-6). He commissioned them to announce the coming of the kingdom and gave them authority over demons, as well as the ability to heal.[10] These accounts prefigure the post-Pentecost ministry of the Twelve.[11] While some of the specific instructions contained in the accounts give the impression of being limited to a particular situation and time, "their preservation by Mark and the other Evangelists indicates that the basic principles in them were regarded as of lasting value for the church."[12]

At a later occasion Luke records the Lord's commissioning of seventy-two disciples to embark on a similar mission (Lk 10:1-23). Again they are told to proclaim the nearness of the kingdom and given authority over demons. In describing their return from the mission, Luke highlights the fact that these disciples were quite thrilled with their supernatural authority: "Lord, even the demons submit to us in your name" (Lk 10:17).

Jesus gave a threefold response to their report. First, he revealed to them that he had watched Satan "fall like lightning from heaven" as they carried out their mission (Lk 10:18). This image does not refer to an ecstatic vision that Jesus had of Satan's fall from heaven either in the past (his initial rebellion) or in the future (either at the cross or at Jesus' Second Coming). Jesus is revealing how their aggressive confrontation with Satan's kingdom was meeting with victory over Satan's power and influence.[13] Satan had stormed from heaven in rage.

Second, Jesus reaffirmed the disciples' authority over the demonic realm. He told them that he had given them authority *(exousia)* to trample on snakes and scorpions—both symbols of demons[14]—and "to overcome all the power of the enemy" (Lk 10:19). Since they had appropriated Christ's authority, the evil one's power could not harm them. In commenting on this verse, Ethelbert Stauffer notes, "As the Father had given the Son authority over the adversary, so the Son gives it to his disciples."[15] The same authority is bestowed on all disciples in Jesus' postresurrection commission. He told his disciples: "All authority *[exousia]* in heaven and on earth has been given to me. Therefore go and make disciples of all the nations" (Mt 28:18-19). It is the promised presence of Jesus himself with them as they fulfill their evangelistic commission that guarantees this authority over their foremost adversary and all the powers of darkness (Mt 28:20). Luke's book of Acts also stresses the role of the Holy Spirit in empowering the disciples to evangelize the world (see especially Acts 1:8).

Surely the disciples needed divine power to give them boldness and zeal in proclaiming the gospel, often to hostile audiences. But their need for supernatural power and authority moves far beyond the mere physical plane of making the gospel known. A supernaturally powerful opponent, who would use every device at his disposal to prevent the spread of the gospel, confronted the early church, which required divine power in order to face this unearthly opposition. From Philip's encounter with Simon the Magician to Paul's confrontation of Elymas and the deep influence of the occult on the church in Ephesus, the book of Acts gives explicit testimony to the magnitude of this powerful antagonism.

At their return from their mission Jesus' final response to the seventy-two was designed to temper their enthusiasm about their new authority and place it in a proper perspective. Jesus said, "Do not rejoice that the spirits submit to you, but rejoice that your names are written in heaven" (Lk 10:20). Joseph Fitzmyer appropriately remarks, "Jesus directs the attention of the disciples away from thoughts about sensational success to a consideration of their heavenly status."[16] Having power to cast out demons is no guarantee that one is a Christian. In the Sermon on the Mount, Jesus said that on the judgment day many will say to him, "Lord, Lord, did we not prophesy in your name, and in your name drive out demons and perform many miracles?" Jesus then explains that he will reply to them, "I never knew you. Away from me, you evildoers" (Mt 7:22-23). The Jewish exorcists at Ephesus (Acts 19:13-16) serve as an example of those who did not know Jesus, but invoked his name in an exorcistic formula. Similar examples can be found in the Greek magical papyri. The most important matter, however, is for a person to be a true disciple and accordingly have their name registered in the book of life.

Interpreters often disagree over the extent to which (or even, if) the mission of the Twelve and the mission of the seventy-two prefigure the ministry of the church and is therefore normative for us today.

Aspects of both missions were clearly situational and unique (e.g., the enjoiner not to go to the Gentiles in Matthew's account). There should be no doubt that at least two important parts of these mission accounts do indeed prefigure the mission of the church for all generations—the fact of a proclamational mission and the authority of the disciples over demons.[17]

The book of Acts and the New Testament Epistles illustrate and confirm both points. During the ministry of Jesus, the disciples were commissioned to proclaim the nearness of God's kingdom. Jesus' death and resurrection later fulfilled the content of the "good news" about the kingdom. After Jesus' resurrection (Acts 1:3), and after he spoke to the disciples for forty days about God's kingdom, the disciples proclaimed "the good news of the kingdom of God and the name of Jesus Christ" (Acts 8:12; 14:22; 19:8; 20:25; 28:23). In fact, the book of Acts ends with Paul in Rome, where "boldly and without hindrance he preached the kingdom of God and taught about the Lord Jesus Christ" (Acts 28:31).

In the book of Acts Luke also gives his readers many inspiring examples of Spirit-filled people overcoming Satanic opposition to spread the gospel. In a complementary fashion the writers of the Epistles spend much effort in affirming the identity of believers in Christ, which entails their authority over the powers of darkness.

It remains for believers today to continue fulfilling their proclamational mission with zeal and to appropriate the power and authority that is theirs by virtue of the very presence of Christ in their lives.

Ultimate Victory for Christ and His People

Each of the Gospel writers speaks of Jesus' announcement of his planned glorious return. Mark writes that all "will see the Son of Man coming in clouds with great power and glory" (Mk 13:26; see also Mt 24:30; Lk 24:27). His return will set in motion a series of events of cosmic proportions. The Lord will gather his people from every part of the earth and inaugurate a time of judgment and condemnation upon all evil (see especially Mt 25:31-46). Jesus specifically says the devil and his angels will be consigned to the torment of an eternal fire that is prepared for them (Mt 25:41).

While Jesus said little else about this doom of the powers of darkness, the Apocalypse of John develops this theme further. The seer's vision of the conclusion of Christ's thousand-year reign includes an account of Satan's doom. Ultimately the devil will be thrown into a "lake of burning sulphur" (also called "the second death"), where he will face an eternal punishment (Rev 20:10).

This message of hope is for all who know Christ. The grievous persistence of evil in the world, largely instigated by the devil and his powers of darkness, will soon meet its end.

PART II
Paul's Teaching
on the Powers

WHAT THE APOSTLE PAUL HAS TO SAY ABOUT THE POWERS OF darkness should be formative for our thinking as Christians. For those of us who regard his letters as containing theology that is normative for belief and practice, Paul's teaching on the powers should shape and refine our world view. A careful assessment of his teaching on this topic is therefore essential, especially since our modern world view is often thought to be at odds with the biblical teaching on evil spirits.

How is Paul to be understood on this issue? Does he disagree with the prevailing cultural assumption that evil spirits do not exist? What does he think about the idea of evil spirits influencing the affairs of humanity and opposing God's plan of salvation? How does Paul instruct his churches to respond to those forces?

These questions are best answered when we see Paul and his letters in their first-century religious and cultural context. After we investigate the source of Paul's teaching and the manner of his response to the early Christians in the light of their setting, we will be able to clarify the extent to which Paul agreed with common conceptions about evil spirits and where he differed. Most important of all, we will be able to see, from his perspective, how believers should view the realm of the powers of darkness in light of their relationship with Christ.

6
What Are the Powers?

S INCE THE ENLIGHTENMENT, MANY SCHOLARS HAVE "DEMYTHOLOGIZED" THE powers of darkness in an attempt to relate scriptural statements that refer to evil forces to modern life. For such scholars the idea of the demonic is a cultural or mythical way of referring to the evil thoughts and actions of an individual person or a corrupt social institution. They claim that principalities and powers are identical to the other hostile forces in Paul's letters, specifically the powers of sin, the law, flesh and death.

What exactly did Paul think? Did he conceive of the powers as spirits having their own independent existence, or did he regard them as mere projections of the abstract notions of personal, corporate and political evil?

They Are Real!
On this issue Paul was certainly a man of his times. In line with popular Jewish and pagan thought he too assumed that the world is filled with evil spirits who are hostile to humanity. He never showed any doubt about the existence of such a realm. Instead, he taught his churches how to live and minister in a world where these powerful supernatural opponents exist.

We need to be more precise, however. It is not enough just to observe that he believed in evil spirits; we need to see what he really thought about them. It is therefore important to discern how much of the popular belief he accepted and what portions he rejected. Part of our answer to this question can be answered by looking at the varied terminology he used for the powers of darkness (see p. 218).

The Source of Paul's Vocabulary for the Powers

An important question we face is whether Paul depended primarily on the Jewish demonology of his time or on an understanding of evil spirits rooted more in pagan popular belief. It is not adequate to say Paul derived his terms for evil spirits exclusively from the Old Testament, although quite a few of the words he used appear in the Greek Old Testament (the LXX, or Septuagint). While the terms "Satan" and "devil" are common in the Old Testament, the name "Belial" never appears (see 2 Cor 6:15). Whereas the word translated "powers" *(dynameis)* is quite frequent in the Greek Old Testament, Paul's most common expressions for the powers, *archai* and *exousiai,* are never used.[1]

Most scholars believe Paul's vocabulary for the powers reflects the Jewish demonology of his own day. All of the terms Paul used for the powers can be found in Jewish documents of the Greco-Roman period. The Judaism of Paul's time had a highly developed angelology, as evidenced by the following citations from Jewish documents that contain many of the same terms used by Paul:

> And he [God] will summon all the forces *[dynameis]* of the heavens, and all the holy ones above, and the forces of the Lord—the cherubim, seraphim, ophanim, all the angels of governance *[archai],* the Elect One, and the other forces *[exousiai]* on earth and over the water. (*1 Enoch* 61:10)[2]

> And I saw there [in the seventh heaven] an exceptionally great light, and all the fiery armies of the great archangels, and the incorporeal forces *[dynameis]* and the dominions *[kyriotetes]* and the origins *[archai]* and the authorities *[exousiai],* the cherubim and the seraphim and the many-eyed thrones *[thronoi].* (*2 Enoch* 20:1)[3]

> There with him [God] are the thrones *[thronoi])* and authorities *[exousiai];* there praises to God are offered eternally. (*Testament of Levi* 3:8)

While all three texts refer to the angelic hierarchy surrounding God's throne, the Jews believed the same hierarchy existed in the kingdom of evil. Furthermore, many of these terms were commonly used to refer to various ranks of human leaders in governmental positions of authority. The angelic kingdom was widely believed to be structured in an analogous way to earthly political kingdoms.

Although Paul used many terms for the angelic powers known to Judaism, this does not mean that what he had to say about the powers of darkness would have been incomprehensible to the non-Jew. While "principalities" *(archai)* and "authorities" *(exousiai)* seem to be uniquely Jewish expressions for the unseen realm, many of the other words he used were also used by Gentiles to refer to the world of spirits and invisible powers. Words like "powers" *(dynameis)*, "dominions" *(kyriotētes)*, "thrones" *(thronoi)*, "angels" *(angeloi)*, "world rulers" *(kosmokratores)*, "demons" *(daimonia)*, "elemental spirits" *(stoicheia)* and "rulers" *(archontes)* were known and used by pagans, as evidenced in their magical and astrological texts.[4]

It is very important to remember that a very thin line separated Jewish and gentile religious belief in many quarters during the first century. On the one hand, many Jews practiced magic, believed in astrology and borrowed religious concepts from the cults of their pagan neighbors. On the other hand, the Gentiles took many religious ideas and cultic terminology from Judaism. This is seen most clearly in the Greek magical papyri, where in a magical recipe Yahweh, Solomon and Jewish angelic names are invoked together with Hekate, Helios, Serapis and a host of other Greek and Oriental deities. It is thus very difficult to separate what is "Jewish" and what is "Hellenistic" when the topic of good and evil spirits is approached. In some ways it becomes an unnecessary question because of the spirit of the times (Zeitgeist). All believed in the existence of good and evil spirits and shared a basically stock vocabulary for referring to it.

The matter of crucial importance then is what Paul believed to be true about this realm. In this respect Paul was deeply indebted to his Jewish heritage and the teaching of Jesus.

What About Gnosticism As the Source?

A few scholars have interpreted Paul's references to principalities, powers and authorities as the angelic rulers who control the seven planetary spheres in the Gnostic belief system. They find a striking similarity in vocabulary between Paul and Gnosticism and assume Paul had taken these terms from Gnosticism. For this and other reasons these interpreters then contend that the readers of Paul's letters were struggling with Gnostic influence, and thus Paul was writing to counteract this encroaching and dangerous teaching. This contention has been especially true in the history of the interpretation of Ephesians and Colossians, which have sometimes been regarded as Paul's teaching against Gnosticism; or, as in the interpretation of a few scholars, the author of these letters (often considered not to be Paul) betrays the influence of Gnosticism on himself!

The difficulty with any Gnostic interpretation is that there is no clear evidence supporting even the existence of Gnosticism prior to the advent of Christianity. One evangelical scholar, Edwin Yamauchi, has presented a very convincing case that Gnosticism did not come into existence as a coherent system of religious thought until after A.D. 70, and perhaps not even until after A.D. 135.[5] A number of scholars are pointing to these two dates because they are convinced that Gnosticism actually arose in Judaism and that the catalyst for its inception came from disappointed Messianism associated with the decisive victory of the Romans in the two Jewish wars.[6]

Rooting the origin of Gnosticism in the second century A.D., however, does not mean that many of the concepts found in the developed Gnostic systems of thought (of the second to fourth centuries A.D.) did not exist in the first century A.D.[7] Gnosticism was not an accumulation of entirely new concepts, but drew from a wide variety of religious traditions. Gnosticism displays an extraordinary eclecticism, or borrowing of ideas. It adopted its central concepts and ideas from the multiplicity of Greco-Roman religions, astrology, magic, Persian and Iranian religion, Judaism, and at many points, even Christianity. The terminology for the angelic powers in Gnosticism probably came from the reservoir of terms for spirits, angels, demons and gods, which virtually all religious traditions shared. In Gnosticism, however, these powers were given well-defined functions as rulers of ascending planetary spheres. This appears to be the unique contribution of Gnosticism to the history of religion (influenced strongly at this point by Mithraism). Therefore, Gnosticism is not as relevant for understanding Paul's references to the principalities, powers and authorities as some scholars suppose.

They Are Part of Satan's Kingdom
Paul's teaching on the powers called for a significant change in outlook for many of his gentile converts. In popular belief, and especially in magic, they were accustomed to thinking there were "good" and "evil" spirits. In magic it was important to know the names of good and helpful spirits who could be called upon to help and provide

protection from evil spirits.

In line with the Old Testament, contemporary Judaism and the teaching of Jesus, Paul taught that there was one primary figurehead of evil, Satan, who commanded a host of "spiritual forces of wickedness." Paul would not have accepted the various distinctions between good and evil spirits made by his gentile converts in their pre-Christian experience. All the spirits called on and revered in magic, astrology and the pagan cults were evil and "demonic."

Satan, or the devil, is "the god of this age" (2 Cor 4:4). While God is ultimately sovereign since he is the creator of everything that exists, Satan has been allowed to exercise a great amount of evil activity on the earth. John recorded Jesus calling attention to the devil's present authority by describing him as "the prince *[archōn]* of this world" (Jn 14:30; 16:11). While Satan's authority is not absolute, neither is it trifling. He wields all kinds of destructive influence over all levels of life and exerts his greatest hostility against God's redemptive purpose in and through the Lord Jesus Christ.

According to Paul, Satan holds unbelieving humanity in his captivity. He "has blinded the minds of unbelievers, so that they cannot see the light of the gospel of the glory of Christ" (2 Cor 4:4). Even at the end of his apostolic career Paul's convictions had not changed. He regarded those opposing the ministry of the gospel as having fallen into a trap of the devil "who has taken them captive to do his will" (2 Tim 2:26). Elsewhere he described Satan's activity as holding unbelievers in "slavery." Prior to the work of God's redemption the Galatians "were in slavery under the basic principles *[stoicheia]* of the world" (Gal 4:3). At this point Paul brought into view Satan's powerful assistants who carry out the same malignant purposes as their leader. In Ephesians Paul described the captivity in terms of unbelievers being "dead" in their transgressions and sins. This was when they followed "the ruler of the kingdom of the air" (Eph 2:1-2).

Through blinding, holding captive, enslaving and keeping people in the sphere of death, the work of Satan and his powers runs counter at every point to the loving, reconciling and life-giving purpose of God in Christ. Satan has a multiplicity of schemes to defraud and take advantage of people even after they become Christians (2 Cor 2:11; Eph 6:11). Although his character is dark and evil, he often presents himself in a very positive light to further his deceitful work (2 Cor 11:14).

They Are Involved in the World Religions

The gentile converts to Christianity faced a very important issue: What kind of perspective were they now to have on their former gods and goddesses? How were the worshipers of Dionysus, for instance, to view their god now that they were Christians? Was he truly a god, but of a somewhat lesser stature than the one God? Or, was he merely a stone image who represented no real divine being?

Paul specifically addressed this issue in his first letter to the Corinthians (1 Cor 8 and 10).[8] Two questions faced the Corinthian church, which elicited the apostle Paul's response. They were concerned with (1) whether they could eat a meal in the temple of one of the local gods, and (2) whether it was permissible to eat meat that had previously been sacrificed to a god or goddess.

There was a difference of opinion among the Corinthian believers on both of these issues. It appears some of the more confident Christians, knowing that an idol has no real existence (8:4), had no scruples with going into an idol temple and eating a meal (8:10).[9] The result of such action, however, was the spiritual demise of other Christians. Seeing their more assured fellow believers exercise this freedom gave the "weaker" Christians the courage to do the same and eat food offered to a god (probably in one of the temples). A crisis of conscience plagued the weaker Christians, with some returning to idolatry. It is very likely that this situation was not merely a potential problem Paul was trying to forestall, but that a few from the Corinthian church had actually returned to their pagan worship.

Since Paul was understandably very concerned about this situation, which was "destroying" (8:11) some of these precious believers, he set forth a lengthy argument advocating that the Corinthians should completely cut their ties with the pagan temples,[10] and that the stronger believers should be willing to waive their right to eat idol food out of sensitivity to the conscience of weaker Christians.

One of the central features of Paul's argument is that there is a demonic character to non-Christian religions. He agreed with the informed Corinthians in principle that an idol has no real, independent existence (8:4). For the Christian, he concurred, there is no God but the one true God; the pagan deities—Apollo, Isis, Sarapis and the rest—are so-called gods. Nevertheless, Paul went on to affirm some kind of real existence for these gods, noting, "indeed there are many 'gods' and many 'lords' " (8:5). In one sense he did believe in the existence of other "gods" and "lords," but in a qualitatively different way than those who worshiped these beings. Paul will later contend that the images represent demons (10:20-21) and not true divinities; they are not to be thought of on the same level as the one God. In another sense, however, they are real gods and lords in that they are subjectively believed to be such by those who worship them;[11] they are "real" to their worshipers. Also, for the "weak" Christians at Corinth, these gods were still quite real in their "conscience" or in their "awareness." Their "intellectual conviction that there was only one God had not been fully assimilated emotionally."[12] The convictions of their hearts had not caught up with their cognitive understanding. We cannot underestimate how difficult it must have been for people accustomed to believing in the reality of many gods suddenly to transform those years of deeply entrenched religious conviction into a monotheistic framework. The fact that these pagan gods really are "nothing," however, does not make them any less dangerous.

Paul later contended that there is a close connection between idolatry and demonic activity. He argued, "Do I mean then that a sacrifice offered to an idol is anything, or that an idol is anything? No, but the sacrifices of pagans are offered to demons, not to God, and I do not want you to be participants with demons" (10:19-20). In Paul's mind there are indeed supernatural beings associated with pagan idolatry—the powers of darkness! In the span of two verses Paul used the word *demon* four times. He saw demons as the actual recipients of the sacrificed meat (10:20). By eating and drinking in the pagan temples, the Corinthians were drinking "the cup of demons" and eating at "the table of demons" (10:21). In essence they were having "fellowship" *(koinōnia)* with demons, a fellowship that should be reserved for their relationship to Christ alone (1:9). Communion with the Lord Jesus at his table should completely replace participation at the table of demons. For Paul, then, there was an intensely demonic character to pagan religions in general.

For Paul this position was not at all novel. It represented the established position of Judaism. Moses' song of praise to God, reflecting on the idolatrous behavior of the Jews while they were in the wilderness, proclaims, "They made him jealous with their foreign gods and angered him with their detestable idols. They sacrificed to demons, which are not God" (Deut 32:16-17). This attitude toward idols is reflected elsewhere in the Old Testament and in the Judaism of the

New Testament period.[13] Jewish belief closer to the time of Paul is well illustrated in a second-century B.C. Jewish document, which, at this point, comments on the idolatry of the sons of Noah:

> And they made for themselves molten images, and everyone worshiped the icon which they made for themselves as a molten image. And they began making graven images and polluted likeness. And cruel spirits assisted them and led them astray so that they might commit sin and pollution. And the prince [of these demons], Mastema, acted forcefully to do all of this. And he sent other spirits to those who were set under his hand to practice all error and sin and all transgression, to destroy, to cause to perish and to pour out blood upon the earth. (*Jubilees* 11:4-5)[14]

Another Jewish document, dating just prior to the time of Christ, connects idolatry to witchcraft and the demonic: "I have much grief, my children, because of the lewdness and witchcrafts and idolatries that you will practice against the kingdom, following mediums, soothsayers and demons of deceit" (*Testament of Judah* 23:1).[15] The Testament of Naphtali speaks of the Gentiles exchanging the worship of the Lord for idolatry, which is also connected with the demonic: "The Gentiles changed their order, having gone astray and having forsaken the Lord and they followed after stones and sticks, having followed after spirits of deceit" (*Testament of Naphtali* 3:1).[16]

In a similar way when Paul wrote to the Romans, he indicted the Gentiles for exchanging the worship of God for a lie. In his eyes they "exchanged the glory of the immortal God for images made to look like mortal man and birds and animals and reptiles" (Rom 1:23). What he said to the Corinthians in no way contradicts his statement to the Romans. Paul went beyond describing pagan gods as lifeless images to affirm that Satan and his powers of darkness have used these non-Christian religions to hold humanity in bondage.

It is perfectly clear why Paul urged the Corinthians to "flee from idolatry" (10:14). By maintaining any kind of involvement with the pagan temples, the Corinthians were exposing themselves to powerful demonic activity and compromising their allegiance to the one true God. Some were being "destroyed" by this involvement (8:11). Those with "knowledge" among the Corinthians failed to take into account the extremely dangerous influence of the hostile powers of darkness that were so closely linked to the non-Christian religions. Their baptism and observance of the Lord's table did not guarantee immunity from the treacherous activity of the demonic powers. Likewise, neither were the people of Israel immune to the deadly effects of idolatry, in spite of the fact that they too had been symbolically "baptized" and had consumed "spiritual food" and "spiritual drink" (10:1-12). Paul did make a distinction between eating in pagan temples (which he regarded as participating in idolatry) and eating in a private home food that had once been sacrificed to a god (10:23-33). For the latter case, sensitivity to weaker Christians should guide the stronger Christian; idolatry was no longer the issue. Paul, on the one hand, advised them to "eat anything sold in the meat market without raising questions of conscience" (10:25). Yet, on the other hand, he urged restraint to the person who, by eating the meat in the presence of another (weaker) Christian at the home of a nonbeliever, may offend the conscience of that weaker Christian (10:27-29).

There is much to learn from Paul's handling of this situation at Corinth that is vitally relevant for the church today, especially as we minister to people from a background of various forms of pagan worship. Gordon Fee provides a very fitting description of its relevance:

> Those who have been involved in the rescue of drug addicts and prostitutes, e.g., or of people involved in various expressions of voodoo and spirit worship, have an existential understanding of this text that others can scarcely appreciate. Many such people must be forever removed from their former associations, including returning to their former haunts for evangelism, because the grip of their former life is so tenacious. Paul took the power of the demonic seriously; hence his concern that a former idolater, by returning to his or her idolatries, will be destroyed—that is, he or she will return to former ways and be captured by them all the more, and thus eventually suffer eternal loss.[17]

One of the main principles that guided Paul's reaction to the Corinthian situation was the conviction that demons animate idolatry. For Paul idolatry consisted of worshiping any handmade image. It involved worshiping and serving anything other than the one true God. Participating in idolatry included everything attached to the service and worship of the gods. For the Corinthians this involved eating in the pagan temple.

By extension the operative principle for us today is that all the various non-Christian religions represent a special manifestation of the work of the powers of darkness to deceive people and turn their attention away from the one true God.

What Paul Does Not Say

While Paul has much to say about the powers of darkness, there is a lot that he does not say, particularly when we read his letters against the background of the Judaism of his day. It would certainly be helpful for us to pin Paul down on a few of the issues regarding the powers; however, we will have to be content with not knowing the full extent of his thinking about evil spirits. Here are a few of the areas where Paul is silent:

1. *An explanation of the angelic rebellion and fall.* Many traditions point to God's judgment on the king of Tyre in Ezekiel 28 and on the king of Babylon in Isaiah 14 as texts that go beyond a mere description of the historical circumstances of those particular kings and impart to us insight into the rebellion of Satan and a host of angels. Much of Judaism during the Greco-Roman period pointed to Genesis 6 and the account of "the sons of God" (interpreted as angels) sleeping with mortal women and giving birth to creatures who became demonic spirits as the origin of the powers of darkness (see, for example, *1 Enoch* 6—11). Paul never endorsed or alluded to either of these traditions (or any others) regarding the origin of evil spirits. He merely assumed the presence of evil supernatural beings in the world who are hostile to God and to the church. Why? "The reason is that these problems of origin are thrown into the background by most pressing and realistic questions about the wiles of the devil in actual life."[18]

2. *The names of the angelic powers.* We have seen that much of the Jewish literature current at the time of Paul (especially the apocalyptic literature) focused on identifying the powers by name, such as Ruax, Barsafael, Artosael and Belbel. Apart from a single reference to Satan as Belial (2 Cor 6:15), Paul has no concern to name the spirits. For him this would likely be a worthless undertaking, since they would all respond to Christ's authority.

3. *The order within the angelic hierarchy.* While Paul used many of the categories for angelic beings found within Jewish apocalyptic texts, he never gave any insight into the relative ranks of the principalities, powers and authorities. The Jewish *Testament of Adam* lists the angelic powers according to their various orders—from the lowest to the highest—giving their respective functions. The Testament gives the lowest

order as the angels, followed by archangels, archons, authorities, powers, dominions, and then the highest orders, thrones, seraphim and cherubim. Paul's varied references to the powers shows no concern at all with the respective ranks or orders. Again, Paul's concern was primarily functional; that is, he wanted his churches to know that there are powerful angelic beings who assail Christians, and they should be prepared to respond to them.

4. *The activities of certain demons and how they are thwarted.* Some forms of Judaism considered it important to know the precise authority that evil spirits had over people and the manner in which they could be overcome. For instance, an evil spirit named "Lix Tetrax" was believed to promote disunity and start fires. Only through the work and authority of the good archangel Azael could the evil activity of Lix Tetrax be thwarted (*Testament of Solomon* 7:1-8). In contrast the apostle Paul pointed to the Lord Jesus Christ alone as the source of the believers' authority over the powers of darkness. He never alluded to the need for invoking angels or possessing special knowledge about the function of the various evil spirits.

5. *Territories ruled by evil angels.* The book of Daniel reveals that good and evil angels have been set over certain countries. Specifically, Daniel spoke of evil angels who exercise influence over Persia and Greece, whereas the good angel Michael fights against these angels on behalf of Israel. Although Paul showed a great deal of dependence on the book of Daniel for some of his terms and concepts (including the term *archōn*), Paul himself never connected the powers of darkness with any specific country or territory. For instance, he never entreated God to thwart the angelic prince over Rome or to bind the demonic ruler over Corinth. This may be explained in part by the fact that he normally spoke in rather comprehensive terms when he referred to the powers; for example, he lumped them all together and spoke of Christ's supremacy or the believer's authority over them. It is likely that, for Paul, it was not a matter of great importance for a believer to identify precisely the evil angel wielding the supreme authority over a territory in the demonic hierarchy. What Paul stressed is the recognition that there are powerful demonic emissaries who attack the church and hinder its mission and that they can be overcome only through reliance on the power of God.

7

The Defeat of the Powers
at the Cross

*T*HE CROSS OF CHRIST IS THE PIVOTAL POINT OF SALVATION HISTORY. THIS is true, not only in the sense that Christ made satisfaction for sin through his blood, but also in the fact that Christ won a decisive victory over the evil powers.

The Ultimate Sovereignty of the Creator

While Christ and the church are represented throughout the New Testament as being in conflict with the powers, never were these opposing forces free and independent of God's absolute sovereignty. God is sovereign because he is the Creator. When Paul prayed, he addressed God as the Father "from whom his whole family in heaven and on earth derives its name" (Eph 3:15). Every member of each division in the angelic hierarchy "derives a name" from God in the sense that its identity and authority comes from him. Every grouping in the hierarchy of angelic beings, both good and evil, receives its life and being from God the Father. He is truly the Father in that he is the source of all life.

Nowhere in Paul's writings is the sovereignty of the Creator with respect to the powers brought out more clearly and forcefully than in Colossians 1:15-20. In this passage all of the Creator's functions are attributed to Christ upon whom "God was pleased to have all of his fullness dwell." Christ is praised for creating the universe and sustaining it as well as moving it toward a time of consummation that will be characterized by universal reconciliation. Paul can legitimately extol Christ's sovereignty over the powers because Christ created them all.

Paul never envisioned a time when the Creator would lose control over his creation. Nor did he reflect upon a time when the forces of darkness would threaten to overwhelm God's providence and authority. God has always retained control, and he remains in control while continuing to unfold his purpose in history. For Paul he is the God "who works out everything in conformity with the purpose of his will" (Eph 1:11). Neither the stars nor the astral spirits—commonly believed to control human destiny—can countermand God's plans. Only the electing and redeeming God, who chose a people to be his own before the creation of the world, has control over history and human destiny.

The Attempt to Ruin God's Redemptive Plan (1 Cor 2:6-8)

Paul gives us a brief glimpse at a moment in time when the powers thought they could forever thwart the redemptive purpose of God. Another Christian writer, the apostle John, revealed that Satan had wanted to speed Christ's journey to the cross by entering Judas so he could betray Christ to the officials (Jn 13:27).[1] Paul confirms John's account of Satan's intent, disclosing that the powers of darkness were convinced they could neutralize God's purposes by precipitating Christ's death. Paul writes:

> We do, however, speak a message of wisdom among the mature, but not the wisdom of this age or of the rulers *(archontes)* of this age, who are coming to nothing. No, we speak of God's secret wisdom, a wisdom that has been hidden and that God destined for our glory before time began. None of the rulers of this age understood it, for if they had, they would not have crucified the Lord of glory. (1 Cor 2:6-8)

This passage contributes three important insights into our understanding of the powers. First, their knowledge of God's plan is limited—they were not aware of precisely how God would inaugurate his method of redemption through Christ. Paul states it plainly, "None of the rulers of this age understood it." God did not reveal to these supernatural beings his "secret wisdom" (literally, his "wisdom in a mystery"). The intricacies of the plan of salvation were kept hidden, not only from humanity, but also from the angelic realm. The satanic opposition thus naively believed putting Jesus to death was the way to do away with the Son of God who had come to fulfill his Father's will and inaugurate his kingdom.

Second, the demonic rulers are facing impending doom (1 Cor 2:6). Paul asserts that the rulers of this age "are coming to nothing" (NIV), "are passing away" (NASB), "are declining to their end" (NEB). Paul here employed a strong word *(katargeō)*, which is generally used to mean "render powerless," "abolish" and "wipe out."[2] Ironically, this is true of the powers because the cross of Christ marked their defeat. Although they may experience temporary victories in their ongoing hostility against the church, their ultimate doom is certain. Paul uses the same word *(katargeō)* later in his letter to the Corinthians, when he says all the hostile powers must be destroyed before "he hands over the kingdom to God the Father" (1 Cor 15:24). The demonic rulers are also described by Paul as being part "of this age." Following traditional Jewish eschatology, Paul conceived of two ages, this age and the one to come. The powers are a part of this present evil age (see Gal 1:4) from which God is rescuing his people. The demise of the powers is all the more certain because the Second Coming of Christ will mark the end of "this age." All the fullness of life in the age to come will then be experienced—and without contending with the devilish influence of the demonic rulers.

Third, the demonic rulers are intimately involved in the affairs of life by working in and through people. From the Gospel accounts it is clear that Jesus was nailed to the cross by humans—Roman soldiers following orders from the proconsul, Pontius Pilate. Jesus had been handed over to Pilate for crucifixion by the Jewish council consisting of the elders, chief priests and teachers of the law, and led by the high priests Annas and then Caiaphas. Furthermore, a crowd of people had assembled for Passover who were shouting to Pilate that Jesus should be crucified. It appears that the guilt for Jesus' death should be assigned to all of these people. Yet in this passage, Paul pointed to demonic responsibility for Jesus' death. Not all interpreters of this passage have seen it in this way. Some think Paul has in mind only the human rulers responsible for his crucifixion, usually Annas, Caiaphas and Pilate.[3] There are a number of good reasons, however, for believing Paul intended his readers to think of demonic rulers when they read this passage. First, Paul used the term "ruler" *(archōn)* elsewhere for Satan. In Ephesians 2:2, for example, Paul described Satan as "the ruler *[archōn]* of the kingdom of the air." On one other occasion, he did use the word for human rulers (Rom 13:3), but the important point to establish here is that the word was part of his vocabulary for referring to an evil spirit-being.

Second, it is more natural to interpret the demonic rulers as being "wiped out" *(katargeō)* than the human rulers. Later in the same letter he said Christ must destroy *(katargeō)* the powers of darkness ("all dominion, authority, and power") before he hands over the kingdom to God the Father (1 Cor 15:24). He also used the word *katargeō* to refer to Christ's slaying of the satanically inspired "lawless one" during the time of great distress at the end (2 Thess 2:8). He never used the word for the ultimate doom of unbelieving humanity. It is significant that the writer of Hebrews also used the word *katargeō* with reference to the evil spiritual realm—by his death Christ "destroyed" the devil (Heb 2:14).

Third, this interpretation best explains Paul's argument in this passage. In the larger context Paul was acclaiming the inscrutable wisdom of God. This wisdom is the essence of Paul's message and is imparted by revelation of the Spirit to believers. He belittled human wisdom as useless for understanding God's ways. He now advances his argument by showing that not even the angelic powers could understand the secret wisdom of God.

Fourth, Paul probably used the word *ruler* for evil angels because it was part of the wide array of terminology for evil spirits in Jewish tradition at the time. Furthermore, it likely carried the connotation of exceptional power and authority in the hierarchy of evil spirit-beings. This is especially true when we realize it was a title for Satan. The use of the word "ruler" *(archōn)* in Judaism for evil angels can be illustrated by its appearance in the second century B.C. Testament of Simeon. In this document Simeon allegedly gave the reason for his jealousy and hatred of his brother Joseph:

> In the time of my youth I was jealous of Joseph, because my father loved him more than all the rest of us. I determined inwardly to destroy him, because the Prince *[archōn]* of Error [or "deception"] blinded my mind so that I did not consider him as a brother nor did I spare Jacob, my father. (*Testament of Simeon* 2:6-7)[4]

This text also illustrates the tendency of later Judaism to rewrite patriarchal history by attributing demonic involvement to events.

Finally, the word "ruler" *[archōn]* was also part of the early Christian vocabulary for the satanic. The "prince *[archōn]* of this world" is one of John's most common expressions for the devil (see Jn 12:31; 14:30; 16:11). An example of its use by the Apostolic Fathers can be seen in the late first-century Epistle of Barnabas:

> There are two ways of teaching and of power, the one of light and
> the other of darkness. . . . On the one are stationed the light-giving
> angels of God, on the other the angels of Satan. And the one is
> Lord from all eternity and unto all eternity, whereas the other is
> Lord *(archōn)* of the season of iniquity that now is.[5]

Paul held the demonic rulers responsible for Christ's death. He assumes that these powers of Satan were working behind the scenes to control the course of events during the passion week. It was not a part of Paul's purpose to explain exactly how these demonic rulers operated. At the very least we can imagine they were intimately involved by exerting their devious influence in and through Judas, Pilate, Annas and Caiaphas, and by inciting the mob.[6]

Demonic victory over God's plan by putting Christ to death failed. The powers did not apprehend the full extent of God's wisdom—how the Father would use the death of Christ to atone for sin, raise him victoriously from the dead and create the church. Least of all did they envisage their own defeat!

Christ's Victory over the Powers (Col 2:15)

Nowhere else in the New Testament is Christ's victory over the powers of darkness given fuller expression than in Colossians 2:15: "And having disarmed the powers and authorities, he made a public spectacle of them, triumphing over them by the cross." The death and resurrection of Christ marks the beginning of their demise. Christ won a once-and-for-all victory over the powers with eternal repercussions. The details of Paul's statements are worth examining.

God Disarmed the Powers. Christ's death and resurrection deprived the evil forces of any effective power against himself or the members of his body, the church. Whereas, prior to the cross the powers could maintain a kingdom and hold humanity in slavery, Christ's work changed that. No longer can these powers exert their compelling influence over people whom Christ has claimed for himself. Christ is able to redeem people from captivity and bring them freedom because he has disarmed the powers.

How did Christ's death and resurrection accomplish this disarming? Precisely because the powers could not deter Christ from making a satisfaction for sin. By offering his life and spilling his blood, Christ could extend forgiveness of sin to his people. The powers thus lost their chief mechanism for holding people in bondage: "You were dead in your transgressions and sins . . . when you followed . . . the ruler of the kingdom of the air" (Eph 2:1-2). God's wrath was propitiated, and the offense of sin was forever taken from his sight. Christ's work gave believing humanity access to God through which they could receive a new nature and be filled with his divine enabling power. The resurrection demonstrated that even death could not be victorious over Christ. The strongest weapon in Satan's arsenal was not sufficient for conquering Christ. Neither will it prove sufficient for destroying his people.

It is doubtful Paul conceived of some lessening of Satan's ability or power by virtue of Christ's work on the cross. With an army of mighty spirits, Satan continues to be a powerful foe. The disarming of the powers occurred with respect to Christ and those who are incorporated into Christ. Satan was shown to possess inadequate power and wisdom to defeat Christ—which brings Paul to his second affirmation.

God Publicly Exposed the Powers. The cross "exposed" the relative weakness of the powers. The word Paul chose could also be translated "make an example of," "disgrace" or "mock." It seems to have been a word commonly used for the exposing and disgracing of anyone who committed adultery. This usage is seen in its only other appearance in the New Testament in Matthew 1:19, which describes the situation where Joseph did not want to "disgrace" Mary; that is, to "expose" her publicly for her supposed adultery. One ancient writer mentions a Cyprian law, "according to which an adulteress had to cut her hair and was subjected to contempt by the community."[7]

As the crucifixion of Christ approached, the powers thought they would finally kill God's own Son and put an end to his merciful saving purposes (1 Cor 2:6-8). Christ's death and resurrection, however, uncovered the foolishness of their plans. E. F. Scott gives an eloquent explanation of this "exposure" in his comments on Ephesians 3:10:

> The hostile powers had sought to frustrate the work of God, and believed they had succeeded when they conspired against Christ and brought about his Crucifixion. But unwittingly they had been mere instruments in God's hands. The Death of Christ had been the very means He had devised for the accomplishment of His plan. So it is here declared that the hostile powers, after their brief apparent triumph, had now become aware of a divine wisdom they had never dreamed of. They saw the Church arising as the result

of Christ's death, and giving effect to what they could now perceive to have been the hidden purpose of God.[8]

Having thought they could destroy Christ, the powers were astonished to find Christ rising from the dead and assuming the position of "head" over a new body of people he was bringing into union with himself. The devices of the powers could now be seen as futile by all. In Galatians 4:9, Paul certainly had adequate reason to describe the "elemental spirits" as "weak" and "miserable."

God Paraded the Powers in a Triumphal Procession. Paul now builds on the idea of a public exposure of the powers by depicting their defeat in terms of a "triumphal procession." Paul used an expression that was common in the context of a Roman military victory. When a general defeated the opposing forces and won the battle, a "triumphal procession" would occur to celebrate the victory. The successful general would lead the procession, followed by his army singing hymns of victory and jubilantly reveling in their conquest. Also in the parade would be the defeated king along with all his surviving warriors. The disheartened and subdued enemies became a public spectacle for ridicule, with their subjugation paraded for all to see.[9] In a similar fashion, God has thus put the principalities and powers on public display, revealing their powerlessness before Christ. New Testament scholar Eduard Lohse comments, "As their devastating defeat is shown to the whole world, the infinite superiority of Christ is demonstrated."[10]

Christ's death and resurrection thus represents his decisive victory over the powers of darkness. This truth is strongly attested elsewhere in the New Testament. The writer to the Hebrews also brings this fact out by highlighting the leader of the powers, Satan: "He [Christ] too shared in their humanity so that by his death he might destroy him who holds the power of death—that is, the devil" (Heb 2:14). In one of his letters, John affirms: "The reason the Son of God appeared was to destroy the devil's work" (1 Jn 3:8).

We would be reading too much into the passages if we imagined some kind of visible battle between the powers and Christ while he was on the cross, which represented the culmination of Christ's conflict with the powers. It was their last-ditch effort to destroy the one on whom the hope for the salvation of the world lay. They were indeed successful in seeing Jesus put to death. In God's infinite wisdom, however, this was his divine method for procuring salvation for all who believe. Little did the evil powers realize that Jesus would rise from the dead.

The Supremacy of Christ (Eph 1:15-23)

The divine exaltation of Jesus Christ soon followed his resurrection. God installed Jesus to a position of power "at his right hand in the heavenly realms, far above all rule, authority, power, and dominion" (Eph 1:20-21).[11] Paul was not abashed to point out that the exaltation of Christ entailed bestowing upon him a position of unrivaled power and authority as a basis for the exercise of his lordship. There is not one evil angelic prince who can be named as a threat to Christ's dominion.

The phrase "every title [literally, 'name'] that can be given" would have communicated in an especially powerful way to people who had formerly been involved in magical practices—like many of the Christians at Ephesus. Knowing the right names and invoking the most powerful names was crucial to the practice of magic. Paul argued for the superiority of Christ in no uncertain terms. There is no conceivable god, goddess, power, spirit or demon who does not fall under the dominion of Christ. Christ alone is supreme. He alone deserves devotion.

Paul also asserts, "And God placed all things under his feet." Everything, including the powers of darkness, now comes under Christ's authority. Paul viewed this as a Messianic fulfillment of Psalm 8:6 ("You made him ruler over the works of your hands; you put everything under his feet") and Psalm 110:1 ("The LORD says to my Lord: 'Sit at my right hand until I make your enemies a footstool for your feet.' "). Just as humanity was given dominion over the physical creation to rule over it (Ps 8:6), Christ has now been given mastery over the entire realm of spirits and angels by virtue of his resurrection and exaltation. Christ's dominion, however, will extend far beyond the spirit realm to include all of creation. In this context Paul stressed Christ's immediate mastery over the angelic world.

Psalm 110:1 was the most frequently cited Old Testament passage by early Christian writers. It was commonly used to interpret God's enthronement of Christ. The "enemies" of this psalm were always identified with the invisible powers whom Christ defeated and subjugated.[12] In his interpretation of the psalm, Paul gave a representative list of the powers Christ has conquered. His subjugation of the powers of evil thus fulfills Old Testament expectation.

Paul gave further explanation of Christ's universal dominion, saying God has appointed Christ to be the ruling "head" over everything for the church (Eph 1:22-23). Although the powers still do not willingly recognize his "headship" and superiority and still continue in their hostile activities, nevertheless, they will ultimately have to answer to Christ and recognize him as their ruler and the Lord (Eph 1:10; Phil 2:10).

For Christians in western Asia Minor who feared the ongoing hostility of the powers, this passage would have proved particularly appropriate and comforting. For Christians today who are sufficiently discerning to see the impact of the evil works of the devil and his powers in its multiplicity of forms, this passage should prove encouraging and inspire confidence.

The Powers As Christ's Captives (Eph 4:8-10)

Using Psalm 68:18, Paul extended his case for Christ's supremacy over the powers of darkness by interpreting them as captives defeated in war. He also used this psalm to introduce a discussion about the gifted people Christ furnishes to the church. As cited in Ephesians 4:8, the psalm reads: "When he ascended on high, he led captives in his train and gave gifts to men." Although the main function of the psalm is to introduce his presentation about gifts, Paul's remarks about ascending on high with captives was not merely incidental.

In his explanation of the psalm Paul spoke of Christ descending to "the lower depths of the earth" (TEV) prior to his ascension (Eph 4:9-10). This description probably refers to Christ's descent to the underworld, given fuller expression in 1 Peter 3:18-22,[13] where he likely proclaimed his victory over all the fallen angels and spirits and warned them of their impending doom. This passage thus gives further evidence for the universality of Christ's lordship.

This passage would have been particularly meaningful to people living in the first century who deeply feared the underworld and worshiped underworld deities.[14] In popular belief, Artemis, Hekate and Selene were goddesses believed to have power over the underworld. In a number of papyri Hekate is even said to hold "the keys to Hades"—a function given to Christ alone in Revelation 1:18.

In this passage Christ is shown to be more powerful than all whom the underworld represents. In Philippians 2:10, where Christ's universal supremacy is praised, Paul expresses the same thought: "Therefore God exalted him to the highest place and gave him the name that is above every name, that at the name of Jesus every knee should bow, in heaven and on earth *and under the earth,* and every tongue confess that Jesus Christ is Lord, to the glory of God the Father" (Phil 2:9-11; italics mine).

Although he was always sovereign because he was the Creator, Christ still needed to defeat those rebellious powers. The cross, resurrection and exaltation of Christ are the basis for his victory over the powers. As we will discuss in the next chapter, the basis for our victory over the powers is also rooted in the death, resurrection and exaltation of Christ.

8
A New Kingdom and Identity for Believers

*A*FEW YEARS AGO WHILE DRIVING ON A FREEWAY, I SAW A BUMPER STICKER on the car ahead of me that caught my attention. It read: "Christians Aren't Perfect, Just Forgiven." For a few years this epigram became rather popular among Christians. It seemed to provide an answer to the accusations of hypocrisy assailing the church from those outside (and perhaps soothing the conscience of the Christian breaking the speed limit!) while conveying a foundational doctrinal truth, the forgiveness of sins.

I do not object to the message conveyed by the bumper sticker. I do disapprove of the simplistic attitude toward conversion that such a statement could engender. Christians truly are people who have been forgiven. But there is so much more that happens behind the scenes at conversion. One who becomes a Christian genuinely becomes a brand-new person and a member of a new kingdom with an all-powerful and all-loving Lord. The new believer is divinely rescued from slavery in a kingdom controlled by evil supernatural forces. And so much more. Far more than just a decision for Christ, becoming a Christian is a divinely powerful redemptive work of God.

Christians are given a new identity. Their new status becomes the basis for renewing their manner of life on earth. A prominent New Testament scholar once said that living the Christian life consists of "becoming what you are." In one sense Christians truly are not perfect, but they are in progress. In another sense, in the presence of our justifying God, Christians are perfect.

As believers we need to know who we are now; that is, we need to know our new identity in relationship to Christ. Knowing this is the basis for our behavior and for resisting the supernatural powers of darkness.

Rescued from the Kingdom of Darkness

Just as God delivered Israel from their bondage in Egypt, Christ has rescued believers from Satan and his powers of evil. To the Colossians, Paul says, "For he has rescued us from the dominion of darkness and brought us into the kingdom of the Son he loves, in whom we have redemption, the forgiveness of sins" (Col 1:13). Behind this statement lies the exodus event as the informing pattern of deliverance. Paul used the same word for "rescue/deliver" that occurs repeatedly throughout the Greek Old Testament to describe Israel's rescue from their bondage in Egypt (see, for example, Ex 6:6; 14:30).

Deliverance from slavery in Satan's kingdom is also at the heart of Paul's concept of "redemption."[1] Again Paul used the same terminology found in the Exodus account to describe Israel's redemption. Exodus 6:6 says, "I will free you from being slaves to them and will *redeem* you with an outstretched arm" (italics mine). Here the concept of redemption appears to bridge the gap between two results of Christ's work on the cross—deliverance from Satan's kingdom and forgiveness of sin. Paul's concept of redemption, important to his understanding of Jesus' death (see, for example, Rom 3:24 and 1 Tim 2:6), is broad enough to cover both concepts. Some segments of Judaism longed for the Messiah to bring redemption from the devil's kingdom. For instance, a second-century B.C. Jewish document states: "He will liberate [or 'redeem'] every captive of the sons of men from Beliar, and every spirit of error will be trampled down" (*Testament of Zebulun* 9:8). Christ is "our redemption" (1 Cor 1:30) by virtue of his work on the cross, where he not only paid the ransom for sin but also destroyed the power of the influence of the evil dominion (Col 2:14-15).

In this Colossians passage Satan is the one described as "the authority of darkness." This expression highlights his rulership over a domain. The domain includes the various powers of darkness mentioned throughout the rest of Paul's letter to the Colossians—powers, authorities, elemental spirits, thrones and so on. It also includes his captives—every person who is not a member of Christ's kingdom.

Darkness and light are the contrasting metaphors Paul chose to describe the nature of the two opposing kingdoms. Paul used this imagery elsewhere to describe the two conflicting kingdoms. In 2 Corinthians, he says, "What fellowship can light have with darkness? What harmony is there between Christ and Belial?" (2 Cor 6:14-15). Here the respective leaders of each dominion are distinguished.

Believers have been uprooted from one domain and transplanted into another. When Paul says God "brought us into" the kingdom of the Son he loves, he used terminology that may have reminded his Jewish readers of political deportation and colonization. According to the Jewish historian Josephus, Antiochus "transferred" several thousand Jews to Asia Minor in the second century B.C.[2]

Followers of Christ truly have a new citizenship. We have been rescued from the clutches of the powers of darkness. This "behind the scenes" action happens at conversion and is symbolized by the rite of baptism. Turning to Christ involves a powerful work of God on our behalf. Conversion for some may only "feel" like a personal decision, but an invisible rescue occurs in the unseen world.

We should not be tempted to think only those people who are involved in occultic activity and Satan worship are slaves to "the dominion of darkness." Paul made it clear that all who are not believers (that is, not in the kingdom of Christ) are in bondage to the hostile powers. This concept is especially difficult for Westerners to grasp, but nevertheless it is true. Even those who are moral, who obeys the laws of the land and appear to be productive members of society, are captive in Satan's domain if they are believers.

In a number of ways Paul explained the new identity of people who have been made members of Christ's kingdom. An understanding of this new status is essential for resisting the ongoing hostile influence of the powers of the old dominion and living according to the new ethical standards of God's kingdom. We will look at a few of Paul's concepts of the meaning of new life in Christ that are especially relevant for gaining the right perspective on the Christian life in light of the opposition we face from the powers of darkness.

In Christ

Paul's favorite expression for describing the position of the believer is "in Christ." The phrase (and its cognates) occur well over 200 times in Paul's writings. It is packed with deep significance for understanding who we are as Christ's redeemed people. Its frequency underlines

Paul's desire for believers to see themselves closely linked to their victorious Lord.

We may begin explaining it by describing what it is not. It should be distinguished from living "in darkness," "in sin," "in the world," "in Adam" and "in the flesh." It is interesting that Paul never referred to the pre-Christian life as being lived "in Satan" or "in the devil." This fact highlights the qualitatively different relationship that occurs between the believer and Christ compared to the nonbeliever and the devil.

The person who is "in Christ" has experienced a fundamental change. Paul says, "If anyone is in Christ, he is *a new creation;* the old has gone, the new has come!" (2 Cor 5:17; italics mine). A divine creative activity occurs in the life of a person who becomes a Christian. Donald Guthrie explains that this refers to "the death of the old creation dominated by adverse spiritual forces, and the emergence of a new creation in which everything is Christ-centred."[3]

Being "in Christ" also reflects an initiation into a new age. Christ's death and resurrection inaugurated "the age to come," consisting of life, righteousness, peace and joy. In contrast, Adam is the representative of life in the present age. Through Adam came sin, condemnation and death (Rom 5:12-14). Paul can therefore say, "For as in Adam all die, so in Christ all will be made alive" (1 Cor 15:22).

Paul's concept of being "in Christ" is not a mystical idea of absorption into a pantheistically conceived deity with a resultant loss of individuality—like a drop of water falling into the ocean. In Christ self is maintained, but unity and relationship with an empowering and directing leader is the distinctive trait. This truth comes out most clearly in Paul's concept of believers being members of "the body of Christ."

Joined to Christ and to One Another
The new identity of the believer must also be understood in connection with what Paul termed "the body of Christ." The work of the Holy Spirit joins every new believer to the body of Christ upon conversion (1 Cor 12:13). The body image is one of Paul's methods for depicting the solidarity of believers with one another and their closeness to Christ. Paul stressed the interdependence of the various members of the body because God has uniquely endowed each person with a particular ability (charisma) to minister to others (1 Cor 12:1-30).

When he wrote to the Ephesians and the Colossians, Paul took the image one step further, describing Christ as the "head" of the body (Eph 1:22-23; Col 1:18). As the "head," Paul implied that Christ functions, not only in a position of leadership, but also as "the inspiring, ruling, guiding, combining, sustaining power, the mainspring of its activity, the centre of its unity, and the seat of its life."[4] The head truly empowers the body and enables it to fulfill its mission in spite of intense demonic hostility. The head is able to accomplish this because God has exalted Christ and placed all of the evil demonic powers under his feet (see Eph 1:22). We believers must respond to the leading impulses of the head and receive his enabling power.

The same thought is expressed with Paul's image of the church as the bride of Christ (Eph 5:22-33). This image, above all others, emphasizes the closeness and intimacy Christ desires to have with his people. Christ not only loves his people and sacrifices his life for them, but he also "feeds and cares" for them (Eph 5:29). Out of his divine resources he gives them all they need for life and godliness.

Dead, Resurrected and Exalted
While the powers rule over a domain of death, all who know Christ have been given life. God can bestow life on his people only through their identification with Christ's work—especially his death and resurrection. Baptism symbolizes this unity with Christ, as Paul explains, "We were therefore buried with him through baptism into death in order that, just as Christ was raised from the dead through the glory of the Father, we too may live a new life" (Rom 6:4).

True freedom comes from identification with Jesus' death—freedom from sin, freedom from death, and freedom from the grip of the principalities and powers. While this freedom is final and absolute insofar as we exist for the age to come, it needs to be appropriated as long as we still live in this present age and possess corruptible bodies. For this reason Paul found it necessary to admonish his readers by attempting to convince them that they are dead to sin. He urged the Roman Christians to "count yourselves dead to sin but alive to God in Christ Jesus" (Rom 6:11) because "the death he [Christ] died, he died to sin once for all; but the life he lives, he lives to God" (Rom 6:10). As believers, sin no longer has a compelling influence over us. Therefore, we can refuse to engage in it.

In a similar way with regard to the demonic powers Christians need to believe they truly do not have to succumb to their influence. Paul has to remind the Colossian Christians that they had died to the demonic powers, arguing, "If with Christ you died to the elemental spirits of the universe, why do you live as if you still belonged to the world?" (Col 2:20 RSV). The Colossians believers were tempted to follow the tenets of a false teaching that Paul believed to be inspired by the evil powers themselves. In whatever way the hostile powers might make their influence felt, believers have the strength to resist. The strength comes from identification with Christ's death. On the cross he defeated sin, death and the powers of darkness.

Some of the difficulty comes in unmasking the influence of the evil powers. It is possible that the Colossian Christians were uncritically accepting the false teaching that was being presented to them, thinking it to be helpful for their spirituality. Paul, however, revealed to them the true demonic nature of the teaching in his epistle to them. We, too, need God's wisdom to enable us to discern critically the nature of all teachings.

Believers' authority over the evil powers is rooted in their identification with the resurrection and exaltation of Christ. This authority is explained most clearly in Paul's letter to the Ephesians, a letter in which Paul was concerned with the issue of the evil powers. In Ephesians 1, Paul extolled God's incomparably great power by which he raised and exalted Christ to a position "far above" every rank in the order of the powers of darkness (Eph 1:19-22). In Ephesians 2, he applied this exalted Christology directly to the believer, saying, "And God raised us up with Christ and seated us with him in the heavenly realms in Christ Jesus" (Eph 2:6). The implication for believers with regard to the powers is clear from the informing context. Just as Christ holds a position of superiority to the powers, so too do believers have a position of superiority and authority over the devil's forces. The power that raised Jesus from the dead is the same power now available to believers. Thus Paul can pray that the Ephesians will grow increasingly aware of this divine resource. He appealed to the Ephesians, saying, "I pray also that the eyes of your heart may be enlightened in order that you may know . . . his incomparably great power for us who believe" (Eph 1:18-19). This truth is especially significant in the larger context of Paul's letter to the Ephesians, since this truth becomes the doctrinal basis for his later discussion of spiritual warfare in Ephesians 6:10-20.

Paul also affirmed the same truth to the Colossians—people who were struggling with the influence of the powers of darkness. He reminded them that they were buried with Christ and raised with him through their faith in God's power (Col 2:12). Based on their identification with Christ's work, Paul could admonish them to regard themselves as dead to the evil powers (Col 2:20) and alive to Christ because they had been raised with him (Col 3:1). To these believers Paul gave one of the most comforting promises found in the New Testament: "For you died, and your life is now hidden with Christ in God" (Col 3:3). In practical terms, Paul's teaching about their relationship to Christ meant that the Colossian Christians had the power to resist the influence of unhealthy false teaching and align their conduct more closely with God's desires. Neither should they continue to fear the influence of the demonic powers, which they dreaded prior to conversion and which their non-Christian friends and neighbors continued to dread.

Identification with Christ in his death and resurrection is an incredibly important truth for all who are struggling with the influence of the demonic in their lives. Becoming a Christian means being linked to a powerful Lord who wields overpowering authority over the realm of darkness.

Filled—Endowed with Power and Authority

Paul taught the Colossians that God had endowed Christ with all of his "fullness" *(plērōma;* Col 1:19). He reaffirmed this thought in his letter to them, saying, "For in Christ all the fullness of the Deity lives in bodily form" (Col 2:9). Paul made this statement here because he wanted to relate it to the Colossian church—it is not merely another laudable truth about the omnipotent Christ, but is something that has great significance for the day-to-day lives of believers. Paul continued by saying, "and you have been given fullness in Christ, who is the head over every power and authority" (Col 2:10).

Notice that Paul connected the Colossians' possession of divine "fullness" *(plērōma)* with Christ's supremacy to the demonic powers. Why? Paul was trying to convince the Colossians that they have been endowed with Christ's power and authority over the demonic realm. Paul could just as easily have left the statement out. It appears that he was specifically applying the significance of their filling with God's resources to their struggle with the powers.

The verb Paul used here is in the Greek perfect tense and is translated "you have been given fullness." In this instance Paul wanted to convey to these believers that when they became Christians they received this endowment, but more importantly, this divine "fullness" continues to be available to them as God's provision for them in their ongoing conflict with Satan's realm.

The word *fullness* indicates far more than just power and authority over the forces of darkness. Most scholars believe it refers to a number of things related to God, including his power, essence, glory, presence and love. It probably has as its background the idea of the Old Testament Shekinah: "I looked and saw the glory of the LORD filling the temple of the LORD" (Ezek 44:4). It comes very close to overlapping with the work of the Holy Spirit who fills the believer.[5]

The believer must appropriate this "fullness." Paul found it necessary to pray that the Ephesians would "be filled to the measure of all the fullness of God" (Eph 3:19). While God's fullness is available to the believer, it must be received and used. Belief and prayer become highly important factors in appropriating these resources.

The Spirit and the Gifts

The hallmark of the Christian life is reception of the Holy Spirit. Possession of the Spirit is what distinguishes Christians from non-Christians (1 Cor 2:10-14). "For Paul the possession of the Spirit is the sine qua non of Christian life."[6] The Spirit is thus the basis for the new identity of the believer.

People living during Paul's time believed in the existence of spirits who could enter into individuals and alter their behavior. In contrast, Paul repeatedly spoke of one particular divine spirit whose indwelling he favored exclusively. This divine spirit is of a qualitatively different nature than the spirits known by the people in the Hellenistic religions and in magic. This one "Holy Spirit" is closely related to the one God and to Christ. This Spirit is, in fact, called "the Spirit of God" (Rom 8:14) and "the Spirit of Christ" (Rom 8:9). He is sent from God and reveals God to us (2 Cor 2:12; Gal 4:6), because he knows the deep things of God (1 Cor 2:10-11). This Spirit is the only spirit-being whom Paul advocated should have a place in a believer's life.

Whereas in popular magic a supernatural spirit ("a divine assistant") was commonly summoned to accomplish the will of the recipient, Paul saw the Holy Spirit as coming to accomplish only the will and purpose of the one God, who revealed himself to Israel as a "holy" God. He had commanded his people to "be holy because I, the LORD your God, am holy" (Lev 19:1). Likewise, the Spirit of God is "holy" and seeks to promote holiness among the people he indwells. The Spirit stimulates such virtues as kindness, love, joy and peace and enables believers to rid themselves of the filthy things that are part of their lives (Gal 5:16-26). The Spirit is, in effect, the divine provision to empower Christians to "put to death the misdeeds of the body" (Rom 8:13).

The Holy Spirit works in the context of the corporate solidarity of believers. It is the Spirit who brings us to God and draws us into the close bond with other believers known as the body of Christ. In reflecting on the unity of believers in the body, Paul remarks, "For we were all baptized by one Spirit into one body—whether Jews or Greeks, slave or free—and we were all given the one Spirit to drink" (1 Cor 12:13). Whenever someone becomes a Christian, they receive the Holy Spirit who incorporates them into the Christian community. The expressive metaphors of "baptizing" and "drinking" emphasize the reality and extent of this divine gift—"immersion in the Spirit and drinking to the fill of the Spirit."[7] This common experience of the Spirit is what constitutes the basis of unity for all who are Christians and makes all believers part of the one body of Christ.

Among believers, mutuality is divinely intended. Christians cannot be individualists. No single believer possesses all of the Spirit's endowments. Rather, each believer is uniquely endowed by the Spirit to help others grow in their Christian lives (1 Cor 12). The regular operation of these Spirit-inspired endowments (*charismata*) by the members of the church is vital for the ongoing spiritual progress of all the members of the body.

In Paul's way of thinking one can never experience enough of the Spirit's inspiring and empowering presence. Paul urged believers always to seek a fuller manifestation of the Spirit's presence and work (Eph 5:18). He wanted them to continually be "filled" with the Spirit, which would make itself felt in the quality of worship in the community—they would "speak to one another with psalms, hymns and spiritual songs" (Eph 5:19). The "filling" of the Spirit would certainly also bring about the continued use of the Spirit's edifying gifts and reinforce the cultivation of Christian virtue. All of this stands in stark contrast to the world from which the Ephesian readers had come.

Paul prefaced all of his comments on the Spirit here with the admonition "do not get drunk on wine." Possibly the drunken and frenzied revelry connected with the worship of the god Dionysus, the god of wine, forms the general cultural background of this statement.[8] The first-century readers were called to turn their backs to alcoholic intoxication and inspiration from any other spirit or deity (such as Dionysus) and yield themselves completely to the Holy Spirit of God. They were to allow themselves to be filled completely with God's Spirit and give thanks to God the Father. He alone can cheer the heart and bring joy. Because of the Spirit's presence, we can "sing and make music in [our] hearts to the Lord!"

Secure and Protected

Paul eloquently attested to the security of all who are "in Christ" in the face of every conceivable hostile power. More than security he portrayed believers as wrapped in the arms of a loving God, forever protected and forever cherished.

At the end of a section where he had described the nature of life in the Spirit, he closed by pointing his readers to the love and power of God in Christ. He remarks:

> For I am sure that neither death, nor life, nor angels, nor principalities, nor things present, nor things to come, nor powers, nor height, nor depth, nor anything else in creation, will be able to separate us from the love of God in Christ Jesus our Lord. (Rom 8:38-39 RSV)

While throughout the book of Romans, Paul had been primarily concerned about the influences of sin, the law, the flesh and death on the believer, he turned his attention here to a more comprehensive list of forces that could separate us from God. His focus was primarily upon the hostile spirits and angelic forces against whom we struggle. This comes out particularly in his references to "angels," "principalities," "powers" and quite possibly in the expressions "height" and "depth."

Principalities and *powers* surface throughout Paul's letters as the spirit beings he saw as hostile to God's people. In this context angels must be regarded as the rebellious evil angels who function in a way similar to the principalities and powers. Paul used the term *angel* in this sense (see 2 Cor 12:7 and Col 2:18), and it was widely used in Judaism to describe supernatural beings in league with Satan.

It appears that Paul may have used the terms *height* and *depth* as a comprehensive way of referring to all of the astral spirits who were commonly believed to control human destiny. In astronomical texts both terms appear technical. They were used to refer to the zenith and nadir of the stars, that is, the highest and lowest points reached by a heavenly body. It may be intentional that Paul's very next expression is, literally, "nor any other creature." Some commentators have thought this reference confirms that Paul had astral spirits in mind when he used *height* and *depth*. J. D. G. Dunn comments on these two terms, "Paul deliberately draws on current astronomical terms to denote the full sweep of the heavens visible and invisible to the human eye, and thus all astrological powers known and unknown which could be thought to determine and control the fate and destiny of human beings."[9]

In Christ nothing can sever us from God's rich love showered upon us. However they are conceived, not even the powers of darkness have the ability to disunite God and his people. This does not mean that the principalities and powers will not try. Our conflict with them continues, but in Christ we have a superabundant supply of divine enabling power and love to sustain us.

In his second letter to the Thessalonians Paul affirmed the promise of divine protection in a much simpler way. In a letter that warned believers about the coming of a satanically inspired "lawless one" (2 Thess 2:8-9), Paul's assurance of divine protection would have proved exceptionally comforting. Paul told them, "But the Lord is faithful, and he will strengthen and protect you from the evil one" (2 Thess 3:3). The promise had already proved true in the experience of the Thessalonians as new believers. In his earlier letter Paul had remarked that he had sent Timothy to check on their progress in the faith because he was afraid that "in some way the tempter might have tempted you and our efforts might have been useless" (1 Thess 3:5). Quite the contrary to his fears Paul learned that the Thessalonians had been growing in their faith, in spite of persecution, and were actively propagating the message of the gospel. The Lord was truly faithful to them. He did indeed strengthen and protect them from the evil one.

Protection from evil spirits was something of great concern to people living in the first century. The word *protect* occurs over and over again in the magical papyri as part of recipes that are designed for bringing protection to those who use them, especially in the form of a magical amulet. This kind of magic is commonly referred to as "apotropaic" magic, which literally means "warding off." It claims to protect people from evil spirits. For Paul only the one true God gives "protection." His protection for the believer extends as far as the rule of all the powers of darkness, including Satan himself.

Although God provides us with protection, becoming a Christian does not mean that one gains an automatic immunity to the demonic realm. Believers need to learn about their position in Christ. This is precisely why the study of Scripture and theology is so important for Christian living. Since Satan is a deceiver and an accuser, we need to know the truth about who we are in Christ. The actuality about our new identity needs to be grasped and appreciated in the depths of our consciousness so that we can live like free people, rescued from servitude to the powers of darkness.

These truths are difficult for people to comprehend and accept. Paul felt the need to pray and ask for the help of the Holy Spirit to guide the Ephesian Christians in opening their hearts to it (Eph 1:17-18). Surely more than a few of Paul's readers in Ephesus had heard many of the same truths being taught by their teachers when they gathered for worship and instruction. After all, Paul had spent nearly three years in the area, personally imparting his doctrine to the people who would become the leaders and teachers of the churches in the area. Many of the people still needed to be convinced. We also need to ask God for the Spirit's illuminating help so that we too may understand the full significance of Christ's work for us and our new identity in Christ.

Once the truth about our new identity in Christ has been grasped, we need to align our lives with this reality. We need to learn to draw on the resources available through our vital union with Jesus Christ. The Spirit's fullness must be appropriated for living in the world on a day-to-day basis. And now is when we need to talk about "spiritual warfare."

9

The Influence of the
Powers on Believers

*T*HE PAINFUL INFLUENCE OF THE EVIL ONE CONTINUES TO BE FELT THROUGH-
out the world. The horrors of war, poverty, financial exploitation and racial discrimination are evident worldwide. Christians do not appear to be immune to Satan's solicitations to evil. Many
succumb. Stories of adultery, financial improprieties, hypocrisy, division and the like are all too typical of the modern church. Many
pastoral counselors are reporting numerous cases of Christians struggling with direct demonic involvement in their lives.

Satan As a Defeated but Active Enemy
Life experience amply demonstrates to us that Satan and his forces are
still quite actively engaged in their malignant activity. Throughout his
letters Paul assumed Satan's continuing powerful opposition to God's
people, and he worked with his churches on how to respond to that
evil. Yet, at the same time, Paul was convinced that Christ's death and
resurrection had defeated and disarmed the powers of darkness (Col
2:15). How are we to make sense of these two seemingly contradictory
points of view?

First, Christ did win a decisive victory over the powers through the
cross. Because of his death and resurrection, Christ broke their compelling grip on humanity, thereby enabling him to rescue people from
Satan's domain and install them as members into his own kingdom.
Because those hostile forces have no power or authority over Christ,
they consequently have no power or authority over members of his
body. Believers acquiesce to the influence of evil powers only in so far

as they do not depend on the resources available to them in Christ. Believers can resist Satan's enticements to sin when they appropriate God's power made available to them through their union with Christ.

Second, a decisive battle frequently determines the outcome of a war. Christ's victory on the cross forever determined the outcome of Christ's conflict with the powers of darkness. The war continues, but every battle is a relatively minor skirmish in comparison to the battle won through Christ's death and resurrection. Oscar Cullmann has drawn a helpful analogy to Christ's conflict with the powers by using the two major events of World War 2—D-Day and VE-Day.[1] No one would doubt that the outcome of World War 2 was decided when the Allied forces landed at Normandy on June 6, 1944 (D-Day). Yet VE-Day, the day of final victory, did not arrive until May 8, 1945, almost a year later. Numerous battles were fought and many casualties were sustained, but the enemy's failure to prevent the successful Allied invasion determined the war. Another scholar relates this to the conflict Christ and his church face with the powers:

> D-Day was but the prelude to V-Day, the Day of Christ, the parousia, the day of the final victory of God in Christ. It is the conviction that though the campaign may drag on and V-Day, the day of final glory may still be out of sight, D-Day is over and the powers of evil have received a blow from which they can never recover.[2]

The church continues to live in this "mopping up" period. Final victory is assured, but it is still a dangerous time, and there are many battles to be fought. Satan and his powers continue to attack the church, hold unbelieving humanity in bondage and promote every kind of evil throughout the world. Believers will continue to suffer the painful effects of the large-scale evil spurred on by the powers of darkness— evils such as war, morally deplorable public policies, crime, gang violence and the like. But the powers can no longer take us captive, separate us from God and keep us in sin. We have freedom in Christ. We have a message of redemption and freedom to proclaim.

The Threefold Nature of Evil Influence

In this book the focus on the theme of principalities and powers could lead one to believe Paul gave a demonological root to all evil. That is not the case. Paul's view of the nature of evil influence on people is very balanced.

In Ephesians 2:1-3, Paul describes sinful behavior as stemming from three compelling influences—to be seen as three strands combining to make one sturdy cable. This cable tightly binds unbelievers, keeping them in slavery to the kingdom of darkness. It may be helpful to depict these three sources of evil influence graphically:

1. *The World:* "the ways of this world"
2. *The Devil:* "the ruler of the kingdom of the air" "the spirit who is now at work in those who are disobedient"
3. *The Flesh:* "the cravings of our sinful nature . . . its desires and thoughts"

In simplest terms we might categorize these influences as "the world, the devil and the flesh." We need, however, to take a closer look at what Paul specifically said.

In this passage Paul was disclosing the nature of his readers' lives before they turned to Christ. Here a set of overriding principles help us to understand how Paul perceived evil as influencing the lives of people in general, Christians or non-Christians. Christians will still need to contend with the same sources of evil influence, but Christians have a new means of overcoming these influences through the power of Christ. Those who are not believers, being apart from Christ, are enslaved to these influences, not having the power or ability to escape.

When he spoke of "the ways of this world," Paul was thinking of the powerful influence of societal attitudes, habits and preferences that are at odds with God's standard of holiness. Literally, the text indicts the character of "the age of this world." There is a stark contrast between the character of "this age" and "the age to come." John R. W. Stott aptly describes the character of "the age of this world":

> Both words "age" and "world" express a whole social value-system which is alien to God. It permeates, indeed dominates, non-Christian society and holds people in captivity. Wherever human beings are being dehumanized—by political oppression or bureaucratic tyranny, by an outlook that is secular (repudiating God), amoral (repudiating absolutes) or materialistic (glorifying the consumer market), by poverty, hunger or unemployment, by racial discrimination, or by any form of injustice—there we can detect the sub-human values of "this age" and "this world."[3]

This influence begins at birth with values that are passed on from the parents and extended family. It is reinforced all throughout life, both formally and informally, through the educational system and the media as well as through peer pressure. It continues to be transmitted through patterns of thinking, traditions, customs and even institutions. This is not to say everything in society is evil. But there is much in society that leads away from God.[4]

"The ruler of the kingdom of the air," the second evil influence Paul delineated, is a powerful supernatural being in charge of a whole host of evil spirits often thought by the ancients to reside in the air. This ruler is more precisely a "spirit," and Paul portrayed his method as very immediate and direct: "He is now at work in [or among] those who are disobedient." It would be inaccurate to say all who disobey God are "possessed" by an evil spirit. Yet Paul was clear that this evil agent and his emissaries exert a very close and personal kind of influence over individuals. This spirit exerts a powerful, compelling influence, although many English translations miss this description. When Paul said the ruler is "at work in," he used a word that was part of his vocabulary of power and could be translated, "The spirit who is now powerfully at work in . . ." The GNB translates the phrase, "the spirit who now controls the people." Notice that Paul emphasizes here the work of the evil spirit in people as opposed to institutions.

The final evil influence that Paul drew attention to is what he termed "the flesh." This is Paul's favorite expression to convey the inner drive of people to act in ways deviant to the standard of God's righteousness. It points not only to the inner motivating force behind actions that are associated with the body, such as sexual sin, but also to aspects of the thought life as well, such as envy and anger. This inner impulse to do evil is set in contrast to the new impulse to live with moral integrity provided by God's gift of the Holy Spirit (see Gal 5:19-23).

Paul, therefore, presented the true character of evil influence in all three of its manifestations. The source of evil tendencies is both internal and external to people as well as supernatural. Individuals possess an internal inclination toward evil, and their environment (peers, media, societal norms, and so forth) also strongly influences them. Such a perspective linking the categories of "the world, the flesh and the devil" was also integral to the thought of James (see Jas 3:15) and John (1 Jn 2:15-17; 3:7-10) and, presumably, common in the early church.

Paul's teaching suggests that the explanation for our behavior is not to be found exclusively in human nature or in terms of the world's influence. Similarly, an exclusively demonic explanation for deviant behavior is unduly myopic. Rather, we should explain behavior on the basis of human nature, environment and the demonic—all three simultaneously. One part may play a leading role, but all three parts need to be considered. Paul's theology at this point has significant implications for those involved in counseling ministries. Yet we also need to see it as extremely relevant for our church life.

The demonic side receives the strongest emphasis in Ephesians and Colossians, while the flesh is more prominent in Romans and Galatians. The general situations of the readers of each book may have something to do with their paricular emphases. If the readers of Ephesians and Colossians tended to need help in dealing with their past involvement in occultic practices, this fact would explain why the demonic side is stressed more strongly in those two letters.

In the final analysis, however, Paul regarded Satan as the chief opponent of Christ and his kingdom. The demonic explanation for evil behavior needs to be seen as the thread that ties together all the evil influences. In practice Satan exploits the depraved tendencies of the flesh and exercises a measure of control over all levels of a social order.

Through the cross of Christ Christians gain their freedom from these compelling and enslaving influences. His death and resurrection resulted in the "age to come," breaking into the present age. Believers now share already in many of the blessings and resources of the age to come. Through the cross of Christ our flesh was crucified, and we can live under the guiding and enabling impulses of the Holy Spirit. Finally the cross of Christ marked a decisive victory by God over the powers of evil. Through union with Christ believers can resist Satan and be victorious over his kingdom.

How the Powers Influence Believers
Paul was primarily concerned with the health and well-being of his churches. Consequently he spent little time reflecting on the influence of the powers over the world at large. He did not, for instance, explain how the powers of darkness exert their control over the Roman Caesars, the economy or the diplomatic relationships among the various Roman provinces. This does not mean that Paul's teaching on the powers has no relevance for understanding their influence on social, political and economic structures. In fact, his thought has significant implications for understanding and responding to those structures. What has been preserved for us, however, are his letters to churches—

churches facing various internal struggles and the ongoing effects of sin. Paul warned his churches to be concerned with the world. But their concern should be expressed chiefly through the proclamation of the gospel of Christ. Paul clearly saw Christians as still susceptible to the deleterious influence of evil spirits. It is not just the temptations of the flesh and the allurement of the world that a person contends with once he or she becomes a Christian. The powerful supernatural work of the devil and his powers sets itself against individual Christians and the church as a whole. The fact that the powers exploit the flesh and exert their influence over the world systems makes the extent of their influence comprehensive.

In addition to drawing the implications of the work of Christ to the powers, Paul's letters are concerned with describing the nature of the influence of the powers on believers. What follows is a discussion of some of the specific ways that the forces of darkness attempt to exercise their control over Christians.

Temptation

The most well-known function of Satan and his powers is the act of temptation. Paul even ascribed to Satan the title of "the tempter" (1 Thess 3:5). Satan entices God's people to behave in ways that are contrary to God's desires. By doing so, Satan hopes to re-enslave them in his dominion (Gal 4:8-9).

Unfortunately Paul does not give us a complete picture of the psychology of temptation. He did not describe in any precise way how Satan tempts believers. Although such information could go far in satisfying our curiosity, Paul apparently felt he had given his readers all the practical information they needed in order to resist the evil influence of the powers.

Based on the tenor of his writings as a whole and our discussion of Ephesians 2:1-3 in particular, it appears Paul saw Satan and his powers as working in and through the internal and external influences on people; that is, Satan uses and exploits "the flesh" and "the world." When Paul wrote to the Corinthians about husband-wife relations, he cautioned husbands and wives not to abstain from sexual relations for an extended period of time. He feared that they might not have adequate self-control and that Satan might tempt them to compromise their marital fidelity, presumably by having relations with another person (1 Cor 7:5). Elsewhere he described sexual immorality as an act of "the flesh" (Gal 5:19). Paul likely envisioned Satan working so as to intensify the human craving for physical satisfaction. As such, it is still a temptation of the flesh, but it is charged with the powerful, compelling, supernatural activity of the powers of darkness. This is partly why self-control only comes through the work of God's Spirit (Gal 5:23, 16-18).

Satan also tempts believers through a wide variety of external influences ("the world") because he is "the god of this world" (2 Cor 4:4) and his angelic lieutenants are elemental spirits "of this world" (Gal 4:3; Col 2:8, 20). The prince of darkness can thus wield tremendous influence over all the structures of existence, including religion. One of the ways that Paul's churches struggled with "the world" was through various forms of false teaching that often came from outside groups (but also from corrupting influences within). In all instances these early Christians faced the pressure of conforming to non-Christian religious traditions, usually the practices and beliefs of their neighbors.

Giving a Foothold to the Devil

Paul never used the language of "demonization" (often described as "demon possession") in his letters, which is so common in the Gospels. The closest he came to "possession" language is his concept of giving a "foothold to the devil" as found in Ephesians 4:27. He warned the Christians in Ephesus, "do not give the devil a foothold."

Topos is the Greek word that the NIV translates as "foothold." It could also be translated "opportunity" (NASB, RSV) or "chance" (TEV; NEB translates it "loop-hole"). Thus this verse can be expressed, "Do not give the devil a chance to exert his influence."[5] In Romans 12:19, Paul used *topos* in a similar way, when he says, "Do not take revenge, my friends, but 'leave room' [literally, 'give a place' or 'give a chance'] for God's wrath."

This is the only time Paul made such a statement in any of his letters. He did not go on to explain what kind of "foothold" he believed the devil can gain in the life of a believer or how the devil operates once a believer gives him a "chance." J. A. Robinson interpreted this passage as referring to an "opportunity for the entry of an evil spirit."[6] I cannot find clear support for this assertion from Jewish tradition, but there are a number of examples of the idea of God's people giving the devil (Beliar) an opportunity to take control of their lives. The *Testament of the Twelve Patriarchs,* written just before the time of Christ, has much to say about the potential influence of the devil and his spirits over God's people. One text in particular links unchecked anger with the devil gaining a foothold, just as in the context of Ephesians 4:27. The *Testament of Dan* 4:7 states, "Anger and falsehood together are a double-edged evil, and work together to perturb the reason. And when the soul is continually perturbed, the Lord withdraws from it and Beliar rules it."[7] In light of this Jewish tradition it is not surprising then to see Paul regarding excessive anger with relinquishing control of one's life to the devil.

Paul is clear about how the believer can give the devil a chance to exert control. His warning about giving the devil a foothold is prefaced by the admonition, "Do not let the sun go down while you are still angry" (Eph 4:26). Paul conceived of excessive anger as one of the means of Satan's entry into a believer's life. He probably did not consider this particular vice as the only point of vulnerability for diabolic exploitation. Paul mentioned quite a number of vices in the larger context of the passage, including lying, stealing, dirty talk, bitterness and malice. It is likely that any sinful activity that the believer does not deal with by the power of the Spirit can be exploited by the devil and turned into a means of control over a believer's life. Therefore, Christians need to resist.

For Paul there is no middle ground. There is no nominal Christianity. Believers either resist the influence of the evil one who works through the flesh and the world, or they relinquish control of their lives to the powers of darkness.

For this reason it is extremely dangerous for believers to harbor bitterness, hold a grudge or pilfer from their place of employment— to name a few examples. Giving in to those temptations does not just confirm the weakness of the flesh, it opens up the lives of believers to the control of the devil and his powers.

Deceived by Servants of Satan (2 Cor 10—13)

Ever since the garden of Eden, Satan has continued to use his diabolical method of deception, causing people to believe a lie. This was particularly true in Paul's churches with regard to the proliferation of false teaching and the deceitful work of false teachers. In writing to the Galatians, Corinthians and the Colossians, Paul warned these believers about the influence of false teaching. In all three cases he explicitly connects the false teaching with the work of Satan and his powers. Paul also instructed Timothy on how to deal with false teachers at Ephesus, who essentially were pawns in Satan's hands. All these forms of false teaching characteristically impugn the true nature of the gospel and the person of the Lord Jesus Christ—always leading to the wrong kind of lifestyle and behavior.

The Corinthians were giving credence to a group of polished orators who had described themselves as apostles and missionaries (2 Cor 11:13). They publicly disdained Paul and tried to present themselves as having a higher level of spiritual authority over the Corinthians. While they had apparently claimed to possess authority from Jerusalem, Paul implied that they were teaching a different Jesus and a different gospel than he had proclaimed to them (2 Cor 11:4). Paul then charged them with being "false apostles, deceitful workmen, masquerading as apostles of Christ." Finally, he unmasked their true identity: They are servants of Satan masquerading as Christians. Paul regarded Satan as the master of masquerade and deceit. Paul said that Satan can even disguise himself as an angel of light (2 Cor 11:14). Some strands of Jewish tradition actually believed that Satan did disguise himself as an angel of light when he tempted Eve in the garden of Eden.[8]

Paul was fearful that these emissaries of Satan would cause the Corinthians to believe a perverted gospel. He therefore cautioned them, "I am afraid that just as Eve was deceived by the serpent's cunning, your minds may somehow be led astray from your sincere and pure devotion to Christ" (2 Cor 11:3). Paul responded to this situation by endeavoring to "demolish strongholds"—that is, he wanted to tear down the wall of hostility that his opponents had erected between himself and his Corinthian converts (2 Cor 10:4). Furthermore, a "stronghold" of false teaching needed to be eradicated from their midst because it was contrary to the truth of the gospel. Ralph Martin comments, "Paul distinguishes the alien intruders at Corinth, whose satanic work (11:13-15) he wants to overthrow and neutralize, from the body of Pauline believers for whom he entertains optimistic hope of their recovery from the snare of deviation and seduction."[9] Paul therefore wrote to them to expose the satanic character of this new teaching and to call the Corinthians to break this yoke with Belial (see 2 Cor 6:14—7:1). He wanted them to commit themselves afresh to the true gospel that he proclaimed as a legitimate apostle of the Lord Jesus

Christ—the gospel of the Christ who suffered and calls his people to manifest divine power in weakness.

Paul exposed other kinds of demonically inspired false teachings that denigrated the gospel of Christ in the church at Colossae and among the churches of the Galatian region. Paul described the new teaching at Colossae as having come to them through human beings, but in reality the "elementary spirits of the world" (Col 2:8) inspired it. It challenged the full sufficiency of Christ for the believers in Colossae.

Slavery to the Elemental Spirits (Galatians)

The novel teaching threatening the church at Galatia struck at the heart of the gospel (Gal 1:6-9). Evidently some zealous persons from Judea were teaching the Galatian Christians that they must be circumcised in accordance with the Mosaic regulations (and perform other legal requirements) in order to be saved. In Paul's eyes, this requirement compromised the true nature of the gospel message, which is that salvation is given without performing any works of the law, a salvation by grace alone.

Paul also spoke of the Galatians "observing special days and months and seasons and years" (Gal 4:10). While Paul had no problem with Christians having personal convictions on such matters (Rom 14:5), he objected to these observances (including circumcision) being viewed as religious obligations, as part of the necessary response to the gospel message. In Paul's mind, to turn to circumcision and legal observances was tantamount to returning to slavery—a slavery to the principalities and powers *(stoicheia;* Gal 4:9)!

For Paul both Jews and Gentiles were in bondage to the powers of darkness prior to conversion. He explained that unredeemed Jews are slaves to the elemental spirits of the universe (Gal 4:3).[10] These hostile forces apparently exploit the law and use it as a tool to hold unbelieving Judaism in captivity. God's redemption through Christ brings freedom—freedom from the law and freedom from servitude to the powers (Gal 4:3-5).

Likewise, prior to their conversion, the Gentiles "were slaves to those who by nature are not gods" (Gal 4:8). At one time they thought they were worshiping real gods and goddesses in their pagan worship, but they were soon to find out that these were mere idols—tools of the devil and his powers of darkness. The Galatians had appeared to have turned their backs on their pagan gods, but they were now tempted to add Jewish legal requirements to the pure gospel of Christ, which Paul had taught them. In Paul's mind this would be trading one form of slavery to the powers for another.

According to F. F. Bruce, Paul was making the point that, "the *stoicheia* . . . not only regulated the Jewish way of life under law; they also regulated the pagan way of life in the service of gods that were no gods. . . . For all the basic differences between Judaism and paganism, both involved subjection to the same elemental forces."[11] He adds, "for those who did not live in the good of Christian freedom the *stoicheia* ['elementary spirits'] were 'principalities and powers', keeping the souls of men in bondage."[12] The gospel is truly a message of freedom. Any form of legalism as a principle of Christian life is contrary to the gospel.

Both pagan religion and the Jewish law surface here as two systems that Satan and his powers exploit to hold the unbeliever in captivity and re-enslave the believer. As such, they function as two aspects of the world, or "the present evil age," and illustrate how the powers operate in conjunction with the world.

Surprisingly, even something that is inherently good—the law—can be perverted by Satan and used to accomplish his own purposes. This evil influence came to the Galatians in the form of a new teaching propagated by people who appeared to them as credible and credentialed. On the surface the new teaching probably looked true and appealing to the Galatians. We might generalize from this that the influence of the powers comes in subtle ways. Only spiritual discernment can detect it. One lesson to be learned from the situation of the Galatians as well as the Corinthians is the importance for every believer to be rooted deeply in sound doctrine, especially Christology. Satan consistently seeks to have us believe a lie about Christ and his redemptive work.

In light of these instances of satanically inspired false teaching, it is not surprising that at the end of his life Paul warned Timothy, "The Spirit clearly says that in later times some will abandon the faith and follow deceiving spirits and things taught by demons" (1 Tim 4:1). He was increasingly aware of this subtle, yet effective, method of Satan for bringing about the demise of the church.

Paul described those who bring such false teachings as having fallen into "the trap of the devil, who has taken them captive to do his will"

(2 Tim 2:26). This statement gives helpful insight into the character of false teachers. They are, in essence, Satan's instruments. Satan and his powers work through these human agencies to deceive the church and lead it astray. All is not bleak, however. There is hope even for those who are the emissaries of Satan. God may still "grant them repentance leading them to a knowledge of the truth" (2 Tim 2:25). This could happen if they listen with an open heart to the leadership of the church. Paul urged the leadership to have an attitude of gentleness as they work with such people, always with an eye toward their repentance.

Direct and Immediate Influence with Physical Symptoms

Scripture gives us a unique and extraordinary example of God allowing an evil angel to inflict some kind of physical malady on a Christian. In this case, the demonic affliction was not the result of sin in the life of the believer, but rather a part of God's providential means of insuring his servant's dependence upon him.

The condition affected the apostle Paul himself. He told the Corinthians, "To keep me from becoming conceited because of these surpassingly great revelations, there was given to me a thorn in my flesh, a messenger of Satan, to torment me" (2 Cor 12:7). No one will probably ever know precisely what the "thorn in the flesh" actually was. It was likely some physical affliction.[13] Numerous specific ideas have been suggested, including defective eyesight, recurring malarial fever, a nervous disorder, defective speech and even epilepsy.

What is clear in this passage is that "a messenger of Satan," literally, "an angel of Satan," produced it. This was not an unusual activity of Satan. Ralph Martin points out that Satan is associated with physical illness in the biblical tradition.[14] God allowed Satan to inflict sickness on Job (Job 2:5), and Jesus accused Satan as the one who had kept a woman crippled for eighteen years (Lk 13:16). Outside of the biblical tradition, evil spirits were often believed to cause sickness.

Paul explained that he explicitly pleaded with the Lord three times for his "thorn" to be removed, but God did not allow it to be taken away. God permitted this demonic agent to hurt Paul so that he would draw on the power of Christ and not on his own strength. God told him, "My grace is sufficient for you, for my power is made perfect in weakness" (2 Cor 12:9). Paul emphasized that God allowed it to continue so that he would not be inclined to assert his independence from

God and become proud. Paul felt especially susceptible to this because of an incredible revelation that God had granted to him (2 Cor 12:1-6).

Paul's example strongly underlines God's desire for humility among his servants. An arrogant, prideful or independent spirit is so contrary to what God desires in us that he may permit a demonic agent to afflict us. This example also warns us that it is not necessarily God's desire for all sickness to be alleviated. God may allow an unpleasant condition to continue to insure our humility and our dependence upon him.

As God's Tool of Discipline

There is a second positive way that God sovereignly uses Satan's forces. Just as God used an evil angel to help instill a proper attitude in the apostle Paul, so too, he can use the forces of darkness to promote the restoration of erring Christians.

In his first letter to the Corinthians, Paul firmly responded to a grievous situation in which the Corinthian church was tolerating one of their members sleeping with his stepmother (1 Cor 5:1-13). Paul chided them for turning a blind eye to the situation of blatant immorality and for their arrogance in spite of the situation. He urged them to excommunicate the man from their church. He told the church to assemble and "to deliver this man to Satan for the destruction of the flesh, that his spirit may be saved in the day of the Lord Jesus" (1 Cor 5:5 RSV).

Notice that the ultimate goal of such action is restoration. It is not an act of "good riddance," but rather a disciplinary measure designed for the person's ultimate well-being. While the intention was for him to be saved in light of Christ's return, Paul likely intended that his repentance be evident to the Christian community before he is restored.

Paul defined the man's expulsion in terms of handing him over to Satan for the destruction of his flesh. It is doubtful that Paul was thinking of a real personal delivery to Satan in which Satan is personally summoned and the man is given to him. What the text says is probably what Paul considered the net result of excommunication to be. Gordon Fee provides an apt explanation of this action:

> In contrast to the gathered community of believers who experience the Spirit and power of the Lord Jesus in edifying gifts and loving concern for one another, this man is to be put back out into the

world where Satan and his "principalities and powers" still hold sway over people's lives to destroy them.[15]
No longer would this man benefit from the caring nurture of the body of Christ. Satan and his forces could inflict their murderous influences on him.

Paul envisioned that this process would produce "the destruction of his flesh." While a number of commentators have thought this means that the man would physically die, it is probably better to interpret the passage as the translators of the NIV, "so that the *sinful nature* may be destroyed" (italics mine).[16] This could very well entail physical illness or even death, but the language does not necessarily make this implication. Unfortunately Paul did not explain specifically how he saw the destruction of this man's carnality to occur. He was optimistic, however, that it would happen.

In a similar way, Paul "handed over to Satan" two other men, Hymenaeus and Alexander (1 Tim 1:20). In this case, Paul was more specific about the goal of their removal from the church; he wanted them "to be taught not to blaspheme." Again, Paul did not let us know what he thought Satan and his powers of evil might do to these two men, but he clearly saw positive value in the process.

It is important for us to adjust our thinking on church discipline in light of these two passages. Church discipline is not merely a social action, it is a spiritual action. It involves the dislocation of a believer from the primary sphere of the Holy Spirit's activity—the body of Christ. These examples also serve to remind us of what vital spiritual importance the regular gathering together of God's people really is.

Hindering the Mission of the Church

Not surprisingly, Satan also seeks to curtail the evangelistic efforts of Christians. Evangelistic activity represents a frontal assault on Satan's dominion. Indeed he makes every effort to frustrate Christians who seek to reveal the redemptive message of the gospel.

Satan is "the god of this age," who "has blinded the minds of unbelievers, so that they cannot see the light of the gospel" (2 Cor 4:4). The church's mission is to bring sight to the blind. The gospel must be proclaimed in the power of the Spirit because the church faces an enemy of supernatural proportions, who commands a host of angelic powers seeking to prevent the spread of the kingdom of Christ.

Paul gives us one glimpse into the satanic opposition he himself faced in his endeavor to preach the gospel to the Thessalonians. According to Luke's account in Acts, Paul barely had three weeks to preach the gospel to people in Thessalonica (Acts 17:1-9). He was forced to leave abruptly because of a violent local outbreak of persecution. Fearing for the spiritual well-being of those who had become Christians, Paul earnestly wanted to return and spend more time with them. He wrote the Thessalonians and told them that he and his companions had tried to come to them again and again, "but Satan hindered us" (1 Thess 2:18 RSV).

Paul did not reveal the specific manner in which Satan had thwarted his efforts, but certainly Paul perceived the course of events preventing his return as the powerful working of Satan and not as the redirecting providence of God through the Holy Spirit (compare Acts 16:6-10). Commentators have made many suggestions as to how Satan worked—through Paul's "thorn in the flesh," opposition from the Jews and restraint by the civic officials of Thessalonica. Whatever the method, Paul perceived Satan's hand as behind it.

Paul taught the church that it, too, would face powerful demonic hostility when it preached the gospel. Consequently, the church would need to depend on God's power in order to make the gospel effectively known. This reliance is essentially the offensive aspect of "spiritual warfare" (Eph 6:10-20).

Paul taught that Satan would actually set traps to malign the church and ultimately hinder its mission in the world. One of the qualifications for an overseer is a good reputation with non-Christians so that the leader would not be slandered and thus cause the church disgrace (1 Tim 3:7). Paul described such a disgrace as falling into "the devil's trap." According to Gordon Fee, "It is a trap set by the devil when the behavior of the church's leaders is such that outsiders will be disinclined to hear the gospel."[17]

Such a disgrace to the gospel could come not only through the church's leaders, but also from the rank-and-file members. Paul saw an opportunity for Satan to slander the church when young widows became idle gossips and busybodies (1 Tim 5:13-16). As a result, he counseled this group to get married, raise a family and manage their households well.

There is a clear lesson to learn from these two passages in 1 Timothy. Unruly or sinful behavior among its members sharply blunts the ability of the church to reach its community with the gospel of Christ.

It is important for believers to resist satanic impulses to displease God, not only for their own spiritual good, but also for the effective evangelistic outreach of the church. Our lives must adorn the good news we proclaim.

10
Christ and No Other

*I*N AFRICA A RECURRING PROBLEM FOR TRIBAL PEOPLE WHO TURN TO CHRIST is what to do with their household gods and the deities whom their ancestors worshiped. Should they forsake them and destroy all their cultic images and paraphernalia? Or should they hold onto them and try to worship Christ together with their tribal deities? This decision is incredibly difficult for a tribal chief who fears that forsaking the gods of his ancestors might mean big trouble, even death, for him and his people.

In Paul's day Christians struggled with the same issue. New converts certainly would have asked: Why not continue celebrating the mystery rites of Cybele or Dionysus? Why not wear an amulet invoking gods and angels for protection from evil spirits? Why not worship Hekate or Selene for the protection they can provide from the astral spirits or dangerous wildlife spirits? Would not spirituality be enhanced by performing the mystery rites of Demeter or by observing the days that are sacred to Artemis or to Yahweh?

The Colossian Christians, in particular, were undoubtedly entertaining many such questions. Living in a valley about 100 miles inland from Ephesus and only eleven miles away from Laodicea, the fledgling church at Colossae was struggling to resist the influence of other religious traditions. In a spiritual environment where syncretism was an accepted part of life, these Christians were tempted to compromise their fidelity to Christ alone.

To all Christians who are tempted to syncretize their faith, Paul gave a very clear response in the epistle to the Colossians. Yahweh continues to be a jealous God. He wants all believers to give their wholehearted and undistracted devotion to him and to his beloved Son, the Lord Jesus Christ.

The Problem at Colossae: Christ Plus Something Else

Paul perceived a dangerous teaching was threatening the health and stability of the Colossian church.[1] Although it is difficult to interpret the details of the aberration with certainty, it appears a group of people within the church were advocating that the rest of the church join them in a number of practices that were not a part of the Christian tradition or apostolic teaching. These practices seemed to be rooted in a syncretistic view of Christianity in which elements of mystery initiation, Jewish ritual observances and magical practices were combined with the gospel. In his letter Paul revealed the demonic nature of this false teaching and its accompanying practices. He called the church to a fresh commitment to the purity of the gospel.

Like all other cities of the Mediterranean world during Paul's time, numerous gods and goddesses were worshiped at Colossae.[2] Since archeologists have never excavated this ancient city, we know little about its religions from inscriptions, temples or cultic images. Fortunately a number of Colossian coins have been discovered bearing the images of a few of the deities worshiped there. Among them were Isis, Sarapis, the Ephesian Artemis, the Laodicean Zeus, Demeter, Men, Selene and Helios. We can assume that magical practices and astrological beliefs were part of the spiritual outlook of the Colossian citizens because they were so deeply rooted in the coastal cities of Asia Minor. There is also evidence for a fairly large Jewish population in Colossae and the neighboring cities of Laodicea and Hierapolis. Thus there was probably a Jewish synagogue in or near the city.

There is also evidence that the false teaching had an explicit connection with mystery initiation. This connection may be seen at a place in the letter where Paul is describing the nature of the false teaching as part of his polemic. Unfortunately this connection is not clear in many of the modern English translations of the New Testament. In Colossians 2:18, Paul warned the Colossian Christians: "Do not let anyone who delights in false humility and the worship of angels disqualify you for the prize. *Such a person goes into great detail about what he has seen,* and his unspiritual mind puffs him up with idle notions" (NIV; italics mine). Years ago, Sir William Ramsay, the distinguished authority on the geography and religions of Asia Minor, suggested that the italicized part of the verse should more precisely be translated: *"what he had seen when he performed the higher stage of the [mystery] ritual"* (italics mine).[3]

The varying translations revolve around the interpretation of one very important word in the verse, which occurs only here in the New Testament. The word is actually quite rare in all of Greek literature, and every translator has had difficulty determining the exact meaning of it in this context. Literally, the phrase reads, "what he had seen, entering." Some have tried to explain the word as "entering" in the sense of "investigating" or "explaining." Ramsay based his interpretation on the appearance of the word in a series of religious inscriptions found just a few years earlier in a cultic sanctuary. The word appeared a number of times and seemed to refer to the climax of the initiation rites to the mysteries of the god Apollo at his temple at Claros on the west coast of Asia Minor. What heightened the significance of this discovery for interpreting Colossians was the fact that one of the groups coming to the Apollo temple was from Laodicea, Colossae's nearest neighbor.

All of this seems to point to the fact that the false teaching at Colossae had a very close tie with initiatory rites into the mystery religions. It is possible a faction in the Colossian church was suggesting that their fellow believers join them in celebrating the mystery rites of a local deity, or perhaps even in establishing a Christian mystery initiation. Ramsay suggested there was a rival leader in the congregation who was introducing ideas that he had brought over from his old belief in the mystery religions, resulting in a mystic form of Christianity.

The dangerous teaching at Colossae also had an explicit connection with magical practices. The phrase "worship of angels" (Col 2:18) offers some evidence for this connection. It is quite possible Paul was denouncing a magical invocation of angels.[4] It is not necessary for us to think only of good angels surrounding the throne of Yahweh. Christians and Jews were not the only ones who used the word *angel* for supernatural beings or spirits. Pagans also used the word *angel* in reference to their deities (such as Hekate) and to refer to intermediary spirits. Understood in this sense, Paul warned the Colossians not to get involved in calling on other gods or supernatural beings for protection or to perform a given task. For Paul this was tantamount to worshiping them. Christ alone deserved their worship.[5]

This disrupting faction was presenting its teaching as a "philosophy" (2:8). This word does not necessarily imply an adherence to the ideas of a particular Greek philosopher or philosophical school of thought. *Philosophy* was a term that was used quite broadly, even in the sense of magical practices. Paul's opposition to it was clear when he described their "fine-sounding arguments" (2:4) as "hollow" and "deceptive" (2:4, 8).

This teaching was not merely intellectual with no impact on the way day-to-day life was lived out. There were quite a number of ascetic practices that Paul alluded to in his characterization of it. The ascetic behavior extended to a "harsh treatment of the body" (2:23), perhaps implying even bodily mutilations. Self-flagellation was typical of the behavior of adherents to the cults of Cybele and Attis, which were known to exist in the area. Food and ritual observances also played a role in this "philosophy." Paul cautioned the believers to allow no one to place upon them ritual demands in the realm of food and drink or with regard to religious festivals, new moons and sabbaths (2:16). Paul also scorned a prohibiting phrase that the adherents of this teaching had apparently cited: "Do not handle! Do not taste! Do not touch!" (2:21).

The rival teaching thus appeared to have elements from the mystery religions, magical practices and even Jewish beliefs (sabbaths). It was unequivocally a syncretistic "philosophy"—Christianity plus something else.

The Connection of the False Teaching with the Powers

Apart from Ephesians, there are more references to the principalities and powers in Colossians than in any of Paul's other letters. Paul used a wide variety of terms in referring to these powers: "thrones," "dominions," "principalities," "authorities," "elemental spirits" and "angels" (RSV). While a few scholars have tried to make a case for interpreting some of these powers as good angels, especially those referred to in Colossians 1:16, the broader context of the letter paints them in a rather dark light. The same "principalities" *(archai)* and "authorities" *(exousiai)* spoken of in Colossians 1:16 are pictured as defeated enemies in 2:15 over which Christ is the head (2:10). It is most likely that Paul intended all of his references to the spirit-powers in Colossians to be understood as the evil powers of darkness.

According to Paul's analysis, the religious "philosophy" menacing the church at Colossae could ultimately be attributed to the inspiration of "elemental spirits" *(stoicheia)*. In Colossians 2:8, Paul states: "See to it that no one makes a prey of you by philosophy and empty deceit [1] according to human tradition, [2] according to the elemental spirits of the universe, and not according to Christ" (RSV).

In the first part of the verse, Paul indicts the obvious human involvement that propagates this erroneous teaching, which human tradition imparts. In the second part of the verse, he points to the true origin of the teaching in a personal, spiritual sense; that is, the evil "elemental spirits" inspire this teaching. He thus connects this false teaching with demonic involvement in much the same way that he characterized pagan religions in general as demonic in 1 Corinthians 10:20-21. A similar situation is envisioned in 1 Timothy 4:1, where believers are warned against demon-instigated teaching: "The Spirit clearly says that in later times some will abandon the faith and follow deceiving spirits and things taught by demons." Those purveying this teaching are described as "hypocritical liars," implying that they claim to be Christians, but are actually Satan's advocates.

The false teaching at Colossae is dangerous precisely because the supernatural opponents, whom Christ died to defeat, inspire it. For this reason Paul can later say, "If with Christ you died to the elemental spirits of the universe, why do you live as if you still belonged to the world?" (Col 2:20 RSV). Through union with Christ and by appropriating his resources, believers can resist the diverse evil influences of Satan and his powers. For the Colossians the perverse influence was especially felt through the rival teaching passed on by people within the context of the church.

Christ Alone Is Supreme

Paul was convinced that the teaching of his opponents at Colossae presented a direct challenge to the absolute lordship of Christ for these believers. By giving credence to the "philosophy," they were transferring their allegiance from Christ and giving it to the principalities and powers. Quite likely fear of the evil supernatural world motivated them in part. They continued to dread the influence of terrestrial spirits who could injure them in day-to-day life, the astral spirits who controlled their destiny, and the underworld spirits who could torment them in the life hereafter. Could Christ truly protect them from those powers? They wondered and were apprehensive. Their doubt compelled them to take the "safest" route—worship Christ *and* the other gods.

In order to restore their confidence in the Lord Jesus, Paul began his letter by including one of the most eloquent and moving pieces of poetic praise of Christ in all of Scripture. Colossians 1:15-20 touchingly affirms the sole supremacy of Christ.[6] The poetic arrangement, choice of words and beautiful expression have caused numerous scholars to refer to it as an early Christian hymn. Possibly Paul quoted a hymn that was known and sung during worship in the Colossian and other churches of Asia. Although Paul could have composed this passage specifically for the Colossians, the rhetorical power of his argument is enhanced all the more if he has cited an already existing hymn. In effect, the Colossians would be guilty of not internalizing what they were reading and singing!

Paul prefaced the hymn by establishing the fact that they are no longer in bondage to Satan's dominion. Paul says, "For he has rescued us from the dominion of darkness and brought us into the kingdom of the Son he loves" (Col 1:13). The hymn then brings out the Son's character in a twofold way: Christ is both Lord of creation and Lord of reconciliation.

As Lord of creation, Christ is described in his unique relationship to the one, invisible God. Christ is not himself an angelic intermediary or one among many. He has a temporal priority over all of creation and is distinctively related to God by being both the "image" of God and possessing all of the rights of a firstborn. Christ is also Lord of creation because he is the Creator. Paul took special pains to point out that he was not only the creator of everything on earth and in heaven, but especially the realm most feared by the Colossians, the invisible realm "whether thrones or powers or rulers or authorities" (1:16). In fact, these powers owe their continued existence to Christ since he is the sustainer of the creation (1:17).

As Lord of reconciliation, Christ is portrayed in the second part of the hymn in his role as bringing ultimate harmony to all of his creation. Marred by rebellion against the purpose of God, the creation faces constant upheaval and distress due to the degenerative impact of evil. The work of Christ provides the basis of hope for the future. At the consummation of the age, all things will be reconciled to God through Christ. Again, Paul stressed that "all things" include the heavenly entities, namely the principalities and powers.

This hymn brilliantly affirms the lordship of Christ over the principalities and powers. How comforting it must have been for the Colossians to be reassured that Christ is superior to the powers they fear and once worshiped. He not only created them, but he is their life-giving sustainer. History is in his control, and the powers will ultimately be brought to their knees before him.

Paul continued to build his case for the supremacy of Christ by declaring later in the letter that Christ is "the head over every power and authority" (Col 2:10). This is based on the fact that "in Christ all the fullness of the Deity lives in bodily form" (Col 2:9), which was also evinced in the hymn (Col 1:19): "For God was pleased to have all his fullness dwell in him." Christ is again portrayed in a unique and close unity with the God of Israel. Tom Wright explains that the incarnation of Christ "was and is the 'solid reality' in which were fulfilled all the earlier foreshadowings, all the ancient promises that God would dwell with his people."[7] God is now truly with his people, indwelling their lives and giving them direction and strength. In verse 10, the emphasis falls on the certainty of Christ's control over the powers—not one evil angelic power stands outside the sphere of his sovereignty. Believers now share in this authority.

The high point of his case for the supremacy of Christ over the powers comes at Colossians 2:15. The principalities and powers were defeated on the cross. This sign of the end for the powers was decisive. They were stripped of their compelling influence over believers. They are now like vicious dogs on a leash. Although they are still active and continue to wreak havoc and promote evil, they are under the control and authority of one more powerful, one they are compelled to obey.

Christ is not one among a number of powers at a certain level of the angelic hierarchy. He is at the top. He is supreme. Despite the claims of other religions and counter to the assumptions of magic, the Colossians could truly worship Christ as pre-eminent. In spite of Paul's eloquent and powerful case to this effect, we cannot minimize the difficulty it would have been for the Colossian believers to believe this truth in the deepest recesses of their consciousness. Years of believing in a multiplicity of gods and spirits and learning how each could be placated is quite different than trusting in one—who is so different.

Christ Alone Is Sufficient

Paul applied his teaching on the sole supremacy of Christ to their situation. He wanted nothing more than to see them conducting their lives with Christ as the focus. He writes, "So then, just as you received Christ Jesus as Lord, continue to live in him, rooted and built up in him, strengthened in the faith as you were taught, and overflowing with thankfulness" (Col 2:6-7). Paul assured them that they have all the resources they need in Christ. Just as God bestowed on Christ all his divine fullness, so Christ imparts to believers the enabling power, love and divine grace for resisting the influence of evil and living according to God's desires. Paul plainly says, "and you have been given fullness in Christ" (Col 2:10). It is no mistake that the very next statement that Paul makes is the description of Christ as the one "who is the head over every power and authority" (Col 2:10). The clear implication of this passage is that part of the divine resources that Christ bestows on believers is his authority over the evil powers.

Christ can impart his fullness to them because of their unique relationship to him, symbolized in the rite of baptism. They have been made alive with Christ by being identified with him in his death and resurrection (Col 2:12-13). Their death with Christ has effectively rendered them dead to the powerful influence of the elemental spirits (Col 2:20). He alone is sufficient to protect them from evil spirits. No phylacteries, amulets or talismans are necessary. Neither is mystery initiation essential for additional spiritual enlightenment since Christ is "the mystery of God" and in him "are hidden all the treasures of wisdom and knowledge *(gnōsis)*" (Col 2:2-3).

The hope and strength of these believers is wrapped up in the fact that Christ actually indwells their lives (Col 1:27). This fact is not to be understood in the sense of a mystical absorption into deity. Christ personally indwells their lives and infuses them with his power, filling them with his love and giving them a blessed hope for the future. This is the essence of the Christian "mystery."

The epitomizing trait of Christianity is relationship with Christ. Given his all-encompassing lordship and his all-sufficiency, the Colossians are left with no legitimate reason to syncretize their faith. Christ is all they need!

Appropriating the Resources in Christ

Having the right concept of Christ is not enough. Giving assent to a creed or a statement of faith does not guarantee victorious living. In practice, theology can easily become severed from ethics, and what one believes about Christ may not necessarily affect the way a person lives. Christology has life-changing implications. It demands a total response and commitment.

The Colossians needed to have their concept of Christ purified, and they needed to be admonished to draw on the resources he provides for day-to-day life. Paul chided them for "not holding fast to the head, from whom the entire body, being supplied and held together by the joints and ligaments, grows with the growth which is from God" (Col 2:19 NASB). It is the "head" of the body that provides what they need, but they have to seek and be willing to receive the nourishment he offers. They also need to endeavor earnestly to live in a way that is consonant with the character of their new heavenly life. They are citizens of two kingdoms. The temptation will be for them to fix their attention on the limitations and problems of life in the present evil age. Paul contended strongly that their focus of attention must be placed on the character of their new life and all the spiritual blessings, security and divine endowments that it brings. For Paul this focus is the secret for overcoming life's obstacles in the here and now; it is the basis for Christian ethics. New Testament scholars refer to it as Paul's "eschatological tension" between the "already" and the "not-yet," which is at the heart of his theology.

Appropriating the benefits of this new life requires that the Colossians set their hearts and minds "on things above" (Col 3:1-2). "Above" is where Christ is seated at the right hand of God. It is also where the lives of the Colossians are "now hidden with Christ in God" (Col 3:3) because of their identification with Christ's death. Part of seeking the heavenly life is through deeply immersing themselves in Christ's teachings. Paul encouraged them to "let the word of Christ dwell in you richly" (Col 3:16). It also involves prayer, an expression of faith in God but also the channel to communicate with God and convey one's needs to him. Paul therefore enjoined them to "devote yourselves to prayer, being watchful and thankful" (Col 4:2). Aware of his own need for divine strength and enablement, Paul requested prayer for himself (Col 4:3-4).

At Colossae the syncretistic impulse facing Christians was strong, especially since a lifetime pattern of worshiping many gods had reinforced it. The pressure from outside the church must have been equally intense. People in Colossian society would not have understood Christ's exclusivistic claims. The false teaching at Colossae was undoubtedly packaged and presented in an alluring way. But for the apostle Paul it was wrong. It was wrong because evil spirits inspired it, and because it detracted from the supreme and sufficient lordship of Jesus Christ.

11
Spiritual Warfare

*F*OR OUR STRUGGLE IS NOT AGAINST FLESH AND BLOOD, BUT AGAINST THE rulers, against the authorities, against the powers of this dark world and against the spiritual forces of evil in the heavenly realms."

Ephesians 6:12 is one of the best-known verses of the entire Bible, yet one of the most misunderstood, misconstrued and practically neglected texts of the Scripture. Immersed in a culture that says evil spirits do not exist, Western Christians struggle even to begin the task of spiritual warfare. We spend more time wondering if we really should believe in demons than grappling with how we should respond to them.

On this topic some of us suffer double-mindedness. Although mental assent is given to the likelihood that evil spirits exists since it is affirmed in the Bible, in reality it makes no practical difference in the way we live our day-to-day lives. When dealing with a personal problem such as illness or depression, medical and psychological services are the only considered alternatives. Little thought is given to the spiritual side. Even in Christian ministry the spiritual dimension is often ignored. Ineffective evangelism, for example, is often attributed to a lack of training or persuasive skill rather than powerful demonic hindrance.

Some segments of Christianity do take seriously demonic existence. They attempt to confront the spiritual dimension. Unfortunately the excesses of a few of these groups sometimes overshadows the healthy aspects of the teaching and practice of others. Ephesians 6:10-20 wrongly becomes a manifesto on exorcism. Or demons are seen behind virtually every problem. The rest of Christianity lamentably writes off the helpful perspective of these groups on the demonic because they appear to be extreme.

We need, more than ever, to gain a revitalized perspective on spiritual warfare. If we are not aware of the subtle and powerful work of our enemy, he will defeat us. Perhaps he already has certain areas of life strongly in his grip, where we have not been aware of his devious work.

Many thinkers believe Western society is on the verge of a major world view shift. Scholars such as Hans Küng are anticipating an epochal move from the "Modern Era" to a "Post-Modern Era," a major paradigm change in the way Westerners view reality. There is no doubt that the rising influence of Eastern thought and the burgeoning impact of the New Age movement will have influence on how Western culture perceives the supernatural. The church needs to be prepared for this new challenge. Few would give the church a strong mark on its preparedness to handle effectively the special problems that arise in ministering to people who have been involved in the "occult." The best way to determine what spiritual warfare means for us now is to discern what it meant for Paul and his readers back then. First of all, spiritual warfare needs to be understood in terms of what it meant to people living in Ephesus and western Asia Minor where occult beliefs flourished and the reality of the influence of the spirit realm was unquestioned. Second, it needs to be understood in the larger context of the entire book of Ephesians.

Spiritism in Ephesus

The city of Ephesus was really not that different from any other city in the Hellenistic world. It did, however, have quite a reputation for being a center for magical practices. Luke reinforces that reputation by his account of the burning of the enormous amount of magical books (Acts 19:13-20). As discussed in chapter one, magic was concerned with manipulating the spirit world. It is based on a world view that sees spirits, both good and evil, involved in virtually every part of life.

Ephesus was also a city famous for its patron deity, Artemis of Ephesus. The Ephesian Artemis was worshiped as a goddess of the underworld. She was also believed to wield effective power over the spirits in nature and wildlife. The signs of the zodiac on her cultic image reassured her worshipers that she was a cosmic deity who had influence over the astral spirits who controlled the unfolding of fate. Ephesus was not only the city of Artemis; at least forty-four other deities were worshiped in this city.

It was precisely these kind of people—magical practitioners and worshipers of Artemis and countless other gods—who were becoming Christians and joining the churches in the area. It is too easy to read the book of Ephesians through our own cultural lenses and fail to grasp the nature and magnitude of the issues facing these young first-century Christians. Although they would have longed to give their devotion to Christ, the pull to syncretize their Christianity with other practices and beliefs would have been intense. With regard to the issue of the demonic, the Ephesian readers had far more in common with non-Western cultures than they do with those of us in the West.

Quite likely Paul intended the epistle to the Ephesians to be read not only in Ephesus but also in a number of churches in the western part of Asia Minor. Ephesus is a good point of reference for us in looking at the Ephesians. It was the capital city of the province with a population of at least a quarter million people. It was a religious center and had strategic influence over all of Asia Minor.[1] It had also been Paul's base of operation during his nearly three-year stay in the province. The basic issues were the same throughout these western Asian churches. These new believers needed help in developing a Christian world view. They especially needed to know how to respond to the gods and goddesses they had formerly worshiped and the various astral, terrestrial and underworld spirits they had feared.

I have written a book-length treatment on Paul's letter to the Ephesians, where I contend that this epistle is occasioned in part by Paul's special concern to address the needs of people coming to Christ from a background of what today we would call "occultic" beliefs.[2] This explains why the principalities and powers and the theme of spiritual warfare receives more attention in Ephesians than in any of his other letters. Ephesians then becomes the pivotal letter in comprehending Paul's thought on the issue of principalities and powers.

Christ, the Powers and the Power of God
Paul wanted his readers to entertain no doubt that Christ is superior to the powers they feared and had once served. Knowing that his

readers would be tempted to doubt the superiority and all-sufficiency of Christ, Paul prayed that God would open their eyes so they could see the incomparably great power of the God of the Lord Jesus Christ. His prayer became an elaboration on the mighty power of God: "That power is like the working of his mighty strength, which he exerted in Christ when he raised him from the dead and seated him at his right hand in the heavenly realms." Paul did not stop here. He went on to draw the implications of the exaltation of Christ to the status of the powers. Christ is "far above all rule and authority, power and dominion, and every title that can be given, not only in the present age but also in the one to come." The powers are especially in view when Paul says, "God placed all things under his feet and appointed him to be head over everything for the church" (Eph 1:19-22).

Anticipating his summons to spiritual warfare, Paul prayed for God's strength to be imparted to all of his believing readers. He prayed that "out of his glorious riches he may strengthen you with power through his Spirit in your inner being" (Eph 3:16). Having prayed for them, he can then admonish his readers at the end of the letter to "be strong in the Lord and in his mighty power" (Eph 6:10). God's power is essential not only for resisting the influence of the powers of Satan, but also for manifesting love in the Christian community and living according to the ethical standards that Paul laid down.

The mighty resurrection power of God is available to believers. Paul encouraged Christians to draw on this power for daily living. In Asia Minor the believers had to develop an entirely new perspective on divine power. Their perverted understanding of the supernatural needed to be purified by growing in the knowledge of the one true God and why he would impart his power to people.

First, the source of this power is new. They have been reconciled to Yahweh, the "one God and Father of all" (Eph 4:5). He is the God of Abraham, Isaac and Jacob, but also the God of the Lord Jesus Christ. He is supreme and has no competitors. All the former deities they once served must be forsaken and regarded as the manifestations and work of the evil principalities and powers.

Second, these believers were directed to a new and unique means of access to divine power. A magical formula or recipe will not manipulate God. He is a personal God who communes with his people and seeks a relationship with his own. This fellowship with God does not come through some mystical absorption into a deity and through a mystery ritual or any other means. It comes by the access made to God through the work of Jesus Christ on the cross (Eph 2:18). Believers have been brought into a very close union with the Lord Jesus Christ, which Paul most commonly refers to as being "in Christ." Such is the closeness and solidarity of this bond that believers can consider themselves to have been coresurrected and coexalted with Christ (Eph 2:6). This is the basis for the new identity of believers and the foundation for their sharing in Christ's authority over the powers of evil.

Third, there is a new purpose for imparting divine power to people. No longer are believers to use supernatural power to inflict harm or for self-centered ends. God's power is imparted to believers to enable them to lead selfless lives. Believers are called to exercise the kind of sacrificial love that was modeled on the cross (Eph 5:2). In the eyes of the world, this is impossible. And, although Satan and his powers will seek to prevent it, God's power strengthens believers even to love selflessly.

The Nature of Evil Influence

In Ephesians Paul was at pains to point out that people cannot respond to life's decisions neutrally. They are deeply affected by a set of evil, determining influences. These influences led people on a path that is directed toward death—life apart from God. In Ephesians 2:2-3, Paul described these influences in terms of the environment ("the age of this world"), an inner inclination toward evil ("the flesh") and a supernaturally powerful opponent ("the ruler of the kingdom of the air, the spirit").

By drawing attention to these three forces, Paul established the inescapability of death for non-Christians and their resultant need to experience God's redemptive work. But an understanding of these three evil influences is also important for Christians as they seek to spread the gospel and live according to its ethical standards. These influences continue to make themselves felt even after someone is saved. A Christian is not automatically immune to temptation, the world's influence or Satan's direct assault.

Although these three influences continue to operate, there is a decisive difference for the Christian. The believer lives in union with the risen Christ and may draw on Christ's power—his victory over temptation, his resistance to the world's allurements and influences, and, above all, his victory and resultant authority over Satan and the powers of darkness. This passage thus forms the essential background to an appropriate understanding of why an orientation about the Christian life as warfare is essential.

The Christian Life As Warfare

The spiritual warfare passage represents the church as facing intense attack by the devil and his powers of evil. Paul used an extended metaphor of a soldier who puts on the appropriate pieces of armor to heighten this image. In this case the soldier puts on a belt, a breastplate, footgear, a shield and a helmet, and then takes up a sword. The main point of this imagery is that Christianity should be understood as warfare and believers should prepare for this warfare just as any soldier would prepare for battle. It is really unimportant to decide whether Paul has a Roman, Greek, Jewish or Persian soldier in mind. Most of the imagery comes straight from the book of Isaiah (see Is 11:5; 52:7; 59:17). Furthermore, one needs to exercise caution in reading too much into each of the material images, such as emphasizing that the helmet protects the brain and the breastplate the vital organs. Paul felt free to vary the spiritual truths he attached to military imagery. For example, whereas the breastplate represents righteousness in Ephesians 6:14, it represents faith and love in 1 Thessalonians 5:18.

In verse 12, the use of the word *struggle* describes a scene of conflict. In the first century this word was commonly used, not in the context of warfare, but as the typical term for the sport of wrestling. It even occurs on inscriptions in western Asia Minor in reference to the wrestling event of the various games held in the regional cities. As such, Paul probably used it to heighten the closeness of the struggle with the powers of evil. The use of the words *evil* and *darkness* also indicate the character of spiritual warfare. The world rulers *(kosmokratores)* are depicted as ruling over "this darkness" and as being "evil." The whole setting is cast "on the evil day," which probably refers both to the fact that "the days are evil" (Eph 5:16) and that there will be intense times of demonic attack. Finally, the devil is depicted in extremely vivid terms as launching flaming arrows at the church (Eph 6:16). The whole tenor of the passage is designed to convey the feeling of extreme danger.

The danger posed to Christians by these organized powers of darkness can be overwhelming—left on our own. Christians, however, are not alone. They are united to the exalted Lord who defeated the forces of evil and now imparts his power and authority to the church. Throughout the letter the apostle has emphasized God's power and its availability to believers. This emphasis now reaches a climax when Paul says "be strong in the Lord and in his mighty power" (Eph 6:10). He strung together three power-denoting terms (*endynamō, kratos* and *ischys*) that have a combined effect of bringing the almighty power of God into bold relief especially in contrast to the weaker powers of darkness.

Paul further defined and clarified God's power by specifying various ways God bestows his power on the church and by relating the means through which God's enabling might is imparted. Paul enumerated seven spiritual weapons. Five of these are objective endowments from God (truth, righteousness, the gospel, salvation and the Spirit/the word of God) and two stress our responsibility (faith and prayer). Our responsibility is also implicit in the five gifts from God (see also the chart at the end of the chapter). While this list of spiritual resources ("weapons") does not exhaust all divine bestowments available to Christians, it represents the essence of all that is vital to waging successful warfare against the powers of darkness.

The nature of spiritual warfare, as Paul portrayed it here, is primarily concerned with Christian conduct and spreading the gospel—not with exorcism or eradicating structural evil. The heart of spiritual warfare could best be summarized as resistance and proclamation.

Spiritual Warfare As Resistance

Four times in the passage Paul used the word *stand/withstand* (same root in the Greek: Eph 6:11, 13, 14). In the larger context of Ephesians it is clear Paul did not want believers to "give a place to the devil" with excessive anger, lying, stealing or succumbing to any other temptation to moral impurity (Eph 4:27). Paul described the devil and his powers as working in concert with the flesh and the world (Eph 2:2-3—see above) to promote sin among Christians and hinder the progress of the gospel. For this reason the Christian needs to appropriate God's enabling power in order to live with moral integrity.

Spiritual warfare is therefore resistance. It is a defensive posture. It involves recognizing the supernatural nature of temptation and being prepared to face it. It also implies appropriating God's power to progress in eradicating moral vices that already have a place in one's life.

The first two spiritual weapons Paul named are "truth" and "righteousness." There appears to be two sides to these weapons. On the one hand, they need to be understood as divine endowments for the task of spiritual warfare. On the other hand, they are to be regarded as virtues that need to be cultivated in the lives of believers. This understanding is quite natural in that the gospel brings with it implications for Christian conduct. Paul saw the gospel as "truth" (Eph 1:13) and as the power of God for salvation (Rom 1:16). In contrast, the devil is the archadversary who uses many schemes designed to misrepresent, deceive and trick. Believers need to be convinced and assured of the gospel's truth and what it affirms about them as God's children. By implication, believers need to conduct their lives in a manner consistent with the truth of the gospel. Lying and deceit can have no place in a believer's life; they are an affront to the God of truth. Consequently, in Ephesians, Paul told each Christian that he or she "must put off falsehood and speak truthfully to his neighbor" (Eph 4:25; see also 5:9).

One of the most remarkable parts of the salvation that God provides is the gift of "righteousness." After informing the Romans that "there is no one righteous, not even one" (Rom 3:10), Paul elaborated on the wonderful news that "this righteousness from God comes through faith in Jesus Christ to all who believe" (Rom 3:22). This righteousness means that those who believe in Jesus have been acquitted of all guilt before God. They are completely forgiven and reconciled to him as friends, better yet, as sons and daughters. The devil and his malicious powers would certainly like Christians to believe otherwise. The powers strive to convince people that God could not possibly forgive them for some of the horrible things they have done in the past. Such a notion could not be further from the truth. Christians have indeed been pardoned through Christ's blood, and as such, can live boldly and confidently, not with guilt, fear and timidity.

Possessing God's righteousness, however, brings responsibility. The apostle admonished his readers to strip off the old self and put on the new self, which is "created to be like God in true righteousness and holiness" (Eph 4:24). The development of personal holiness and integrity is part of the preparation for engaging in victorious spiritual warfare. Conversely, a lack of integrity and personal holiness will certainly hinder a believer's ability to resist the onslaught of Satan's minions successfully.

Another very important aspect of a believer's resistance is "salvation," which is linked to the helmet as the fifth piece of armor (Eph 6:17). Salvation needs to be understood as Paul explained it in the larger context of the letter. In Ephesians 2:5-10, Paul twice reaffirmed to his readers that "by grace you have been saved," eloquently describing the concept of salvation. These two occurrences are the only occasions in all of Paul's letters where he used the Greek perfect tense to refer to salvation. The perfect tense stresses the results of a decisive action in the past. Paul wanted his readers to be very secure in their identity in Christ. They are people who are saved and enjoy the benefits of being saved.

Paul clarified what he meant by salvation in that same context with three powerful thoughts: (1) believers have been made alive with Christ, (2) they have been raised up with Christ, and (3) they have been seated with him in the heavenly realms (Eph 2:4-6). For Paul it is vitally important that believers know who they are in Christ in order to resist the influence of Satan and his forces on their lives. Only through their salvation and union with Christ will they be able to resist.

Finally, the believer is given a "sword" to fend off the attacks of the evil one. The sword is linked with the Spirit and the Word of God. Just as Jesus used Scripture to resist Satan's temptations while he was in the wilderness (Mt 4:1-11), Paul called on believers to use God's Word to resist the devil in their own situations. This is not to be understood as a semimagical use of Scripture, quoting it out loud as a means of thwarting the devil. It involves gaining a thorough familiarity with Scripture and an accurate understanding of its relevance for any given situation. When Jesus was tempted, the devil applied Scripture inappropriately and out of context; Jesus responded to the devil by applying Scripture appropriately and according to its proper intent in conveying the mind of God on specific matters. The thorough, systematic study of Scripture on a regular basis is vital for all believers. It is an integral part of engaging in effective spiritual warfare.

Spiritual Warfare As Proclamation
Spiritual warfare is not only defensive; it also takes the offensive. Paul

of Christ to advance on enemy territory by pro-
l of the Lord Jesus Christ. Just as Christ bound the
er to plunder his house, so too the body of Christ
kingdom by proclaiming the promise of divine
n the kingdom of darkness.
rt of the soldier's gear that is not a weapon, but it
.t enables the soldier to take an offensive posture
l footwear. A typical soldier would journey for miles
:ed to the battlefront and then pursue the enemy
true when Xerxes led his armies all the way from
ɔt to conquer Greece!). The footgear of the Chris-
ɪe readiness to announce the Good News of peace"
lievers need to be prepared to share the good news
God may lead them.

Many commentators have correctly observed that the only offensive
weapon in the entire panoply is the sword (Eph 6:17). While it is used
as a part of a believer's resistance, it is also a weapon of aggression.
The Word of God and the work of the Spirit are the means by which
the people of God step out in defiance of Satan and rob his domain.
They are the means by which God draws people to himself, transform-
ing their lives and bringing them into relationship with himself.

Thus, according to Paul, the primary aggressive action the Christian
is called to take in the world is to spread the gospel—the good news
of salvation through the death and resurrection of Christ. The gospel
represents "God's power to rescue people from [the devil's] tyranny."[3]

The whole course of Paul's ministry is a model of this aggressive
proclamation. The church should follow Paul's lead. Luke seemed to
understand this point and wrote his account of Paul's missionary
outreach in a way that would inspire zeal and courage among the
believers who read it. At the same time, Luke did not minimize the
amount of conflict Paul faced in his proclamational mission. Luke
interpreted much of this conflict, as described in chapter one, as
powerful demonic opposition. Yet the Christian who depends on
God's power, as Paul did, will overcome enemy hostilities, and the
gospel will continue to advance, with more and more people being
saved out of the dominion of darkness.

Even here, in the context of Ephesians, Paul personally was concerned with the mission of the church in spite of his imprisonment.
He wanted God's enabling power to be imparted to him through

prayer, not necessarily for a demonstration of the gospel's supernatural character through miraculous events. He sensed a need for God's touch so he could proclaim it fearlessly and boldly! Even after all the years of successful preaching, Paul still felt a great need for a divine infusing of power to give him the nerve to proclaim the gospel fearlessly. He pleads, "Pray also for me, that whenever I open my mouth, words may be given me so that I will fearlessly make known the mystery of the gospel, for which I am an ambassador in chains. Pray that I may declare it fearlessly, as I should" (Eph 6:19-20). Paul's incessant readiness to proclaim the good news was a hallmark of his life. Likewise, it should be of paramount importance to believers in subsequent generations. This is the mission of the church!

Prayer As the Primary Weapon

If Paul were to summarize the primary way of gaining access to the power of God for waging successful spiritual warfare, he would unwaveringly affirm that it is through prayer. Prayer is given much greater prominence in the spiritual warfare passage than any of the other implements. Prayer is also the only spiritual piece of armor that is not given a corresponding physical weapon (like a breastplate or a shield).

When Paul spoke of prayer, it was closely related to his concept of faith. He also mentioned faith for its role in engaging in spiritual warfare. He associated it with the shield. It is mentioned explicitly as the means of overcoming intense diabolic attack: "Take up the shield of faith, with which you can extinguish all the flaming arrows of the evil one" (Eph 6:16). Prayer became for Paul the practical manifestation of faith. By these means, Satan is effectively resisted.

Throughout Ephesians, Paul stressed the role of faith in appropriating the power of God. The faith he called for is based on the objective fact of Christ's resurrection and exaltation over the supernatural powers. God's power is not imparted to Christians by wearing a magical amulet or even a crucifix. Neither does one gain access to it by performing a rite or by chanting certain words. God's power is given through simple trust in him.

This trust finds expression most commonly in the act of prayer. Paul consequently summoned believers to pray "at all times" and "for all the saints" (Eph 6:18). Paul himself modeled this to the readers in this letter, telling them the essence of what he has prayed for them—their increased awareness of God's power and for God to strengthen them with his power (Eph 1:15-23; 3:14-19).

The spiritual warfare passage is often viewed in individual terms; that is, each individual Christian should pray and ask God for strength to do battle. Paul actually depicted the arming in corporate terms. The whole church is involved in the process of arming. In fact, each believer is responsible for arming other believers. All of Paul's admonitions in this passage are in the plural. More important, however, is the fact that Paul urged believers to pray "for all the saints" (Eph 6:18). Since this exhortation is part of Paul's explanation of prayer as the final piece of armor, it is most natural to understand it as his recommendation as to the prerequisite and means of acquiring divine enablement. This fact is supported when he requested prayer for himself in the verses immediately following. In essence, he is asking his readers to arm him for spiritual warfare, particularly in his offensive act of proclaiming the gospel. Certainly the two prayers of Ephesians 1 and 3 model this fact. Through those two prayers, Paul deployed God's armor for the protection and use of his readers. By leaving aside the metaphorical language of spiritual warfare and putting it into the simplest terms, one could say Paul prayed that God would endow them with his power so they could successfully resist Satan's temptations and be divinely enabled to proclaim the gospel fearlessly in spite of demonic hindrance and hostility.

Spiritual warfare, therefore, is more proactive than reactive. It is the preparation before the storm. In practical terms it involves praying for "the healthy" in addition to praying for "the sick"; that is, praying specifically for individuals to resist temptation in their personal areas of vulnerability. It involves praying for the progress of the gospel in light of localized and intense demonic hostility to the ongoing mission of the church. This concept has the potential of rejuvenating prayer groups and prayer meetings in the church today.

Today's church needs a stronger sense of the mutuality of the body of Christ. The Western church, in particular, is guilty of an "individualistic Christianity." Instead of condemning the brother or sister who falls into sin, we need to look first to ourselves. Did we pray for God's grace to enable that person to resist Satan's solicitations to evil? Spiritual warfare is a call to corporate prayer.

Responding to the Powers of Darkness

Interpreting the Armor of God

☐ You cannot succeed on your own. Draw on the strength that Christ promises to supply.

☐ Realize that you cannot count on life to be a smooth, easy path. There are evil supernatural forces out to destroy you.

1. *Put On Your Trousers: Wear Truth*

☐ Know the truth of who you are in Christ (for the powers of darkness will try to deceive you).

☐ Practice honesty and live with moral integrity.

2. *Put On the Breastplate of Righteousness*

☐ Realize your status before God as one who has been acquitted of all guilt.

☐ Acquire personal holiness and develop good character.

3. *Put On Your Boots: Prepare the Gospel of Peace*

☐ Prepare yourself for sharing the gospel wherever God calls you.

4. *Take the Shield of Faith*

☐ Do not doubt! Believe that God will help you overcome.

5. *Put On the Helmet of Salvation*

☐ Be secure in your identity in Christ—as one who has been saved, united with Christ, made alive, coresurrected and coexalted.

6. *Take the Sword of the Spirit, the Word of God*

☐ Devote your life to aggressively spreading the gospel.

☐ Know the Scripture and apply it to every difficult situation.

THE BOTTOM LINE: PRAY!

☐ Ask God to strengthen you to resist temptation and share the gospel effectively.

☐ Ask God to strengthen your fellow believers to resist temptation and share the gospel effectively.

12
Christ's Final Defeat of the Powers

*P*AUL GAVE CHRISTIANS A REASON FOR HOPE IN THE FUTURE. GOD IS MOVING history to a climax that will result in the eternal and absolute reign of his glorious son, the Lord Jesus Christ. This is "the blessed hope," which believers await (Tit 2:13).

People living in the first century were gripped with great fear of the hostile supernatural powers that controlled the unfolding of history and their own personal destiny. Hans Dieter Betz gives a clear expression of the prevalent world view:

> The common understanding was that man is hopelessly and helplessly engulfed and oppressed by these forces [i.e., powerful demonic entities]. They play capricious games with man from the time of his entering into the world until his departure. While working inside of man, they make up the body, yet they also encounter him from the outside, in that he has terrible and traumatic experiences of whatever "Fate" *(Tyche)* has in store. Under such conditions life is not life at all but a daily death.[1]

In order to cope with day-to-day life, Betz observes that "in many ancient cults, cultic measures were developed in order to soothe and pacify the demonic forces. These included prayers, rituals, sacrifices, astrology, magic, and theurgy."[2] In part one of this book much of it has been discussed.

Standing in stark contrast to their non-Christian neighbors, the early Christians had no reason to fear the malignant powers. They were united to the one true Lord, who had defeated all of the hostile forces by his death and resurrection. They realized that their future was wrapped up in the one who is bringing this age, filled with every form of evil, to an end. All of the powers of darkness will be abolished. The early Christians could therefore be a joyous people, full of hope, thankful to God the Father who had chosen them to be his own people before the foundation of the world (Eph 1:3).

Ongoing Hostility and One Final Rebellion

Throughout his letters, Paul strived to prepare his readers for a long period of conflict with Satan and the forces of darkness (especially in Eph 6:10-20). In the midst of all the struggles and battles Paul held out a significant promise: "The God of peace will soon crush Satan under your feet" (Rom 16:20). Paul here has in mind God's curse of the serpent given in Genesis 3:15: "He will crush your head, and you will strike his heel." This passage was present in contemporary Jewish Messianic expectation as illustrated by the *Testament of Levi* 6:5-6: "The Lord God is the mighty one of Israel, appearing on earth as a man and saving Adam through him. Then all the spirits of deceit will be given to be trodden under foot and men will rule over the evil spirits."[3] For Paul it was the Lord Jesus Christ who would accomplish this task. Satan and all of his powers will be devastated at the Second Coming of Christ.

Paul made it clear that an intensification of satanic activity will precede Christ's return (2 Thess 2:1-12). He spoke of a widespread rebellion against God, spearheaded by a major evil figure he called "the lawless one." Satan himself will infuse this person with supernatural power, and he will be capable of performing all kinds of signs and wonders (1 Thess 2:9; see also Rev 13:2). The major thrust of his activity will be deception: He will claim to be superior to the one true God and every deity whom people worship in their various pagan religions. He will seek to have all people worship him, turning their attention from the true God. During this time, God will even permit evil spirits of deception to delude non-Christians and confirm them in their belief in the "lawless one's" great deceit (2 Thess 2:11).[4] This "antichrist's" coming on the scene will in many ways intentionally parallel the manner of Christ's coming, in order to make the deceit more alluring. This final onslaught of rebellion, however, will not occur until God allows the present "restraining force" to be removed.

In Paul's estimation, this great human emissary of Satan will prove to be no obstacle to Christ when he returns. Paul proclaimed the triumphant note that "the lawless one will be revealed, whom the Lord Jesus will overthrow with the breath of his mouth" (2 Thess 2:8).

Paul's teaching here underlines the darkness of the days just prior to Christ's coming. How difficult it will be for those who do not know Christ in those days to turn to him! Believers need to be aware of the character of life in those days so they will not be deceived. This passage also gives further insight into the characteristic features of Satan's method of operation: He works through people, he imitates the truth, and he seeks above all to deceive people, leading them away from the one true God.

Christ's Final Subjection of the Powers

The evil principalities and powers, together with their leader Satan, face a definite point in history when their tyranny will be brought to an end. They now function like vicious dogs on a long leash. When Christ returns, he will tighten the leash to such an extent that they will not be able to cause any harm or instill any fear whatsoever. They will be completely pacified.

Paul saw the consummation of history in Christ's act of handing over his kingdom to God the Father. Prior to this, Paul envisioned two major events: (1) the resurrection of the dead and (2) the "destruction" of Christ's enemies. The first enemy to be vanquished is the host of spirit powers. Paul explains, "Then comes the end, when he [Christ] delivers the kingdom to God the Father after destroying every rule and every authority and power" (1 Cor 15:24 RSV). Uppermost in Paul's mind are all of the supernatural evil spirits and angels with whom the church has struggled throughout its existence. These are precisely the same terms that Paul used elsewhere for such powers (see Eph 1:21). They are the evil forces that have made their influence felt in every kind of human opposition to God and every form of structural evil.

Paul likely did not intend to convey the thought that these powers will be destroyed in the sense of being annihilated. Rather, what is probably meant by the term "destroy" *(katargeō)* is the thought of robbing them of their ability to work evil, that is, to pacify them.[5] The death and resurrection of Christ marked the beginning of their demise, as Paul described in 1 Corinthians 2:6-8. This passage implies that Christ will accomplish this in one final act. They will forever be deprived of their ability to engage in hostile coercive activity against

God and his people.

Death is then named as the final enemy who will be robbed of its ability to betray people of life. Death and the powers of darkness together constitute the enemies whom God will subject to Christ, that is, "put under his feet" in fulfillment of Psalm 110:1 and Psalm 8:6. Christ's resurrection is the guarantee for believers that they too will have life, even after experiencing physical death. Believers are so closely united with their risen Lord that they not only participate in a limited way in his resurrection life now, but they will be raised from the dead at his coming (parousia).

In Ephesians and Colossians Paul expressed the same promise of Christ's ultimate subjugation of the powers of darkness in different terms. In Ephesians 1:10, Paul spoke of the consummation of the age in terms of bringing "all things in heaven and on earth together under one head, even Christ." The comprehensive scope of Christ's reign is strongly in view here; there is no part of the creation that will continue to work in open rebellion against Christ. His reign especially includes all of the principalities and powers.

In Colossians Paul described the end of the age as a universal reconciliation. He says, "For God was pleased to have all his fullness dwell in him [Christ], and through him to reconcile to himself all things, whether things on earth or things in heaven, by making peace through his blood, shed on the cross" (Col 1:19-20). Certainly the powers of darkness will not be redeemed in the same sense as Christians and thus experience a reconciliation with God as friends. Paul made it clear later in the letter that the powers were defeated on the cross as enemies (Col 2:15). They are subjected against their will. The emphasis of this passage is on ultimate universal harmony and the absence of any personal or structural evil. As one commentator puts it, "the alternatives, whether these powers have been subjected or redeemed, are falsely put. It is decisive that the new world will be a world of peace and reconciliation and Christ will be its ruler."[6] Heaven and earth will no longer experience the jolting dislocations and degeneration brought about by evil. They will be brought back into their divinely created and determined order through the resurrection and exaltation of Christ.[7] In this context Paul especially focused attention on the cross of Christ as God's primary vehicle for insuring ultimate peace and harmony through all of creation.

The powers of darkness will finally have to admit that Jesus truly is the Lord, as Paul indicated to the Philippians: "At the name of Jesus every knee should bow, in heaven and on earth and under the earth, and every tongue confess that Jesus Christ is Lord, to the glory of God the Father" (Phil 2:10-11). Whatever kind of supernatural powers exist—astral spirits, terrestrial spirits, underworld spirits—all will be forced to recognize Christ's sovereign lordship. Christ will end their hostility.

Although he did not elaborate on it, Paul indicated that believers will execute judgment with him over the world system and all of the evil angels at the end of the age (1 Cor 6:3). Other New Testament writers also pointed to this future judgment of the angels (2 Pet 2:4; Jude 6). Non-Christians will face the same judgment and doom as the devil (1 Tim 3:6). The Revelation of John envisions the devil and his powers being thrown into a pool of fire, where they will be tormented throughout eternity (Rev 20:10, 14).

Paul's first-century readers would surely have found such passages to be a great solace in light of their fears of the hostile powers and the invisible forces of fate. History is in the hands of a loving God, who purchased redemption with the blood of his only Son. We, too, have the confidence that whatever forces of evil are afflicting us have a limited number of days. Christ will soon reign supreme and restore the world to its created splendor.

PART III
Interpreting the Powers for Today

WE FACE TWO LOOMING OBSTACLES IN INTERPRETING THE RELE-vance of Paul's teaching on the powers for the church today. First, there is the problem of the perception of myth. As pointed out in the introduction, Western society does not give credence to the notion of spirits, be they good or evil. To introduce the idea of evil spirits would be regarded by many as a reversion to primitive myth. We therefore need to grapple seriously with how to draw out the contemporary relevance of the biblical testimony on this theme.

The second major obstacle we face is the wide variety of interpretations of the powers. Traditional Christian interpreta-tion has stressed the influence of the powers on individuals. The bulk of popular charismatic books on this topic have dealt primarily with ministering to people who are demonized. Both of these views, of course, assume that evil spirits really do exist.

More recent interpretations of the powers, in contrast, have stressed the influence of the powers on a broad scale; that is, the powers work primarily through the structures of our exis-tence. Such things as economic and political structures are most often cited (capitalism, socialism, nationalism), but also other factors enter in, such as social patterns, cultural norms, group habits (like the development of a mob spirit in a soccer match). These "structures of existence" are then viewed as the objects of our spiritual struggle and may be regarded as demonic. Many who hold to this view would regard the biblical references to the powers as symbols of nonpersonal realities.

For most Christians, however, the issue of the pervasive in-fluence of the powers has not been a matter of careful reflec-tion. The following section will address the problem of how to interpret the powers for the twentieth-century setting and lead us into thinking more deeply about the influence of the powers on individuals and on a much broader scale. The remarks are limited to the implications we can draw from the apostle Paul's teaching on the principalities and powers. Much more can be gained by a careful study of the life of our Lord, the book of Acts, the rest of the New Testament epistles and the book of Revelation.

13
Reality or Myth?

*I*N COMMON PARLANCE THE WORD *MYTH* CONVEYS THE IDEA OF UNREALITY, a story with no factual basis involving human and superhuman characters having no objective reality. We might say the land of Oz, the wizard and the wicked witch of the West are mythical because they are imaginary creations having no verifiable existence. This fact does not imply that the story has no meaning for us; it certainly does. We can all identify with Dorothy's fear of the wicked witch and her desire to return home.

Many would say evil spirits are mythical in a similar sense. They are imaginary superhuman characters from a story that has meaning for us, but they should not be perceived as actual beings possessing a real existence.

In contrast the apostle Paul never showed any sign of doubt regarding the real existence of the principalities and powers. He saw them as angelic beings belonging to Satan's kingdom. Their aim is to lead humanity away from God through direct influence on individuals as well as through wielding control over the world religions and various other structures of our existence.

We cannot forget, however, that Paul was a man of his times. He lived in a culture, indeed in an era, that affirmed the existence of the spirit world. It would never have occurred to a person living in the first century to ask whether or not these forces were real. People living then were more concerned with how to deal with the influence of the powers.

Belief in the real existence of these powers continued through virtually the entire history of the church, including the Reformation. Martin Luther, like all his contemporaries, had no doubt about the terrible power of the devil and his hosts of darkness, as is evident from his classic hymn "A Mighty Fortress Is Our God" and his many writings.

The Modern World View
The Copernican overthrow of the dominant Ptolemaic view of an earth-centered universe was the catalyst for a new scientific spirit that swept through Europe in the seventeenth and eighteenth centuries— an age known as the Enlightenment.[1] The advances made in the sciences were astounding. They were made possible through the development of a scientific method based on reason, observation and experiment.

The thinkers of this age began to apply this scientific method, not only to science and technology, but also to the humanities. The enthusiasm for the method produced a distrust of authority and tradition in all matters of intellectual inquiry. This, of course, included the traditions of the church and the authority of Scripture. Consequently, many of the Enlightenment scholars rejected religion, with the majority becoming deists and some even espousing atheism.

The period brought about a deep-seated and lasting change in the way we perceive reality in the West. The new supremacy of a materialistic and rationalistic world view now called into question the reality of the miraculous and supernatural, even that which was recorded in Scripture. The references to demons and angels now became regarded as "myth," perhaps important for conveying theological truth but devoid of any historical substance. We continue to live in the shadow of the Enlightenment. This is why in educational institutions all throughout the West the idea of the actual existence of evil spirits is disavowed.

Biblical Scholarship and the Problem of Myth
In the religious academic community the eminent Marburg theologian Rudolf Bultmann has significantly influenced the present generation of scholars. Nurtured in an academic environment that spurned the belief in devils and demons as antiquated and useless for moderns, Bultmann too regarded them as part of the mythical language of the New Testament. For Bultmann, however, myth has an essential

role to play in early Christianity because it explained the other world (the divine and spiritual) in terms of this world. Nevertheless, Bultmann considered this prescientific view of the world as obsolete. He notes, "Now that the forces and the laws of nature have been discovered, we can no longer believe in spirits, whether good or evil."[2]

Bultmann and many other scholars since him relegated the references to principalities and powers in the New Testament to the mythology of Jewish apocalyptic, that is, Jewish accounts of a cataclysmic end of time.[3] Such interpreters regarded Jewish apocalyptic as an eschatological (endtime) myth that influenced Paul in a profound way. While it is true that Paul shares many ideas with Jewish apocalyptic, including the notion of evil spirits wreaking evil throughout the earth, Jewish apocalyptic was not the only view of the world during Paul's time that attributed evil to the work of hostile spirits. As already shown, the Gentiles to whom Paul preached also believed in personal evil forces who influenced humanity on many levels. While some of the terms Paul used for evil spirits are found in Jewish apocalyptic, the same terms and others are also used in magical writings and other pagan literature for supernatural spirits. Regardless of the particular world view (with regard to cosmogony—that is, origins or eschatology), both Jews and Gentiles could understand what Paul had to say on the topic of evil spirits. The concept of evil spirits was something agreed upon by all in the first century.

In addition it is significant to note that Paul only spoke once of the role of the powers in connection with the endtime triumph of God (1 Cor 15:24). The majority of Paul's references to the powers appear in ethical contexts or in terms of the work of Christ on the cross. One therefore cannot dismiss the Pauline references to "principalities and powers" as Paul's dependence on mythical imagery merely because Jewish writers in the apocalyptic literature used the same terms.

Many moderns are content merely to discard either the whole New Testament or the statements in the New Testament that allegedly reflect the outmoded mythical view of the world. Bultmann, however, wanted to take the message of the New Testament seriously and sought to find contemporary meaning in the references to the powers. Consequently, Bultmann suggested a program of "demythologizing" Scripture, that is, stripping off the elements of its outmoded world view as a means of hearing what it has to say for the present day. In his view myth does not give us an objective picture of the world, but an expression of one's understanding of self in the world.[4] Bultmann understood the Holy Spirit, for instance, not as a personal being distinct from the Christian, but the possibility of a new life that can be lived on the basis of an individual's personal and deliberate resolve. Bultmann's overall approach is "existentialist." He repeatedly emphasized the need to escape the constraints of the New Testament world view by discovering the meaning of the existence that stands behind it. He found this meaning in the heart of Christian preaching, which he interpreted as finding personal meaning in the context of one's concrete life decisions.

Many of the followers of Bultmann have tried to demythologize the powers by interpreting them as structures of our existence. Some interpreters suggest that we should understand the powers more in the sense of other Pauline categories such as sin, the law, flesh and death. Others argue that the powers should be seen as social structures, political ideologies and the like. This kind of interpretation has been particularly prominent among liberation theologians. Still, the bottom-line issue is the motive for demythologizing the powers—a denial of the real existence of evil spirits.

Some scholars point to the political dimensions of Jewish apocalyptic as a warrant for demythologizing the New Testament references to the powers by interpreting them as political structures. They correctly point to the fact that political events in the history of Israel influenced and partly motivated the writing of the apocalyptic literature—Israel had lost its struggle for autonomy in the two centuries before Christ. In his interpretation of Jesus' parable of the strong man (Mk 3:20-30), for example, Ched Myers recounts how the Jewish religious leaders accused Jesus of casting out demons by the ruler of demons. Myers then contends that since this terminology echoes the principalities-and-powers language found throughout the New Testament, "the semantic field is obviously that of apocalyptic, and the discourse is therefore specifically political."[5] For Myers, Jesus' attacks on demons through exorcism really represent an attack on the scribal establishment that Jesus intends to overthrow. The language of demons and unclean spirits becomes for Myers the code words to refer to the prevailing social and political structures. Myers sees Jesus' example of "binding the strong man" as therefore a relevant example for his followers today. It is a call to challenge the American government by "unmasking and resisting the institutionalized lies and hidden crimes of imperial domination and violence."[6]

Such a political reading falls short of an accurate interpretation of the terminology used for evil spirits in the New Testament. Simply because the terminology for evil spirits appears in the apocalyptic writings does not mean that all parts of the apocalyptic drama need to be interpreted as political events. It is also a fallacy to assume that since the word *demon* or *ruler* occurs in a piece of writing that was prompted by a political situation, the word must have a political interpretation. There is no doubt that Jews living in the first century believed that real angelic functionaries would carry out the events recorded in their apocalyptic writings. For Myers, as well as for many other interpreters, the root issue centers on a presupposition that the language of demons, evil spirits, and principalities and powers is mythical and needs to be interpreted.

The Modern Understanding of Myth

According to contemporary academic studies of religion, however, the primary function of the term *myth* is not to pass judgment on the factuality of an event or the metaphysical reality of a spirit. Myth has a vital role to play in society by giving an account of its sacred origins. "It reports realities and events from the origin of the world that remain valid for the basis and purpose of all there is. Consequently, a myth functions as a model for human activity, society, wisdom, and knowledge."[7] As Paul Ricoeur points out, myth is distinct from history in that it narrates the founding events that occur before time.[8]

According to this modern definition of myth, every society has a narrative of its origins, that is, a cosmogonic myth. For most people in the West the myths of evolutionism and materialism have replaced the creation story of Genesis. As people relate the experiences of their own time to their understanding of their origins, the myth becomes the basis for explaining present experience. For instance, a Western physician may diagnose someone suffering a severe stomach illness as having a virus, whereas a Zande tribesman would suspect an evil spirit. World view is thus closely tied to myth. Belief in evil spirits is necessarily linked to one's understanding of the origins of existence.

The apostle Paul revealed his own indebtedness to the Old Testament account of creation. His conversion to Christ did not force a paradigm shift to an entirely new mythology, but caused him to rethink his Jewish heritage in terms of the person of Jesus Christ. Fundamental to Pauline theology is his description of Christ in terms of the "new Adam." What is difficult for us to know is the extent to which Paul subscribed to the various Jewish interpretations of the Genesis account (for example, were demons the offspring of the cohabitation of angels and women?—see Gen 6:1-4). Paul is not enamored with such speculation. The fact of their existence and hostility to the church was what occupied his attention.

Those who hold to the modern understanding of myth do not want to demythologize the New Testament (as Bultmann advocated). Rather, they emphasize the importance of discerning the role and function of a given myth in its social setting.

From Projections to Collective Unconscious: Jung and Wink

In his scientific exploration of the unconscious, psychologist Sigmund Freud came to the conclusion that the devil was nothing more than the expression of individual repressions, that is, projections. His associate Carl Jung agreed with him but took the mythological element of religion more seriously than Freud. Jung did not come to the point of accepting the metaphysical reality of the powers, but he did see religious myths involving evil spirits as powerful psychological realities that should not be discarded. His concept of the "Shadow"—the negative side of personality[9]—comes close to the idea of an evil power. The Shadow could also be understood collectively. A group or social order could manifest a collective personality characterized by evil, such as racism, exploitation and violence.[10]

In his recently published studies on the language of power in the New Testament, Walter Wink adopted this Jungian framework for interpreting the powers of darkness. He interprets demons and evil spirits as the psychic or spiritual power ("the inner essence") of an individual, organization, society or government.[11] (Because of the significance of his work, I will give a focused assessment of it in chapter fifteen.)

The Inadequacy of "Myth" to Explain Evil Spirits

Building on the modern understanding of myth, Wolfhart Pannenberg contends that one needs to make a necessary distinction between world view and myth. He argues that belief in demons by people in the New Testament era was part of their world view, but it should not be identified as specifically mythical.[12] Arguing against Bultmann,

Pannenberg contends that belief in demons (indeed, also, the under-standing of the Christ event) is tied neither to Jewish apocalyptic nor to a Gnostic redeemer-myth. He rightly observes that scholarship sub-sequent to Bultmann has thoroughly discredited Bultmann's idea of a Gnostic redeemer-myth influencing Christianity. He also argues that eschatological themes in the New Testament that correspond to Jewish apocalyptic must not necessarily be regarded as mythical. Pan-nenberg's comments are made in the context of advancing a nonmy-thological understanding of the Christ event. The historical work of Jesus, according to Pannenberg, was not a tale derived from some other primitive myth, but an actual event that came to function as a "new myth" for the Christian church.[13]

Pannenberg effectively opens the door to the possibility that the supernatural realm may directly reveal itself to people in some tangible way. He appropriately asks, "Can the other-worldly make its reality known in any other way than by manifesting itself within the world?"[14] Endorsing Pannenberg's approach, Anthony Thiselton argues similar-ly that "belief about supernatural interventions in the affairs of men . . . is not necessarily primitive or pre-scientific, as the Enlightenment view of myth would imply."[15] Pannenberg notices that every religious understanding of the world fundamentally accepts the idea of divine intervention in the course of events.[16] Consequently, it is possible to hold to the real existence of evil spirits without necessitating recourse to interpreting them as part of a larger mythical drama (whether of the creation of the world or of the end of the world).

This seems to provide a very helpful perspective on the ancient (and contemporary) understanding of evil spirits. While Paul may have been working from a specific cosmogonical myth (a story of origins), the details of the myth were neither obvious in his writings nor did they appear to be important to Paul. He evinced concern only about the fact of hostile supernatural interventions in the daily affairs of Christians.

In a similar way it is difficult (if not impossible) to piece together any mythical drama standing behind the numerous Hellenistic mag-ical texts. For those who used these texts, it was the common assump-tion that extradimensional beings existed and that they could be con-trolled. Magic was then concerned with learning how to manipulate these spirit-beings either for personal good or for someone else's misfortune.

We are now back to the question of world view. Can we accept a world view that believes in the metaphysical reality of spirits, demons and angels?

The Clash of World Views

Christians face a dilemma. If we accept at face value the Bible's affirmation of the reality of evil spirits, we create an unbridgeable gulf between our world view and the prevailing Western world view. How can we accept the overthrown premises of a prescientific world view by believing in the real existence of demons and evil spirits?

The crux of the issue for all interpreters is the degree to which we should allow our Western scientific world view to determine our conclusions. Modern hermeneutical theory has convincingly demonstrated that none of us are objective interpreters. We all approach the texts with individual pre-understandings (especially our culture and theological tradition) that influence the results of our analysis of Scripture. This bias should not make us despair of finding the truth and its relevance for our situation. Rather, it should force us to undertake a careful examination of our own presuppositions and assumptions while at the same time attempting to interpret the meaning of Scripture in its own language, cultural, religious and social setting. We then engage in what Anthony Thiselton speaks of as "an ongoing dialogue with the text in which the text itself progressively corrects and reshapes the interpreter's own questions and assumptions."[17] All three parts of this hermeneutical process are essential in finding the meaning and relevance of Scripture in our own day.

As was demonstrated in part one of this book, there is no question that people living in the first century believed in evil spirits, including all of the New Testament writers, particularly Paul. At this point the modern scientific world view stands in direct contradiction to the first-century world view and also the biblical world view. In his recent book on Jesus, Marcus Borg is certainly aware of this interpretational difficulty. He notes:

> Within the framework of the modern world view, we are inclined to see "[demon] possession" as a primitive prescientific diagnosis of a condition which must have another explanation. Most likely, we would see it as a psychopathological condition which includes among its symptoms the delusion of believing one's self to be possessed. Social conditions also seem to be a factor. . . . But what-

ever the modern explanation might be, and however much psychological or social factors might be involved, it must be stressed that Jesus and his contemporaries (along with people in most cultures) thought that people could be possessed or inhabited by a spirit or spirits from another plane. Their world view took for granted the actual existence of such spirits.[18]

Although Borg does not give us help in overcoming the clash between the two cultures, he frames the nature of the issue quite clearly. For us the question now becomes whether the New Testament view of evil spirits should reshape and correct the prevailing Western world view on this particular point.

In the first volume of a projected trilogy on the powers, Auburn Seminary professor Walter Wink reveals the controlling influence of his cultural presuppositions in thinking about the biblical references to the powers. He candidly remarks:

We moderns cannot bring ourselves by any feat of will or imagination to believe in the real existence of these mythological entities that traditionally have been lumped under the general category "principalities and powers." . . . It is as impossible for most of us to believe in the real existence of demonic or angelic powers as it is to believe in dragons, or elves, or a flat world.[19]

He then proceeds to demythologize the language of power in the New Testament, ending up with an interpretation of the powers as the abstract "inner essence" of social systems, political structures and institutions (see the next chapter). Wink's views have already had a significant influence on evangelical thought with regard to the powers.[20]

Critiquing the Modern World View

Should the academic community begin to rethink the part of the Western world view that denies the actual existence of spirits, demons, angels and supernatural powers? I am convinced that we should for the following reasons:

1. On the issue of the actual existence of evil spirits, science is unable to decide the question. Bultmann, together with many modern thinkers, did not frame the question about the real existence of evil spirits in terms of competing world views. For Bultmann the question hinged on whether one accepts a mythical view of the world or an accurate scientific understanding of the world. He whimsically quips, "It is impossible to use electric light and the wireless [note: he is

writing in the middle forties] and to avail ourselves of modern medical and surgical discoveries, and at the same time to believe in the New Testament world of spirits and miracles."[21]

This kind of view, ever so present in our modern world, elevates science to a pedestal where it is given authority to make judgments on questions that it has no ability to judge. Just as it is beyond the scope of science to adjudicate on matters of morality, so it is also beyond the parameters of science to make a decision on the question of the real existence of the devil and evil spirits. J. B. Russell has rightly commented, "The fact that most people today dismiss the idea as old-fashioned, even 'disproved,' is the result of a muddle in which science is called on to pass judgment in matters unrelated to science."[22] If spirits do not have a tangible physical existence, modern science does not have the tools for verifying or denying their real existence. This makes the question of their existence depend not on scientific observation, but upon revelation, world view and human experience.

My interpretation of the Old and New Testament affirms that these writers believed in the actual existence of the powers. Significantly, there are not two schools of thought within the biblical revelation, one affirming and the other denying the reality of the powers. All the writers of sacred Scripture spoke with a common voice on this issue. The tradition of the church also corroborates it. As will be shown, the world views of many societies give credence to the idea of evil spirit beings.

2. Purely naturalistic explanations are not adequate for describing many forms of evil in the world. Even in the West many people experience phenomena in their lives that are difficult to explain scientifically, either through physical or psychological analysis. Australian scholar Graham Twelftree develops this point quite convincingly in his book *Christ Triumphant.*[23] He notes that T. K. Oesterreich, in his monumental study on the concept of "possession" among primitive and modern people, reached the conclusion that possession is a psychological compulsion. Nevertheless, Oesterreich admitted that "an important unexplainable residue remains, for which there is as yet no psychological explanation, and which continues to leave the question open as to whether certain happenings transcend nature."[24] While the field of psychology was only in its infancy when Oesterreich wrote, Twelftree demonstrates that psychologists and counselors to-

day are still faced with an "unexplained residue." Even anthropologists face the same unexplainable phenomena in the interpretation of their fieldwork. Twelftree explains:

> From this we cannot go on to conclude that there are no medical, psychological or rational explanations for the anthropologists' and sociologists' observations of an unexplained residue but it still does suggest that the question [of demonic influence] remains open. It also means that even where diseases may be considered to have a natural or regular explanation the demonic need not be ruled out.[25]

It was in the process of his lifelong quest to find an explanation for horrific evil in the world that Jeffrey Burton Russell became increasingly convinced of the real existence of the traditional devil—"a mighty person with intelligence and will whose energies are bent on the destruction of the cosmos and on the misery of its creatures."[26] For Russell the potential global annihilation insured by nuclear war, the untold suffering and killings of an Auschwitz, and the fact that a mother could put her four-year-old child in an oven and burn her to death (Auburn, Maine, 1984), cannot be explained by mere human destructiveness. There must be a powerful force leading humanity to destruction.

3. Those of us in the West need to place our attitude toward the supernatural into the broader sweep of human history. The last 300 years in the West represent the only time in human history that the existence of evil spirits has been treated with widespread skepticism. Certainly one can point to a variety of ancient philosophers throughout the centuries who doubted the reality of the gods and displayed a skeptical outlook toward supernatural interventions in human history. Such writers are, by far, more the exception than the rule. On the popular level, in particular, never was there a time of such widespread skepticism than in the West over the past three hundred years. This consideration by itself is not sufficient justification to engage in revisionary activity, but it should provoke a questioning of the prevailing world view.

4. The West also needs to realize that it is the only contemporary society that denies the reality of evil spirits. The field of anthropology reveals that throughout Asia, Africa, the Pacific islands, among folk Muslims—virtually anywhere the Western world view has not permeated—the idea of evil spirits is an integral part of the world view of many people groups.

African or Korean Christians, for instance, have no difficulty understanding Jesus' exorcisms or Paul's references to principalities and powers. In fact, Christians from these regions often express disappointment that the Western church has not been able to help them develop a Christian perspective on the realm of spirits.

For many Westerners, unfortunately including even Christians, such world views that continue to give the demonic a place are discounted as prescientific. Often there is an assumption that once these people are educated, they will eventually see that their ways of perceiving reality were skewed. It is supposed that they will eventually begin to think of evil in "correct" abstract terms.

A number of Christian scholars, however, have begun to question the Western world view. As a result of teaching over a ten-year period in an Indian theological college, New Testament scholar Peter O'Brien grew increasingly convinced of this Western cultural anomaly. He remarks, "A number of those from southern Asia who were studying in the college expressed their dissatisfaction with some Western commentaries on the Gospels and the Epistles because of their failure to take seriously the accounts about demons, exorcism, or Christ's defeat of them. The biblical and Pauline world view did not present a stumbling block to these younger third world scholars."[27] O'Brien argues forcefully for taking the realm of evil spirits seriously.

Anthropologist Paul Hiebert made a similar observation as a result of ministering the gospel in India. He came to the conclusion that Western culture has a significant blind spot when it comes to the question of spirits and evil powers—a blind spot he has termed "the flaw of the excluded middle." He describes Western evangelicalism as answering questions of life experience either in empirical (scientific) or theistic (divine) terms, but neglecting the middle zone of spirit forces that are believed by non-Western cultures to influence life. He paints the results of this dichotomy in rather startling terms for its implications for missions: "When tribal people spoke of fear of evil spirits, [Western missionaries] denied the existence of the spirits rather than claim the power of Christ over them. The result, as Newbigin has pointed out, is that Western Christian missions has been one of the greatest secularizing forces in history."[28] Hiebert's article has begun to have a significant impact on many evangelical thinkers.

New Testament scholar Gordon Fee also reacts to the undue amount of influence the Western world view has exerted in our reading of Paul. Commenting on Paul's reference to "demons" in 1 Cor 10:20, he remarks:

> It is fashionable among modern scholars to "exonerate" Paul at this point as being a man of his times. He believed in demons as did all his contemporaries; but we do not because we have "come of age." But that takes neither biblical revelation nor spiritual reality seriously. Bultmann's "modern man," who cannot believe in such reality, is the true "myth," not the gospel he set out to "demythologize." The cloistered existence of the Western university tends to isolate Western academics from the realities that many Third World people experience on a regular basis."[29]

5. The naturalistic world view of the West has never convinced the entire populace on the issue of evil spirits. The occult has found many devotees throughout Europe and North America over the past 200 years.[30] With regard to the phenomenon of spirit-possession, London anthropologist I. M. Lewis observes:

> Although the increasingly liberal treatment by the Church of possession that was assigned to the work of Satan, and the rise of secularism and modern science in the nineteenth century, naturally fostered a widening of skepticism regarding peripheral spirit-possession, the phenomenon did not entirely disappear.[31]

Lewis calls attention to the irony of an upsurge in spiritualism in the Victorian era, especially after the publication of Darwin's *Origin of Species* in 1859.

Many Christian groups have continued to affirm the real existence of evil spirits. Protestant Pentecostal and charismatic groups unanimously believe in the reality and power of the evil spirit forces and minister to people on the basis of that assumption. Numerous other Protestant denominations, subgroups, independent churches and individuals within some of the mainline churches affirm the existence of this realm. Even the Roman Catholic church continues to maintain an office of exorcist. It should also be noted that the pope, supported by a number of theologians, including Cardinal Ratzinger, have reaffirmed their belief in the objective reality of the devil and his demons.

In recent years evangelicalism has grown increasingly open to the idea that evil spirit emissaries do exist and need to be reckoned with on a spiritual basis. This concern is evidenced in part by the vast number of books and pamphlets published over the past decade on the topic of "spiritual warfare." Much of this literature is coming from the pens of evangelicals who are neither Charismatic nor Pentecostal. The formation of the "International Center for Biblical Counseling" (Sioux City, Iowa) is representative of this growing concern to factor in principles of "spiritual warfare" into the counseling ministry of the church. A recent symposium at Fuller Theological Seminary also brought together forty participants from a wide variety of traditional evangelical institutions (only seven participants represented classic Pentecostal/charismatic institutions) to discuss the issue of evil spirits in relationship to local church ministries and world evangelization; all the participants assumed the reality of the demonic.[32]

The "Western world view" therefore does not represent everyone in the West. Nevertheless, an antisupernatural bias still characterizes the academic community in the West and perhaps also a majority of the populace, although change is on the horizon.

6. Popular Western culture is changing. I noted in the introduction how the West is experiencing an "occult explosion," which the rapid growth of the New Age movement is now fueling. The end result is that more and more people are opening themselves up to believe in the supernatural, the paranormal and the realm of spirits. Western culture (quite apart from the influence of Christianity) may very well be far down the road of change. It is quite possible that Hans Küng is correct in his assessment that we are on the verge of a new epoch, a change in paradigms (world view), that will distance us from the "Modern-Enlightened" age.[33]

In conclusion, I want to stress that I am not advocating a complete paradigm shift that would take us back to a prescientific era. I do not believe in a flat earth or a geocentric universe. I laud the utility of the scientific method for helping us to discover innumerable secrets about our world.

What I am suggesting is that we engage in a critical re-evaluation of our Western world view on one important issue—the actual existence of good and evil spirits. There are many reasons we should not only accept Paul's affirmations regarding the existence of evil spirits, but also directly appropriate his suggestions for responding to this realm as Christians.

As citizens of the West, however, we must first strive toward making this as important a part of our world view as it was for Paul. The powers of darkness are real, we need to be conscious of their influence, and we need to respond to them appropriately.

14
The Powers and People

*T*HE BULK OF WHAT PAUL HAD TO SAY ABOUT THE POWERS HAD TO DO primarily with their influence on individuals and the church. This is mainly because he wrote to Christian congregations needing help in responding to particular situations and problems. Paul did not engage in writing a comprehensive systematic theology. For our topic, however, this is a significant advantage. We can see firsthand how Paul applied his theology, particularly his theology of the powers, to the variety of difficulties facing the respective churches to whom he wrote. Paul thus has given us help in determining how to apply the biblical teaching on the powers to the contemporary church.

The starting point for determining how the powers operate should be taken from Ephesians 2:1-2, where Satan is described as the ruler of a host of forces who hold humanity in a slavery apart from God. He creates this bondage by supernaturally influencing individuals to disobey God—that is, by inciting them to sin. The passage suggests three ways that Satan accomplishes this aim: through direct and immediate influence, by exploiting the inner impulse to do evil, and by influencing the environment and social structures. The first two aspects will be discussed in this chapter and the third in the next.

Direct and Immediate Influence
While the Gospels and Acts are full of detailed accounts of people who were demonized, Paul never used the terminology of "demon possession" as found in the Gospels. We should not conclude from this that he did not believe in demonization and thus the need for

exorcism. Assuming that Luke has given us an accurate account of Paul's ministry in the book of Acts, we know Paul himself engaged in the casting out of evil spirits. Surprisingly, Paul never took the occasion to speak about this concern in his letters.

The closest Paul came to the language of demonization is in the epistle to the Ephesians, where he cautioned his readers not to give the devil a "foothold" (Eph 4:27). We cannot know if he would have equated giving the devil a foothold *(topos)* with being demonized *(daimonizomenos),* the term so frequently translated "demon-possessed" in the Gospels. At the very least, "foothold" indicates the relinquishment of a great deal of control of one's life to an evil spirit; and in this case it refers to a Christian. Thus, while Paul never said a Christian can be "demon-possessed," he did say the devil can make significant inroads into a believer's life.

Since Paul never discussed the problem of demonization, he consequently had no occasion to discuss the principles and procedures of exorcism. Again we must be cautious not to draw the unlikely conclusion that Paul was averse to the notion of exorcism. When Paul wrote to his Christian readers, what he did relate to was the importance of resistance and identity. For a Christian who gives in to the temptation to steal, for instance, Paul would urge the person simply to quit, to resist. If this pilfering appetite, fueled by Satan, is left unchecked, it can lead to a greater measure of demonic influence in that individual's life. Behind such an injunction of refraining from a certain unethical behavior is a whole theology of identity. Christians not only have the obligation to eradicate such unseemly patterns of behavior, but they also have the ability to do so. This capacity to resist is an integral part of what it means to be a Christian—experiencing forgiveness, being on good terms with God, receiving a new nature, having a real oneness with the resurrected Jesus, experiencing the power of the new age and so much more.

The Powers Exploit Our Inclination to Do Evil
Paul believed a penchant toward violating God's standards of holiness characterizes all of humanity. This inclination, which he often called "the flesh" or "the old self," is adequate in and of itself to prevent people from pleasing God. Yet Satan and his powers strike where we are most vulnerable. Our powerful supernatural opponent takes advantage of our bent toward doing precisely what God would not want

us to do. He exploits our flesh in his ongoing effort to interrupt God's redemptive purposes.

In some fashion, not explained by Paul, evil spirits entice individuals to carry out the depraved notions and desires that surface from this inner impulse. Paul described unredeemed humanity as incapable of resisting these base desires because of their demonically enhanced appeal. We need to have God's own Spirit and to appropriate his power in order to resist the enticement to do evil. This is why Paul can describe unredeemed humanity as being in slavery to sin or the devil. People do not have the inherent ability to overcome such powerful enticement.

We must be careful not to misinterpret Paul by creating a caricature of what he meant when he referred to non-Christians as being in slavery to sin. He clearly did not intend to convey that all unbelievers are engaged in thievery, murder, sodomy and all the other gross forms of ethical degradation. For Paul any pattern of action motivated by and centered on anything other than God's express will qualifies as sin. Thus he indicted his unbelieving kinspeople as living apart from God, although they claimed to follow God's law. They followed the law neither in the way God had intended nor by the means he provided. A person who appears outwardly moral—and who is kind, philanthropic and generous—may therefore be just as much a part of Satan's kingdom as a person sold out to the occult. That person may have a motivation for performing good deeds that indeed runs counter to the pure and selfless motive that Christ would expect.

According to Paul, unless a person is a member of Christ's kingdom, that person is a member of Satan's kingdom. Becoming a member of Christ's kingdom does not involve making an effort to obey God's revealed law. Rather, it involves a rescue act performed by Christ himself and an initiation into his kingdom through receiving the gift of his Spirit.

Becoming a Christian neither removes the internal impulse to do evil nor deters the powers from trying to exploit it. Indeed, Paul envisioned the believer as coming under rather intense pressure from the hostile spirits to displease God, especially during vulnerable times (as in periods of depression or crisis). For Christians the main difference now is that they can draw on the enabling power that God offers as the means to resist these influences. Ultimately, Satan seeks not only to prevent the development of the virtues within the lives of

Christians but also to undermine faith in God.

The Powers and Sickness

In the New Testament world it was common for people to believe the agency of an evil spirit causes sickness (a belief that is also characteristic of many contemporary non-Western cultures). Such a belief is reflected in the Gospels. Like the issue of exorcism, Paul did not address this topic in any detail except for a brief description of his "thorn in the flesh," which he said in actuality was an evil angelic power (2 Cor 12:7-10). For Paul this spirit exerted its hostile power in a way that produced some unknown physical malady. Paul resigned himself to live with the physical discomfort and hindrance because he interpreted it as a situation that God designed to insure humility and divine dependence in his life. It may seem odd to us that God would permit an evil spirit to hurt his devoted apostle. Paul, however, was familiar with the Old Testament and therefore aware of God's past use of the realm of evil to accomplish his purposes. It is instructive for us to note three things about this situation:

1. Paul had an infirmity, and he was able to identify its origin, assigning the cause to the work of a spirit entity. Sickness and infirmity can have a direct demonic cause. Although Paul did not divulge his diagnostic procedures, his example should challenge us, not only to leave open the possibility of an infirmity being inflicted by a demon, but also to develop a keen sense of discernment.

2. Paul sought God's release from this manifestation of the evil one. This is natural since believers, through union with Christ, share in his authority over the powers of darkness. Paul demonstrated that Christians do have the right to pray for healing from illness, whether the infirmity is produced by the direct work of a demon or occurs simply because people are still earthbound creatures. Sickness and suffering are characteristic of the present evil age; they are not a part of God's kingdom. As citizens of the heavenly kingdom, therefore, we should ask for this special appropriation of the power of the new age, and then God might grant healing. It is important to stress that if we ask God for healing, we should believe he is perfectly capable of performing it.

3. Paul was not healed. Surely it would have been tempting for him to conclude that he did not pray with an adequate amount of faith. Rather, Paul apparently assessed the complex circumstances and de-

termined that his continued affliction was a part of God's sovereign purpose. In fact, Paul was certain that he knew precisely why God was allowing his condition to continue; it was to keep him from exalting himself. We do not have a guarantee from God that we will always be healed if we ask him. We cannot assume that God desires his kingdom to so invade the present evil age that sickness will be progressively eliminated. Our bodies are in the process of decay, and we will all die. The causes of our deaths will be evil—whether through an automobile accident, pneumonia, heart disease or by cancer. Part of our existence is still rooted in the present age. God, however, may use our sickness or handicap to accomplish some specific purpose in our lives or the lives of those with whom we have contact—even if we do not have the ability to discern what that purpose might be.

4. Paul's failure to be healed did not devastate him as a person or cripple his ministry; on the contrary, it enhanced his ministry. God revealed to him that weakness (which includes illness or handicap) is all right since it forces the child of God to depend on God's own enabling power and grace. Paul did not continue to seek God's healing touch. He learned to be content in enduring the illness or handicap he suffered.

Because we have been immersed in an antisupernatural world view, Western Christians tend to have an easier time accepting illness and not expecting healing. On the one hand, we should remember that God is capable of healing and does work healing today. On the other hand, if God does not choose to heal, we need to realize that our faithfulness to God in suffering (or in persecution) is also a moving demonstration of God's power that could lead people to respond to Christ.[1]

Discerning the Demonic

How can a person detect the direct influence of evil spirits as opposed to it being a societal influence or one's own inclination toward doing evil?

In the Gospels and Acts it appears that Christ, the apostles and ministers had little trouble detecting the immediate work of evil spirits in the lives of demonized people. Their physical conditions (unusual muscular strength, physical debilitation or illness), bizarre behavior (like living among tombs), extreme reaction to Christ or the use of his name and authority, and the direct response of the demon using the person's vocal apparatus in reply to Christ (or a follower of Christ) appear to have been foremost among the evidences. Many would contend that the same evidences of intense demonic influence can be seen in certain people today. Some argue that people involved in Satanism and the occult open the door to this kind of severe demonic control; in most instances such people specifically seek communication with demons and the prince of evil.

Yet we should not limit our perception of Satan's activity to these more dramatic forms. We need to be wary of too readily restricting the devil's work exclusively to murderous Satanic rituals, scenes similar to those in the *The Exorcist,* and witchcraft. Satan and his spirits can influence people even if they do not experience voices in their heads and roam graveyards. It is the broader activity of Satan and the principalities and powers that the apostle Paul appeared to stress in his letters.

While Satan may often work in a direct and immediate way in people, he also asserts his sway more indirectly through exploiting "the world" and reinforcing the appetites of the flesh (our inclination toward evil). Thus we need to speak of varying levels of his influence.

First, as "the prince of this world," Satan attempts to exert his polluting influence on all aspects of societal life and culture. When biblical ethics are portrayed in a negative light in society, Satan has been successful in extending his evil influence on a broad scale. For instance, when pilfering from one's employer is rationalized, Satan becomes victorious. When vengeance is regarded as the best course of action against a person who wrongs us, Satan has successfully twisted our moral conscience. In short, Satan can pervert societal morals, traditions and customs. (The next chapter will develop this aspect of Satan's activity in more detail.)

Second, Satan works in concert with an individual's inclination toward evil ("flesh"). If a person is naturally inclined toward anger and bitterness, in some way an evil spirit may directly encourage that attitude. If the malice continues and intensifies, demonic involvement in the person's life may become more direct. This situation is what Paul referred to as giving "a place" to the devil. In principle, it appears that those who persistently and willfully continue in certain patterns of sinfulness may experience increasing amounts of direct demonic influence.

Paul did not speculate about how these powers precisely work their evil influence of temptation. He merely said the powers do exert this kind of influence as his way of motivating and preparing believers to face the impending trials.

During World War 2, Oxford Medieval scholar C. S. Lewis wrote an imaginative account of a series of letters, penned by an older seasoned demon to his younger inexperienced nephew. In this little book, entitled *The Screwtape Letters*,[2] Lewis envisioned each of the powers of darkness as having an assigned "patient" for whom the demon is given the responsibility of using every possible means to direct the patient's attention away from anything that would lead that person toward God's kingdom. Throughout the book Lewis depicted the younger demon (Wormwood) as keeping careful track of everything in his patient's train of thinking and then working to influence the subject's thoughts in the areas the demon considered him to be the most vulnerable. In describing the elder demon's instructions to the younger, Lewis used such phrases as: "make him think," "fuddle him," "tempt," "keep everything hazy in his mind," "keep his mind off . . . ," "turn their gaze away from Him [God] toward themselves," and "let an insult or a woman's body so fix his attention outward . . ." The power of Lewis's presentation is in his ability to balance the "patient's" free will with the compelling power of the incessant supernatural temptation that vies with the ever-wooing, enabling and encouraging Spirit of God. Lewis provokes his readers into thinking about Satan's potential involvement in the hour-to-hour mundane affairs and decisions of everyday life.

While Lewis's account moves far beyond the few insights given to us in Scripture, I do not think he contradicts what we know about the work of the powers in Paul's writings. I am convinced that the apostle Paul would have gone far down the road with Lewis in agreeing with him that the powers of darkness entice unbelievers and believers alike. Lewis has served the Christian community well by heightening the awareness of the demonic in a stirring way that calls for vigilance and dependence on the Lord.

The Issue of Responsibility

If we are duped, exploited or driven to do something by a powerful supernatural opponent—"the devil made me do it"—does that not lessen the level of our personal responsibility? Some theologians fear that this is the case. They are concerned that the belief in a literal devil and evil spirits may lead people to remove responsibility from themselves and locate it somewhere outside of themselves.

When three high-school boys in Carl Junction, Missouri, claimed that the voice of the devil prompted them to kill one of their companions as a sacrifice to Satan in 1987, the courts held the boys responsible and sentenced them to life in prison without the possibility of parole.[3] Is there a possibility that such a ruling was unjust? If a power much greater than themselves compelled them to bludgeon the victim, how could they be held responsible?

It is important to reaffirm that Paul, and the entire testimony of Scripture for that matter, always held people accountable for their decisions and actions. Although Satan can tempt and deceive, God will judge people on the basis of their actions: At "the revelation of the righteous judgment of God," he "will render to every man according to his deeds" (Rom 2:5-6 NASB; see also Ps 62:12 and Prov 24:12).

Nevertheless, there is another sense in which the powers determine the lives of people, indeed all people. Paul envisioned humanity as being enslaved by the evil one and in need of redemption. Held in tension with this concept is that every person has the opportunity to respond to the liberating message of the gospel. When a person believes in Christ, he or she is divinely rescued from the captivity of Satan and made a child of God. In a sense, Paul presented life as a choice between lordships. One can serve Satan and the powers, or one can serve God. This fundamental choice is all-important at the final judgment. Paul explained that Christ will "punish those who do not know God and do not obey the gospel of our Lord Jesus. They will be punished with everlasting destruction and shut out from the presence of the Lord and from the majesty of his power" (2 Thess 1:8-9).

Christians have the ability to resist Satan's temptations to do evil. The ability to resist is mediated to them through their dependence on an all-powerful Lord who strengthens their innermost beings through the presence of his Spirit. For this reason Paul can enjoin his Christian readers to resist the devil ("do not be deceived") and to desist from all kinds of evil practices.

In Paul's view non-Christians do not have the ability to withstand the appeals of the devil. This does not mean that every person consistently engages in the grossest forms of moral evil; each individual still bears God's image (albeit ever so tarnished) and is capable of high standards of morality. Nevertheless, Paul ardently believed every person has violated the ultimate standard of morality, God's law as revealed in the Old Testament.

Furthermore, in spite of Satan's compelling solicitations, Paul argued that each person is accountable to God on the basis of their behavior (Rom 2:1-11). He warned of God's impending judgment: "There will be trouble and distress for every human being who does evil" (Rom 2:9). There is a sense then in which a person can legitimately appeal to the argument "the devil made me do it." God, however, still holds people responsible for their actions. And people have a choice to obey God's law based on their nature as people created in his image; or better, they can respond to Christ's offer of redemption and then base their lives on Christ's ethical demands and appropriate his power to fulfill them.

The Powers Assail the Purity of the Church

This past decade has witnessed perhaps one of the greatest discreditings of the church in its history. Evangelical ministers have succumbed to temptations of sensual lust, pride and wealth in unparalleled proportions. This fact is so well known it needs no documentation or quantification. In the West the purity of the church has been disgraced.

Ostensibly falling victim to the temptations of the "flesh," numerous evangelicals have also been victimized by intense demonic attack. In the apostle Paul's way of thinking, it is really unnecessary to separate the cravings of the inner impulse from the simultaneous activity of Satan who exploits these desires. Just as Satan attacked Jesus in the desert at the outset of Jesus' earthly ministry to thwart him from his redemptive mission, so too Satan assaults the church—the body of Christ—to deter it from fulfilling its mission. Satan entices people at the points of their greatest vulnerability to act in ways displeasing to God, whether it be through engaging in a sexual tryst or by using unethical means to acquire wealth. The results of sin are never isolated to the individual; an entire congregation, a denomination or the churches of an entire region feel the implications.

Not only overt acts of sin, but also idolatry hinders the growth and ministry of the church. The early Christians faced the great temptation of combining their worship of Christ with devotion to other gods and goddesses. This was the spirit of the times (commonly known as syncretism). Paul was thoroughly convinced that worshiping other gods was tantamount to worshiping demons. From his perspective the powers of darkness were deeply involved in the non-Christian religions. This tendency to syncretize continues to be a serious temptation faced by Christians in polytheistic, non-Western cultures. It takes a major step of faith to destroy the household gods and give one's entire devotion to Christ alone.

An inadequate Christology is behind the desire to syncretize. Jesus has been exalted high above the other gods and all other angels, spirits and demons. Christ seeks wholehearted devotion from his people, and he deserves nothing less.

Paul also had a broader view of idolatry that extended to an undue devotion to material possessions. He warned one group of Christians to "put to death . . . greed, which is idolatry" (Col 3:5). Paul was keenly aware of how the desire to accumulate could so grip a person's devotion and attention that it is comparable to worshiping an idol. Many evangelical thinkers have pointed to the culpability of the West in this regard—and rightly so. As our culture continues to become so consumption-fixated, the attitude permeates the church. While this mindset is something that comes from within (the flesh), it is a disposition that Satan exploits and uses to his advantage to blunt the work of the church and its devotion to Christ.

The Powers Seek to Hinder the Mission of the Church

The proclamation of the gospel consumed the apostle Paul in his desire to work toward the intensive growth of the church through conversions. For Paul conversion was directly related to the kingdom of Satan and the powers of darkness. He described conversion as God's rescue act of plucking the individual out of slavery from the dominion of Satan and installing him or her as a member into the kingdom of Christ (Col 1:13). Evangelism, with the goal of conversion, represents a frontal assault on Satan's kingdom.

Just as Satan thundered with fury when the seventy engaged in their mission during the ministry of Jesus, Satan worked mightily against Paul and the early church in their evangelistic efforts. This is perfectly understandable. The kingdom of Satan decreases in direct proportion to the increase of the kingdom of God. Centuries after the death of Paul, the church continues to engage in this proclamational activity. So also Satan continues to rage and work with all his ability and schemes to thwart the mission of the church. As we saw in the previous section, Satan successfully hinders the mission when he discredits the church in the eyes of the nonbelieving public. Who wants to associate with hypocrites, swindlers and the immoral?

Satan's multifaceted ways of harming the outreach of the church are innumerable. What needs to be stressed is his opposition against evangelism. The church today must recognize that it will face powerful demonic opposition whenever it mobilizes to make known the good news of Jesus Christ to its community. It is therefore imperative that the church responds to its evangelistic task through appropriate spiritual preparation and dependence upon the power of God.

15
The Powers and Society

*I*N THE PAULINE LETTERS THE EMPHASIS IS ON THE THREAT THE POWERS POSE to the individual Christian and to the church. This threat comes in a large measure from the temptation of the flesh. It also comes from a larger organized front, which Paul characterized as "the world." We will now look closely at the nature of "the world" as Paul envisioned it and determine how the powers influence the world and work in conjunction with it to lead humanity astray.

Recent Interpretations of the Powers

Since World War 2, there has been a growing trend among scholars in the West to interpret Paul's references to principalities and powers almost exclusively as the structures of our existence.[1] The powers of darkness are "demythologized" and described in terms of religious structures (especially tradition), political and economic structures (as, for example, imperialism, nationalism, dictatorship, socialism and capitalism), the set of values held by a given social grouping (accepted morality, public opinion and interest, ideas of social status, concept of justice and so on) and intellectual structures (*ologies* and *isms*). All of these structures and values exert a controlling influence on society. They are also capable of becoming evil ("demonic") and may stand in the need of redemption.[2] Many of those who interpret the powers along these lines emphasize political structures. Responding to the powers thus becomes a mandate for political activism. In commenting on Ephesians 3:10, for instance, one writer remarks, "Announcing Christ's lordship to the powers is to tell governments that they are not sovereign . . . to witness in a biblical way to the principalities and powers is to engage in dangerous, subversive political activity."[3]

For many of these interpreters a major factor that leads them to a "structural" interpretation is the modern Western world view, which denies the reality of the actual existence of evil spirits. In chapter thirteen, I attempted to show that there is ample reason for revising the modern world view to affirming the actual existence of evil spirits and angels. If this premise is accepted, there is no need to demythologize the powers in order to interpret their meaning for us. Our task needs to be focused on determining how the powers influence "the world" in its variety of expressions; that is, through political structures, values, traditions and so on.

Evangelical scholars identifying the powers with structures often express their concern to grapple with the question of structural evil as part of a quest to develop a biblical basis for social ethics. This is a commendable goal and one that evangelicals have neglected. I would suggest, however, that it is erroneous to equate the powers with the structures. As I will argue, we ought to distinguish between the powers of darkness and the structures of our existence. The two categories are ontologically distinct. One is personal, the other is nonpersonal; one possesses intelligence and the ability to will, the other does not. Truer to Paul's letters is to say that the powers exert their influence over the structures of our existence than to make the powers coextensive with the structures.

Not all evangelicals writing on this topic equate the powers with structures. In his book on social ethics Robert Webber contends that the powers are spiritual beings at work in the world, that they are nonmythological, and that they have an ontological point of reference in time, space and history.[4] In the course of his discussion of the powers, however, their ontological distinction from the structures of existence becomes blurred. At the end of his analysis he states that there really is no firm distinction, but rather a dual reference at each occurrence: "The word *powers* is used in two different ways: it may refer to the spiritual powers of evil or to the powers which we have called 'the structures of existence.' "[5]

For Webber the powers even have a positive side: "We know that the powers are God's creation which serve as agents to provide order, guidance, and meaning."[6] In this latter comment he is clearly referring to the structures of our existence, not evil spirits. But the problem with this view is that he confuses the terminology and inaccurately identifies Paul's "principalities and powers" terminology with the concept of structures. This problem is not just with words; it is also a conceptual problem. An evil spirit is not nationalism; a demon is not a tradition; the principalities and powers are not structures. I would contend that there may be a relationship, however, between an evil spirit and nationalism, in that an evil spirit may incite excessive patriotism.

The primary practical danger in limiting our interpretation of the powers to the structures is that it is reductionistic. It unreasonably restricts how we understand the work of the devil in Paul's day and in our day. Specifically it overlooks the direct and immediate work of an evil spirit in the life of an individual—either through overt demonization ("giving a place to the devil") or the devil's classic work of directly tempting people to sin.

Evangelicals (especially Pentecostals and Charismatics) have traditionally had a much easier time reckoning with the work of Satan on an individual level as opposed to a societal level. In light of this problem the many recent works dealing with the topic of the relationship between the powers and the structures of our existence is a necessary corrective to an individualistic outlook.

In my analysis of various writers on this topic, I have found two Pauline texts that surface as crucial to the debate but which are frequently misunderstood. They are Ephesians 2:2 and 3:10. I offer two necessary correctives to some of the current discussion about the relationship between the powers to the structures of our existence.

1. The references to "air" and "spirit" are not references to "spiritual climate." When Paul spoke of "the ruler of the kingdom of the air, the spirit who is now at work in those who are disobedient" (Eph 2:2), a number of interpreters have assumed he was speaking of something like "the climate of opinion." Some would go so far as to suggest that Paul was referring to culture or world view. This view does not have a long history in the interpretation of this passage. The origin of this idea can be traced back to an essay written by Heinrich Schlier in 1930, later translated into English and published as a small book.[7] Schlier explained that the "air" and "the spirit" of this passage is "the general spiritual climate which influences mankind." He said it exercises a control, a domination that usually begins "in the general spirit of the world, or in the spirit of a particular period, attitude, nation or

locality. . . . Men inhale it and thus pass it on into their institutions and various conditions. . . . It is so intense and powerful that no individual can escape it."[8]

This view has had an undue amount of influence on the course of subsequent treatments on the theme of principalities and powers. The single greatest difficulty with this view is that it would have been unintelligible to a first-century reader. I have argued in detail in another context[9] that Paul is using *spirit* here in the sense of a personal being. Likewise, Paul intended *air* to be understood in a literal sense; both Jews and Gentiles commonly regarded the air as a dwelling place for evil spirits. The following lines from various Greek magical papyri illustrate this perspective:

> For no aerial spirit which is joined with a mighty assistant will go into Hades.
>
> Protect me from every demon in the air.
>
> I conjure you by the one who is in charge of the air.[10]

A first-century A.D. Jewish document aligns itself with this concept: "For the person who fears God and loves his neighbor cannot be plagued by the aerial spirit of Beliar since he is sheltered by the fear of God" (*Testament of Benjamin* 3:4).

In Ephesians 2:2, the reference to spirit is simply a reference to a personal evil force, and the reference to air is representative of the common belief that demons inhabit the air. One simply cannot press the reference to air in this context to find a precise metaphysical description of the dwelling place of an evil spirit.

2. *The church is not called to proclaim a message to the powers.* In Ephesians 3:10, some have seen a divine mandate for the church to preach to the powers. In this passage Paul explained that God's "intent was that now, through the church, the manifold wisdom of God should be made known to the rulers and authorities in the heavenly realms." This passage is not a warrant for raising a prophetic voice against the corrupted structures of our existence. In the context of Ephesians and of Pauline theology as a whole, the passage is merely asserting that the very existence of the church testifies to God's wisdom.[11] This passage confirms that God has foiled the wisdom of the demonic powers, who thought they could end God's redemptive plans by inciting the political and religious leaders to put Jesus to death (1 Cor 2:6-8). God raised Jesus from the dead, and he became the head of a worldwide body of believers who would spread the good

news of his offer of salvation everywhere. As 1 Corinthians 4:9 asserts (as well as numerous Jewish documents), the angels carefully observe the affairs of humanity. The evil angels, the principalities and powers, now see Jesus actively redeeming the lost through the church.

The only message the church is called to proclaim is the gospel, and that gospel to people all around the world who have not heard its good news of liberation and deliverance from captivity in Satan's kingdom. Both the existence of the church and the continued evangelistic growth of the church demonstrate to the powers that they are in fact powerless to impede the redemptive work of God.

The Recent Work of Walter Wink

Walter Wink, professor of biblical interpretation at Auburn Theological Seminary, is currently undertaking an extensive analysis of the powers in a projected trilogy of books.[12] Wink's study represents the quest of a person intent on discerning the nature of structural evil in light of the biblical evidence. His experience of living for a period of time in Latin America and witnessing extensive social and political oppression appears to have moved him profoundly. In the process Wink has neither abandoned the modern world view nor adopted a belief in the real existence of personal evil spirits and angels. Rather, he endeavors to probe more deeply into the meaning of the spiritual and reaches the conclusion that principalities and powers are "the inner and outer aspects of any given manifestation of power." He continues, "As the inner aspect they are the spirituality of institutions, the 'within' of corporate structures and systems, the inner essence of outer organizations of power. As the outer aspect they are political systems, appointed officials, the 'chair' of an organization, laws—in short, all the tangible manifestations which power takes."[13]

Wink's interpretation of the powers is already wielding significant influence on evangelical thinkers, especially those working in the area of social ethics.[14] His thought-provoking and influential work demands a focused critique. I have provided a substantive response to Wink's position in another context.[15] I will summarize a few important observations here.

First, as we saw in chapter thirteen, Wink admits the bias with which he approaches the text. He concedes he cannot bring himself to believe in the actual existence of evil spirits. This bias constrains him to find another explanation for the phenomena that Paul refers to as "principalities and powers." Discontent with the inadequacy of the "structures" interpretation to explain the invisible inner aspect of material reality that is associated with the principalities and powers, Wink applies the unique understanding of myth as explained by psychologist Carl Jung to interpret the powers. By doing this he preserves something uniquely "spiritual" to the powers. He describes the ontological status of the principalities and powers, not as real angelic or spirit entities, but as "an inner spirit or driving force that animates, legitimates, and regulates its physical manifestation in the world."[16] For Wink the heavenly powers are not merely human projections of material existence that serve to validate institutions. They are real and are experienced in the sense that they are the interiority or the spirituality of earthly institutions, systems and forces.[17]

If I could agree with Wink at his starting point of denying the real existence of evil spirits, I would find his explanation to be quite plausible. Since I do believe in the real existence of this realm, however, I find his explanation of the powers unnecessary and even erroneous. If the powers are indeed creatures with intelligence and will, they are not part of myth (in the sense propounded by Wink). Therefore, it is inappropriate to apply the Jungian psychological category of myth to interpret their meaning.

Second, Wink has suggested that Paul himself had already taken key steps toward demythologizing the language of demons, spirits and devils by interpreting them into the abstract categories of sin, law, flesh and death.[18] In my analysis of the language of power in the New Testament, I can see no basis for suggesting that Paul was intending his readers to understand his references to the powers in a symbolic sense. When he spoke about the principalities and powers, he was referring to real, living entities who brought terror and inflicted harm. On this topic all his readers, regardless of religious affiliation, would have understood him. Furthermore, if Wink is right, then the church has misunderstood Paul through the time of the Reformation.

Third, Wink arrives at his interpretation of the powers partly based on his analysis of the language of power in the New Testament. Noticing that a word like *authority* can be used by the same writer in reference to Satan and also with reference to human authorities, he concludes that the language of power in the New Testament is imprecise, liquid and interchangeable. In fact, he later argues that one term can be made to represent all the uses. In applying these preliminary conclusions to the powers, Wink sets forth the following thesis: "Unless the context further specifies (and some do), we are to take the terms for power in their most comprehensive sense, understanding them to mean both heavenly and earthly, divine and human, good and evil."[19] Consequently, as he approaches a text like Colossians 1:16 or 1 Corinthians 2:6-8, he concludes that both the human and demonic are intended.

I am quite uncomfortable with his treatment of the language of power. His method of analysis sidesteps the concerns of modern linguistic theory. I believe that he commits a methodological error known as an "illegitimate totality transfer."[20] This error occurs when a total series of relations in which a word is used in the literature is read into a particular case. Each context must determine which meaning, among the range of possible meanings, is appropriate to that context. In other words, if my wife says, "Look at those animals!" on the one hand, she may be referring to a display of lions in the zoo. On the other hand, she may be at home looking out the window at a group of rowdy kids across the street. She could never have both in mind at the same time. In this instance, the same word is used with reference to two distinct categories of species. I believe a similar use of language occurs in the New Testament with the words for principalities and powers.

Wink has not produced any context that clearly demonstrates that an ancient writer could have in mind both the human and demonic at the same time when that writer used power language. On the contrary, contexts outside the New Testament seem plainly either-or and never both-and. The Jewish intertestamental literature has a lively concept of the demonic (in the sense of personal spirit-beings) as does the Hellenistic magical tradition (which Wink neglects).

Fourth, although his final volume dealing with how to engage the powers has not yet appeared (at the time of this writing), Wink does provide some insight in his first two volumes on how Christians should respond to the powers today.[21] He appears to move the discussion beyond the mere physical response to the powers, which many interpreters who take a purely "structural" interpretation of the powers emphasize. Wink suggests that both the outer and inner aspects of the powers need to be addressed; Christians need to respond to the powers both on a physical and a spiritual plane. For Wink there is still the need for social struggle through protest marches and boycotts to engage the powers. Yet at the same time, Christians need to challenge the "within" of a system or institution. At this point Wink suggests that Christians pray and exercise faith in God, trusting him to change the spirituality of the institution. Nevertheless, he still places a greater emphasis on our physical response to the power structures. He comments, "It is precisely the outer changes we make that challenge, lure, and goad the oppressor toward inner change."[22]

Reasserting the Pauline Emphasis

I am thus hesitant to use the Pauline references to the "principalities and powers" as the fundamental basis for developing a theology of society. On the one hand, a different foundation to social ethics is needed than that which is provided by those who take a structural interpretation of the powers. On the other hand, I believe it is essential to take the principalities and powers into careful consideration when discussing social evil. Robert Webber is correct when he notes, "A theology of society needs to deal with the problem of the demonic."[23]

There is no doubt Paul envisioned the work of evil spirits to extend beyond their hostile influence on individuals and the church. In Paul's letters, however, the emphasis is clearly on their malevolent activity in preventing people from becoming Christians and hindering their growth in Christian virtue. The major issue of concern for Paul, therefore, is not so much the relevance of the powers with regard to social justice, but their implications on salvation history and Christian behavior.

In Paul's eyes the powers unleash their greatest hostility when they hinder the proclamation of the gospel. They use the flesh and, indeed, the structures of the world to blind people from discovering the truth about God's redemptive work in the Lord Jesus Christ.

Paul's concept of ministry included no injunction for Christians to work toward reforming the social or political order. As E. Earle Ellis explains it, "As a reality of the resurrection age Christian ministry has for Paul an evangelical, Christ-imparting relationship to the community of the dying."[24] The proclamation of the gospel takes on decisive importance because it has other-worldly, eternal implications. Those who affirm faith in Christ are rescued from the deadly clutches of Satan's kingdom and delivered from the community of Adam, which is moving toward its death.

This consideration does not mean that Christians are released from any obligation to society at large. Second to Jesus' command to love God with full devotion is his command to love our neighbors. Paul reiterated this command when he called Christians to love their neighbors (Rom 13:8-10) and to do good to all people (Gal 6:10).[25]

The Influence of the Powers on the World

The question we now ask is specifically how do the powers influence the world system with its manifold structures? I suggest two ways of describing the evil work of the powers on the social order.

First, it is essential to return to Paul's emphasis on the direct work of the powers in the lives of individuals. According to Paul, spiritual warfare involves direct demonic enticement to individuals to violate God's standards of holiness and act in ways contrary to his revealed will. Extrapolating from this explicit principle of operation to a larger scale, we must remember that people control governments, corporations, media and various other structures of our existence. If the powers of darkness can gain significant influence over the lives of key people, through them they can create oppressive dictatorships, evil drug rings, exploitative multinational corporations and all kinds of horrific, destructive mechanisms bent on destruction and terror.

The powers are not merely "up there" in the heavens waging war among themselves. They are here, very close to us, trying to influence our affections and our decisions.[26]

Paul's Jewish predecessors and contemporaries thought in these terms. For example, the first-century A.D. section of a Jewish document, entitled Ascension of Isaiah, reflects on why one of the kings of Judah was able to lead the whole city into apostasy:

> And Manasseh abandoned the service of the Lord of his father [Hezekiah], and he served Satan and his angels, and his powers. . . . And he rejoiced over Jerusalem because of Manasseh, and he strengthened him in causing apostasy, and in the iniquity which was disseminated in Jerusalem. And sorcery and magic, augury and divination, fornication and adultery, and the persecution of the righteous increased through Manasseh. (*Ascension of Isaiah* 2:2-5)

In this text it is clear that the powers of darkness are viewed as independent agents who worked directly on the leader of a country to create a regime of terror and evil. Many similar references could be cited, but this is adequate to illustrate the simple concept of an evil spirit working through an individual who wields significant civil authority. The same principle could be applied to many different spheres and social/political structures.

In the twentieth century we have witnessed the extensive repression and exploitation that corrupt rulers can wield over millions of people. Mention the names of Adolf Hitler, Nicolae Ceausescu, Idi Amin, Manuel Noriega and Saddam Hussein, and one easily sees images of untold atrocities. Certainly, Satan and his forces make people of such power the objects of particular attack because of their political authority. Could it be more than coincidental that reports of these leaders' involvement in the occult so often surface after they have fallen from power? Certainly, Satan has only to exploit the desires of their depraved natures to bring about his destructive aims. More direct Satanic influence, however, can sometimes be observed.

Second, I suggest that Paul's concepts of "world" *(kosmos)* and "this age" *(aiōn)* correspond most closely with what many modern interpreters describe as structural evil. Paul described unredeemed humanity as trapped in a pattern of transgression and sin against God because "the age *(aiōn)* of this world *(kosmos)*" so heavily influences them (Eph 2:2). Becoming a Christian involves being crucified to the world (Gal 6:14) and being rescued from the present evil age (Gal 1:4). When Paul spoke of "the world" in a moral sense, he was thinking of the totality of people, social systems, values and traditions in terms of its opposition to God and his redemptive purposes.[27] The structures of our existence, to a large extent, represent the composite result of human ideas, affections and activity. Both people and their ideas can have an evil bent. Yet they are also capable of redemption and purification. In his insightful book on social ethics Stephen Mott draws the correct distinction between the powers and the world. He notes, "The kosmos, a more pervasive theme in the New Testament than the powers, represents the social structuring of evil without necessitating recourse to the symbolism of supernatural personages."[28] He draws attention to the fact that the principle of sin has a serious impact on our social order: "If sin is as pervasive as we say that it is, . . . then it will affect not only our personal motivations, decisions, and acts, but also our social life. It will powerfully influence our customs, traditions, thinking, and institutions. It will pervert our kosmos."[29]

Not only does sin have a degenerative effect on the social order, but so also do the powers of darkness. The powers exert their influence to corrupt the various social orders of the world as a further means of drawing humanity away from God. Working through people, the powers can pollute a society's traditions and values. They can influence authors, television producers, political thinkers and analysts, pastors, university professors, composers, artists, screenplay writers, economic policy makers, architects of defense strategies and journalists. Through a unified networking influence, it is not difficult to imagine how the powers can influence the direction of an entire culture. In one decade something may be considered morally outrageous and in the next morally acceptable through a changed public opinion.

The powers themselves, however, are not the structures. Although the powers do their best to influence the structures, evil still resides in the structures only insofar as the people involved are evil. Just as a glove has no ability on its own to carry out a task, ideologies, economic systems and the like have no power apart from the people who subscribe to them and enforce them. A tradition ceases to be a tradition when people no longer pass it on.

It is with good reason that Paul calls Satan "the god of this age *(aiōn)*" who "has blinded the minds of unbelievers, so that they cannot see the light of the gospel" (2 Cor 4:4). We could legitimately say "Satan is the god of many of the structures that order our existence." Through coordinating the activity of his innumerable powers of darkness, Satan attempts to permeate every aspect of life in his indefatigable attempts to oppose God and his kingdom. The work of the evil one moves far beyond the simple notion of tempting an individual to sin. Satan appears to have a well-organized strategy. He aims strongly at the people with power and influence. The moral lapse of one pastor can send one church reeling. Inciting the moral lapse of numerous prominent ministers devastates Christians all over the country and makes society perceive the fragrant aroma of the gospel as a stench to be avoided.

The powers do indeed influence society and its institutions. We must be careful not to assume, however, that the demonic has polluted all institutions, social structures, traditions and philosophies. As Stephen Mott points out, there is a battle for the control of God's creation. Institutions are integral to human life. "Institutions function both to enslave and to liberate human existence. The powers are always present along with enslavement and death in small or large degree; but their real existence is behind the scenes in a system of hostile values vying for control of the life of the world."[30]

According to Paul, God calls Christians to be rescuing agents. The evil-infected institutions of this present age have trapped people, who are blinded from seeing Christ's redeeming love. Since the institutions of this world *(kosmos)* and the structures of the present age *(aiōn)* are destined to perish, our highest priority is to help people find ultimate freedom from the deadly constraints and terror of the present age and experience the untold blessings of the age to come, and to be liberated from the world and its hellish prince and be inundated with the love, joy and peace of God's kingdom.

By no means is this an encouragement for Christians to escape completely from the present world and withdraw from involvement in the social order and the structures of our existence. Jesus called us to be salt and light, to show the same loving compassion for our neighbors that led him to lay down his life for the lost. God demands that Christians engage in social action based on their love for humanity, their call to be salt and light, and their responsibility to be careful stewards of the creation.

Christians still live in the present evil age—in fact, they live in two ages. The kingdom of God and the blessings of the age to come have broken into the present age in the Lord Jesus Christ. The Spirit and the gifts, the grace of God and the power of the age to come are bestowed on us through relationship with the Lord Jesus. We are called to carry on the redemptive mission that Christ called us to and that Paul modelled for us by his own life and ministry. We are called to demonstrate Christ's love.

The Recent Work of Frank Peretti

In his recent best-seller *This Present Darkness,* Frank Peretti unveils the strategy and networking of those hostile opponents who come from the realm of spirits, demons and powers.[31] He depicts these forces of darkness mobilizing to gain control of a typical small town in America. They try to accomplish this takeover through a variety of means, but primarily through a plot to draw people away from Christ via an organized expression of the New Age movement.

Peretti moves the drama back and forth between the human and the spiritual plane. He discloses the demonic activity behind human struggles and difficulties. His conceptual framework is much the same as that of Lewis's *Screwtape Letters*. Demons exert a direct influence on individuals. For instance, after portraying the evil activities of one of his human characters, Peretti gives his readers further spiritual insight into this person: "a deep and seductive voice spoke thoughts to her mind." This character later turns out to be a university professor who is disseminating occultism through her teaching. Through similar demonic influence on key people throughout the university, the institution itself becomes perverted and is a major staging ground for this new philosophy.

While C. S. Lewis gave the Christian community a thought-provoking assessment of how an evil spirit may exert influence over a person in day-to-day life, Peretti builds upon this insight to help us imagine how the powers might work in concert to attain a much larger diabolical goal. He describes the individual workings of demonic powers, but he also shows their unified collective purpose. Assuming a well-defined hierarchy with a chain of command, Peretti depicts various ranks of powers carrying out their orders as part of a large-scale plan to usher in an occultic philosophy first to one strategic city, and from that base of operations, to the entire country.

As with any fictional representation of the unseen world, a few parts of his work are hard to swallow and perhaps do not seem to match biblical emphases. For instance, why is there so much said about the countermanding work of God's angels and so little about the work of the Holy Spirit? Overall, however, Peretti gives us an account that is not only captivating but also imaginatively represents how the powers of darkness might actually work.

Those who appreciate Peretti's novels will need to remember that the powers of darkness work through a multitude of ways to draw believers into sin and hinder the mission of the church. Satan may very well find his best line of attack against a church through something other than an organized conspiracy like the New Age movement. In fact, is it not more often the case that sexual impropriety, ethical misconduct, deeply entrenched feuds between church members and matters such as these do more to dim the light of the church's testimony in its community than the inroads of occultism or Satanism? This is certainly not to minimize the danger of aberrant (or satanic) teaching, but it does emphasize Satan's use of a wide variety of schemes *(methodeia* Eph 6:11).

The general impact that Peretti's book has had on the life of the church has been quite positive in two respects: First, the book has effectively challenged people to factor the existence of the hostile demonic realm into their world view; and second, the comment I hear almost invariably from people who had read the book is, "It has prompted me to pray." The soaring sales of his book and its sequel, *Piercing the Darkness,* indicate that much of evangelicalism was ready for this challenge.

Structural Evil: One First-Century Case Example

In many ways Paul's demonology reflects the common early Jewish understanding of evil spirits. In particular Paul apparently believed that pagan religions have close ties with the work of demons (see especially 1 Cor 10:19-20). We concluded earlier that the various non-Christian religions represent a special manifestation of the powers of darkness to deceive people and turn their attention away from the one true God.

According to Luke, Paul spent more time in Ephesus than anywhere else during his missionary journeys, which is understandable since Ephesus held strategic importance for reaching Asia Minor with the gospel. Some of Paul's correspondence was written either from Ephesus (1 Corinthians) to Ephesus (Ephesians, 1 and 2 Timothy) or to nearby cities (Colossians and Philemon).

In some ways it is surprising that Paul never explicitly referred to one of the principal opponents of Christianity in Ephesus—the cult of the Ephesian Artemis.[32] Artemis was the patron deity of Ephesus, and her cult wielded significant influence over the social, religious, economic and political lives of people throughout Asia Minor. Artemis, however, was not the only deity worshiped at Ephesus; up to fifty other gods and goddesses are also known to have had their cults in Ephesus during Paul's time.

It appears Paul had not completely by-passed an issue of major importance to first-century Christians in Ephesus, that is, how to respond to the cult and the opposition it presented. In his letter to the Ephesians Paul provided a framework for a Christian response to the root issue: how to respond to the invisible realm of principalities and powers that stand behind it. The principles would therefore apply not only to the cult of Artemis, but also to any other pagan cult.

In chapter eleven, we discussed Paul's concept of spiritual warfare. Here we will consider the cult of the Ephesian Artemis itself. An understanding of this cult provides one example of the multiplicity of ways that the powers exercised their hostile influence on people in Asia Minor as opponents of Christianity. This examination, in turn, may provide a model of the variety of levels of influence the powers exert on us today.

1. *Through the Occult:* The magical substructure of the Artemis cult brought individuals into direct contact with what we would call the occult. (I have documented and illustrated this point elsewhere.)[33] The powers of darkness appear to gain direct access into the lives of people through involvement in magic, witchcraft and sorcery. It is little wonder the roaming Jewish exorcist Sceva found plenty of business in Ephesus (Acts 19:13-17).

Evangelical ministers today are giving numerous accounts of counseling severely demonized people who have had a background of involvement in the occult. Such people need the wise help of mature Christians to lead them to freedom from the bondage they experienced at the hands of the powers of darkness.

2. *Through Counterfeit Religion:* The term *counterfeit* implies a standard. For the early Christians there was only one true God—the God of Israel who is *the* God and Father of the Lord Jesus Christ. Throughout the biblical revelation of both the Old and the New Testament, all other so-called gods are called "false gods."

In the Artemis cult much evidence points to the celebration of mystery rites.[34] A common trait of many religions throughout the Hellenistic world, the mystery rite normally involved a ritual that culminated in symbolic union with the deity. Satan might very well have used the worship of Artemis to satisfy the spiritual yearnings of people and their longing for "salvation" through counterfeit experiences.

There is still only one God and one way of approaching him— through the Lord Jesus Christ. Paul's writings give no precedent for a positive view of obtaining salvation through any of the non-Christian religions.

3. *Through Political, Economic and Civic Structures:* The Artemis cult controlled major economic and civic structures of western Asia Minor. The cult was the major savings and loan institution for the entire region. Athletic contests were held in her honor, and even one of the months of the year was named after her. Christians would have been forced to decide on such questions as whether they should refuse to borrow money from the cult and whether they should decline from

participation in the "Artemisian games." The eyes of Christians would certainly have seen the pervasiveness of her influence on their society.

The demonic is able to influence any existing human structure. The cult of Artemis is merely one example of a first-century structure that Satan used to delude people and lead them away from devotion to the one true God.

Through all of these means, which the principalities and powers inspire and maintain, the Christian gospel faced an all-pervasive and supernaturally powerful opponent. In his letter to the Ephesians Paul gave stressed that the principal opponent is not "blood and flesh": it is not something material and tangible, perhaps like the cultic paraphernalia, the temple of the goddess, the banking structure or the Artemisian games. The opponent is what stands behind the Artemis cult and all structures, institutions, traditions and values that keep people from responding to the good news of Jesus Christ and the kingdom of God. The opponent is Satan and his powers of darkness.

We too need to develop the ability to discern the true nature of the opposition and respond accordingly. Satan and his powers are still alive and use many of the same methods to deceive, oppress, destroy and, ultimately, blind people to the redemptive message of the gospel.

Conclusion:
Contending with the Powers

*I*N THE LAST THREE CHAPTERS WE HAVE EXAMINED THE REALITY OF THE POWers of darkness and seen how they operate. It now remains to consider how to respond to these hostile opponents. Frequently Christians have turned to the Gospels for learning how to detect demonic influence and how to deal with it (based on the exorcism accounts). I have attempted to show that the apostle Paul's letters also speak to this issue in a relevant manner. Here is a suggestive summary of the relevance of Paul's teaching on the powers of darkness stated in a prescriptive way for the church today.

Re-evaluate Your Own World View in Light of Scripture
Many evangelicals remain skeptical about the actual existence of the powers of evil. For some an overly narrow theological tradition or an atmosphere of doubt in their churches perpetuate disbelief. For everyone the skepticism can be traced to the constraints of our rationalistic post-Enlightenment age.

Although my own early theological nurture and training was not in a church (or a theological tradition) that denied the real existence of the powers or their work in day-to-day experience, my secular education, the influence of my peers, the media and many other sources have had their effect on my views in this area. It has taken a concerted effort on my part to rethink reality apart from the world view I inherited from society.

What is your perception of reality? Does it include the conviction that evil spirits are working behind the scenes to promote evil, or do you think of evil in purely abstract terms? To what extent do you see the powers of darkness at work in prompting lust? In influencing thoughts? In sickness? In church strife? In the exploitation of the poor? In civil unrest and war?

Having opened the door to sensing the reality of the demonic and seeing its influence on many levels, we need to sharpen our sense of discernment. We need to avoid the "swing of the pendulum syndrome"—that is, the tendency to move to the opposite extreme. We should seek a balanced approach to life and ministry. For instance, not every sickness can be attributable to direct demonic attack; it may represent merely the natural constraint of possessing a decaying body that is heading for eventual physical death.

Reflect on Where the Powers May Influence You

Ask God for discernment to help you determine where the powers might be effectively working their deceptive and ungodly control over an area of your life.

Direct Influence: Have you ever participated in any occultic activities or in the direct worship of Satan? Many credible Christian writers and counselors can point to involvements in popular witchcraft and sorcery, channeling, the heavy-metal culture, parapsychology (including ESP, clairvoyance, telepathy, etc.), the cults and an assortment of other activities as an entry into the more direct and immediate forms of satanic involvement in life. For those who come from non-Western cultures, involvement in tribal religions, worshiping household gods, and various magical and mystical practices could provide an opportunity for the powers to gain a significant foothold. What are your own past, or present, involvements?

The Flesh: As I have already pointed out, the powers not only work in the more dramatic forms (like the occult), but also in the more subtle, but equally effective, ways. They take advantage of our inner tendency to disobey God; that is, they exploit what seems to come natural to us. Remember, Paul associated behavior like lying, excessive anger, stealing and dirty talk with the activity of the devil. What aspects of your own behavior are you struggling with at this moment?

The World: Carefully assess where "the world system" might be influencing your values and behavior in a negative way. Is public opinion and peer pressure determining your moral choices? Is there a tradition in your church ("we have always done it this way") that may be hindering its responsiveness to the Spirit for more effective ministry in a climate of change? Does your inherited economic philosophy prevent you from giving sacrificially of your financial and time resources for the mission of the church? These questions are merely suggestive of many similar questions we should honestly put to ourselves about the degree of influence the "structures" may be having on us and our fellow believers.

No doubt some might accuse me of "seeing a demon under every bush." This criticism is fine to the extent that I reflect Paul's view of the pervasive nature of the influence of the powers of darkness over many areas of life. We need to take more seriously Paul's emphasis on the variety of ways the powers of darkness operate *(methodeiai—* Eph 6:11). This certainly does not mean that exorcism, prayers for "binding" and direct authoritative denunciations of the devil are appropriate responses in all instances where his activity is perceived. Paul emphasized a "resistance" model of response based on one's relationship with Christ.

The net result of exposing the extent of demonic activity in the affairs of day-to-day life should force us to a deeper dependence on the power of God.

Know Who You Are in Christ

Christians have truly been rescued from the kingdom of darkness and have been made members of Christ's kingdom. The person who has come to know Christ has also been forgiven, acquitted by God of all guilt, reconciled to God, and will experience no condemnation either now or after death. All of these things—and so many more—are true of Christians, but they are so often disbelieved in practice.

Many Christians have a difficult time internalizing their forgiveness, and their new freedom and liberty in Christ. At my church I have found this difficulty to be true in my ministry to new Christians. Nevertheless, the simple meaning of Christ's work on the cross and the nature of new life in Christ bring refreshing experiences of freedom and release. These experiences often result in times of joyous tears as the weight of guilt and Satan's exploitation are broken. Satan surely wants to deceive Christians into believing lies about themselves— "God cannot really forgive you for that," "you will never be able to overcome that habit," "you couldn't possibly ever love that person," and on and on. Christ has broken the power of Satan and evil over his people. Not only are they capable of change, but also Christ calls them to change.

In his classes and seminars on spiritual conflicts and counseling, my colleague at Talbot School of Theology, Dr. Neil Anderson, regularly encounters Christians struggling with problems often related to some kind of demonic influence. Almost invariably, he finds that for Christians facing direct demonic opposition, they have a profoundly inadequate understanding of who they are in Christ. Based upon Paul's teaching that Christians are called to appropriate God's power and resist the devil, Anderson helps these troubled Christians discover who they really are in terms of their new nature and new life in Christ. As a caring facilitator, Anderson prepares them to deal with the hostile influence of the powers through their own volition and their own appropriation of the power and authority available to them in the Lord Jesus Christ.

It is hard to fathom, but Christ wants us to think of ourselves as so closely united to him that we can consider ourselves as having already died to sin and having been resurrected and exalted. We share in his authority over the principalities and powers. Not only that, we are his dearly loved adopted children whom he has made his heirs!

We cannot forget that our new identity as Christians is not only individual but also corporate. We have been joined to fellow Christians in the solidarity of a corporate body. Christ has created the church as the primary vehicle for his grace to resist and overcome the powers of darkness.

Receive and Appropriate God's Enabling Power

We now need to move beyond knowing we have access to God's power into actually using it. Paul stressed the role of faith in appropriating God's power, that is, the powerful work of his Spirit who indwells us. This kind of faith is based on the objective fact of Christ's resurrection and exaltation over the powers of darkness. Wearing a magical charm or even a crucifix does not impart God's power to Christians; nor should we expect God's power through some magical use of Jesus' name. God cannot be manipulated. His power is bestowed on his people through simple trust in him.

Prayer is one of the most natural expressions of trust in God. The apostle Paul modeled this activity throughout his letters. This kind of communication with God acknowledges his sovereignty and our dependence on him for all of life.

One distinct advantage of having a revised world view that gives credence to the real existence of evil spirits is the impact that it can have on our prayer life. If we live in something other than an entirely mechanistic universe, if there really is an ultimate reality who has revealed himself to us in the Lord Jesus Christ, if hordes of evil spirits do exist who constantly scheme and attack us seeking our destruction, then there is great reason to pray. God is there. He hears, he understands, and he wants to help us survive in the context of rampant supernatural hostility.

Perhaps the greatest service that Frank Peretti has rendered to the church in his fictional accounts *This Present Darkness* and *Piercing the Darkness* has been to lift the veil hiding the unseen world. He startles us with his vivid and grotesque depictions of the powers of darkness and forces us to consider afresh the real and pervasive hostility of this evil spiritual domain. Not only do Peretti's heroes survive against this horrific backdrop of other-worldly evil, but they accomplish many remarkable things for the kingdom of God. Why? Because they pray. God hears and responds. One comes away from reading Peretti's novels with a renewed incentive to pray because, if he is anywhere close to the truth in his fictional depictions, what else can one do but turn to God? God will fight for his people.

The Christian life is carried out in community, in dependence on other people. The apostle Paul especially stressed this point through his analogy of the church as the body of Christ. God has chosen to strengthen and build up individual Christians through their relationships with other Christians, particularly when the church assembles for worship and edification. God's Spirit is active in different ways in different people with the ultimate goal of strengthening the entire group through what each individual member is divinely enabled to contribute. Active involvement in the ministry of a local church is therefore vital to receiving the enabling power of God to resist the attack of the forces of darkness.

Praying together with other Christians is essential if we are to appropriate God's power. As we saw in the chapter on spiritual warfare, Paul regarded prayer as the essence of putting on the armor of God. Although we often think of deploying the armor of God in individualistic terms (that is, this is something I pray for myself in my private times of prayer), Paul presented it in corporate terms (that is, this is something we pray for other people while we are gathered together). We are responsible for arming our fellow believers with the power of God.

In preaching Paul's "spiritual warfare" passage, I have sometimes entitled my message "Praying for the Healthy." My goal has been to guide the content of small group prayer into prayers for each other, not just for those who are physically ill or who have some sort of problem (though that is a very important part). I want people to realize that Scripture teaches that we have a responsibility to prepare our brothers and sisters—even in the seemingly "good times"—to face demonic assault and come through unscathed. Prayers like:

Father, I pray for Tom. I ask that you will give him a fresh glimpse of all the resources that are his in the Lord Jesus Christ. I pray that you will strengthen him in his innermost being with the power that your Spirit can supply in abundance. O Father, you are aware of the areas he is most vulnerable to Satan's attack. Strengthen Tom and protect him with your grace to resist the devil's solicitations to evil.

Father, you know Sheila's desire to make the gospel known at her workplace. We anticipate Satan's rage at her plans to communicate this message of deliverance and redemption. Impart to her boldness, just as you did for the apostle Paul, that you can work through her to overcome the obstacles that the evil one will place in her way.

Paul modeled such prayers throughout his epistles, particularly in Ephesians, where he was especially concerned about the matter of spiritual warfare. We will do well to follow his example.

Resist the Evil One

Paul showed incredible concern for the cultivation of Christian virtue into the lives of the people to whom he ministered. Christian virtue, or "the fruit of the Spirit," stands quite apart from worldly vice, or "the deeds of the flesh." The powers of darkness are utterly opposed to the development of Christian virtue. These demonic powers represent everything that is evil, fleshly and worldly.

For Paul resisting the evil one is closely related to putting to death the deeds of the flesh or stripping off the old nature. These are similar activities viewed from different angles. The goal is to recognize when you face temptation—whether the source of the temptation is viewed as coming from the flesh, the old nature or Satan's enticement—and to resist it by the power of God. According to Paul, spiritual warfare is primarily resistance. It involves taking a closer look at the supernatural nature of temptation and preparing yourself to face the spiritual onslaught in a spiritual manner.

One cannot "simply" resist the evil one. It is not as easy as just saying no. Satan and his forces are supernaturally powerful foes. One must be a Christian and appropriate the resources that are his or hers in the Lord Jesus Christ. Following Jesus, knowledge of the truth, faith and prayer are all prerequisites to resisting the devil and making progress in the Christian life.

Join God's People in the Redemptive Mission

The Christian life is not a "holding pattern" until the day of our death. Nor is it something designed by God merely to freshen our lives until we are joined with him in heaven. The church is called to a task, to reach out into the unredeemed world with the good news of the gospel. Christ has given the church the task of "proclaiming release to the captives" of Satan's kingdom. In the context of Paul's teaching on spiritual warfare, this represents the offensive part of that warfare.

The Father suspends the Second Coming of Christ to provide time for the church to engage in this mission. Paul urged his readers to "redeem the time" which God gives for this task. It is furthermore the task of the entire church, each individual member, not just those perceived to be uniquely gifted to carry it out.

Expressed in these terms, the threat of evangelism to Satan and his kingdom is clear. It is little wonder that he opposes this activity with all his might.

Let us engage in a moment of speculation about Satan's "game plan" for the West. How might he best work to blunt the zeal for the mission of the church? If he were to oppose it in a direct way where people could clearly perceive his hostile intention, it might prove counterproductive. People would rally to the occasion.

If he were to use subtle measures, perhaps his strategy would prove more effective.

What if he were to . . .

☐ make Christians think that everyone has already heard the gospel?

☐ promote so many problems in the church that the resolution of conflict would sap all their energy and attention?

☐ cause Christians to believe only missionaries and evangelists should be concerned with outreach?

☐ make Christians think how extremist they might appear to their friends by "forcing their faith" on other folks?

☐ point out everything repulsive about the non-Christians whom they know and with whom they might be willing to share the gospel?

☐ convince Christians that there is a fair chance that everyone will be saved ultimately anyway, given such a loving God?

☐ cause enough "visible" Christians to fall on such a regular basis that Christians appear no different from any other people?

In the West at least, I am convinced Satan has used such devices (and many more) to hinder the redemptive mission of the church. As part of our resistance strategy to Satan and to fulfill our redemptive task, we need to unmask these false pretensions and redirect our energy toward outreach. This call is at the heart of what it means to be evangelical.

The obligation of Christians to the world does not end with the proclamation of the gospel. We are called to be "salt and light" and to demonstrate love to the world. While Paul did not give us an agenda or an example for social activism, his ethics (influenced by Jesus) provide us with a foundation for developing Christian social ethics. Because the powers, through people, work to influence the structures of our existence, we do have a responsibility to countermand as much as possible their polluting sway. The lesson to be learned from Paul, however, is that Christians should place the primary focus of their energy on changing people. Society can change only to the extent that the hearts of the people are changed.

References to the Powers of Darkness in Paul's Letters

Word RSV (NIV)	Greek Term	Occurrences
Satan		
satan	*satanas*	Rom 16:20; 1 Cor 5:5; 7:5; 2 Cor 2:11; 11:14; 12:7; 1 Thess 2:18; 2 Thess 2:9; 1 Tim 1:20; 5:15
devil	*diabolos*	Eph 4:27; 6:11; 1 Tim 3:6, 7; 2 Tim 2:26
evil one	*ponēros*	Eph 6:16; 2 Thess 3:3
prince (ruler)	*archōn*	Eph 2:2
spirit	*pneuma*	Eph 2:2
Belial	*belial*	2 Cor 6:15
the enemy	*antikeimenos*	1 Tim 5:14
the serpent	*ophis*	2 Cor 11:3
the tempter	*peirazon*	1 Thess 3:5
the god of this world (the god of this age)	*ho theos tou aiōnou toutou*	2 Cor 4:4
angel	*angelos*	2 Cor 11:14
Principalities and Powers		
principalities (rulers)	*archai*	Rom 8:38; 1 Cor 15:24; Eph 1:21; 3:10; 6:12; Col 1:16; 2:10; 2:15
powers (authorities)	*exousiai*	1 Cor 15:24; Eph 1:21; 2:2; 3:10; 6:12; Col 1:16; 2:10; 2:15
powers	*dynameis*	Rom 8:38; Eph 1:21
dominions (powers)	*kyriotētes*	Eph 1:21; Col 1:16
thrones	*thronoi*	Col 1:16
angels/messengers	*angeloi*	Rom 8:38; 1 Cor 4:9; 6:3; 11:10 (?); 2 Cor 12:7; Gal 1:8 (?); Col 2:18
world rulers (powers)	*kosmokratores*	Eph 6:12
spiritual hosts (spiritual forces)	*pneumatika*	Eph 6:12
rulers	*archontes*	1 Cor 2:6, 8
elemental spirits (basic principles)	*stoicheia*	Gal 4:3, 8; Col 2:8, 20
demons	*daimonia*	1 Cor 10:20-21; 1 Tim 4:1

Notes

Introduction
[1]This particular advertisement appeared in the *National Examiner*, December 8, 1987.

[2]Mircea Eliade, in a paper he delivered at the twenty-first annual Freud Memorial Lecture, held in Philadelphia on May 24, 1974, and published as "The Occult in the Modern World," in *Occultism, Witchcraft, and Cultural Fashions: Essays in Comparative Religions* (Chicago: University of Chicago Press, 1976), pp. 58-63.

[3]Eliade, "Some Observations on European Witchcraft," *Occultism, Witchcraft, and Cultural Fashions*, p. 69.

[4]For helpful assessments of the movement from an evangelical perspective, see Douglas R. Groothuis, *Unmasking the New Age* (Downers Grove: InterVarsity Press, 1986), and his second volume, *Confronting the New Age* (Downers Grove: InterVarsity Press, 1988). See also Russell Chandler, *Understanding the New Age* (Dallas: Word, 1988), and Elliot Miller, *A Crash Course on the New Age Movement* (Grand Rapids: Baker, 1989).

[5]See Groothuis, *Confronting,* chapter eight, "New Age Business."

[6]Cathleen Decker, "The L.A. Woman," *Los Angeles Times Magazine,* February 21, 1988, p. 13.

[7]Otto Friedrich, "New Age Harmonies" (Cover Story), *Time,* December 7, 1987, pp. 62-72.

[8]See especially Miller, *Crash Course,* pp. 31-32. He provides a very helpful analysis of the New Age concept of channeling (see chapters eight and nine).

[9]For a summary of the content of a number of "spiritual warfare" classes that are being offered in evangelical colleges and seminaries, see F. Douglas Pennoyer, "Trends and Topics in Teaching Power Evangelism," in *Wrestling*

with Dark Angels, ed. C. Peter Wagner & F. Douglas Pennoyer (Ventura: Regal, 1990), pp. 339-57.

Chapter 1: Magic and Divination

[1]Arthur Darby Nock, "Studies in the Graeco-Roman Beliefs of the Empire," in *Arthur Darby Nock: Essays on Religion in the Ancient World,* vol. 1, ed. Z. Steward (Oxford: Clarendon, 1972), p. 34. The article was originally published in 1928. Hans Dieter Betz of the University of Chicago concurs: "The religious beliefs and practices of most people were identical with some form of magic, and the neat distinctions we make today between approved and disapproved forms of religion—calling the former 'religion' and 'church' and the latter 'magic' and 'cult'—did not exist in antiquity except among a few intellectuals" (Hans Dieter Betz, ed., *The Greek Magical Papyri in Translation,* vol. 1: *Text* [Chicago: University of Chicago Press, 1986], p. xli).

[2]*PGM* 4.2695-2704.

[3]For a detailed discussion of the history and usage of the word *daimon,* see Frederick E. Brenk, "In the Light of the Moon: Demonology in the Early Imperial Period," *Aufstieg und Neidergang der Römischen Welt* II.16.3 (Berlin: Walter de Gruyter, 1987), pp. 2068-2145.

[4]Philostratus, *Life of Apollonius of Tyana* 3.38-39. See the text and discussion in Georg Luck, *Arcana Mundi: Magic and the Occult in the Greek and Roman Worlds* (Baltimore: Johns Hopkins Univ. Press), pp. 155-56.

[5]The text is published with critical notes by Dierk Wortmann, "Neue Magische Texte," *Bonner Jahrbücher* 168 (1968):60-80. The English translation of the text here depends on D. R. Jordan, "A Love Charm with Verses," *Zeitschrift für Papyrologie und Epigraphik* 72 (1988):245-49.

[6]*PGM* 36.231-55.

[7]David Aune, "Magic; Magician," in *International Standard Bible Encyclopedia,* vol. 3 (Grand Rapids: Eerdmans, 1986), p. 218.

[8]For the texts and a discussion, see Chester C. McCown, "The Ephesia Grammata in Popular Belief," *Transactions of the American Philological Association* 54 (1923):128-40.

[9]English translation from A. F. Segal, "Hellenistic Magic: Some Questions of Definition," in *Studies in Gnosticism and Hellenistic Religions* (Leiden: Brill, 1981), p. 358.

[10]*PGM* 1.1-2.

[11]*PGM* 1.96-116.

[12]For one evangelical's assessment of the contemporary practice of channeling, see Elliot Miller, *A Crash Course on the New Age Movement* (Grand Rapids: Baker, 1989), chapters eight and nine.

[13]*PGM* 12.153-60.

[14]*PGM* 7.348-58.

[15]The Acts of Peter is available in an English translation; see Edgar Hennecke, *New Testament Apocrypha,* vol. 2, ed. W. Schneemelcher (Philadelphia: Westminster, 1964), pp. 259-322.

[16]See Susan R. Garrett, *The Demise of the Devil: Magic and the Demonic in Luke's*

Writings (Minneapolis: Fortress Press, 1989). In her superb study of the theme of magic and the demonic in Luke-Acts, Garrett clearly demonstrates Luke's concern to proclaim Christ's triumph over Satan, the force behind all magic.

Chapter 2: Greco-Roman and Oriental Religions

¹On the influence of the Oriental religions, see Franz Cumont, *The Oriental Religions in Roman Paganism* (New York: Dover, 1956). Some, such as the eminent historian of Greek religion Martin P. Nilsson, believe that Cumont has overstated his case, however.

²For a good concise overview of the religious life of Corinth at the time of Paul, see Victor P. Furnish, *II Corinthians*, Anchor Bible 32A (New York: Doubleday, 1984), pp. 14-22.

³For numerous pictures of the extant images of these and other Hellenistic deities, see *Lexicon Iconographicum Mythologiae Classicae* (Zürich und München: Artemis, 1984).

⁴Jonathan Z. Smith, "Hellenistic Religion," in *Encyclopaedia Brittanica*, vol. 8 (Chicago: Encyclopaedia Brittanica, 1979), p. 749.

⁵The entire myth is told in the seventh century B.C. Homeric Hymn to Demeter. For a clear and more complete presentation and interpretation of the myth than I have provided, see Luther H. Martin, *Hellenistic Religions* (Oxford: Oxford University Press, 1987), pp. 62-72.

⁶Herbert J. Rose, "Hades," in *Oxford Classical Dictionary*, 2d ed. (Oxford: Oxford University Press, 1970), p. 484.

⁷As cited in Franz Cumont, *The Oriental Religions in Roman Paganism* (New York: Dover, 1956), p. 66.

⁸Cumont, *Oriental Religions*, p. 67.

⁹For a thorough overview of the cult of Asclepius, see Emma J. Edelstein and Ludwig Edelstein, *Asclepius: A Collection and Interpretation of the Testimonies*, 2 vols. (New York: Arno Press, 1975).

¹⁰Edelstein and Edelstein, *Asclepius*, vol. 2, p. 189.

¹¹*P. Oxy.* 11.1381.1-247.

¹²As cited in Edelstein and Edelstein, *Asclepius*, vol. 2, p. 132.

¹³See Sarah I. Johnston, *Hekate Soteira: A Study of Hekate's Roles in the Chaldean Oracles and Related Literature*, American Classical Studies 21 (Atlanta: Scholars Press, 1990), chapters three ("The Mistress of the Moon") and nine ("The Chaldean Daemon-dogs").

¹⁴Alois Kehl, "Hekate," in *Reallexikon für Antike und Christentum*, vol. 14 (Stuttgart: Anton Hiersemann, 1988), p. 315 (translation mine).

¹⁵Kehl, "Hekate," p. 320.

¹⁶Theodor Kraus, *Hekate: Studien zu Wesen und Bild der Göttin in Kleinasien und Griechenland*, Heidelberger Kunstgeschichtliche Abhandlungen 5 (Heidelberg: Carl Winter, 1960), pp. 50-51.

¹⁷See Johnston, *Hekate Soteira*, p. 146.

¹⁸Johnston emphasizes this theme in *Hekate Soteira*.

¹⁹For the most comprehensive treatment of the Dionysiac cult, see Martin P.

Nilsson, *The Dionysiac Mysteries of the Hellenistic and Roman Age* (Lund: C. W. K. Gleerup, 1957).

[20]Livy *History of Rome* 39.13 as cited in Martin, *Hellenistic Religions,* p. 97.

[21]Livy *History of Rome* 39.8 as cited in Marvin W. Meyer, ed., *The Ancient Mysteries: A Sourcebook. Sacred Texts of the Mystery Religions of the Ancient Mediterranean World* (San Francisco: Harper & Row, 1987), p. 82. See also Nilsson, *Dionysiac Mysteries,* pp. 15-16.

[22]Livy *History of Rome* 39.13 as cited in Meyer, *Ancient Mysteries,* p. 86. See also Martin, *Hellenistic Religions,* p. 97.

[23]Nilsson, *Dionysiac Mysteries,* pp. 45, 95-96.

[24]In a paper addressed to the Greco-Roman Religions Group at the 1988 annual meeting of the Society of Biblical Literature in Chicago, Illinois, entitled, "Dionysos at Pompeii: The Villa of the Mysteries," Professor Marvin Meyer argued convincingly that the well-preserved wall friezes at the Villa of the Mysteries in Pompeii should be interpreted as a celebration of the mystery of sexuality.

[25]For a helpful overview of each of these instances, see Robert M. Grant, *Gods and the One God,* Library of Early Christianity (Philadelphia: Westminster Press, 1986), chapter one, "Gods in the Book of Acts."

[26]F. F. Bruce, *The Book of Acts,* New International Commentary on the New Testament (Grand Rapids: Eerdmans, 1954), pp. 525-26.

Chapter 3: Astrology

[1]For a discussion of the deification of the luminaries, see Franz Cumont, *Astrology and Religion Among the Greeks and Romans* (New York: Dover, 1960), pp. 64-76.

[2]From Manilius 1.25-112 as cited in Georg Luck, *Arcana Mundi* (Baltimore: Johns Hopkins Univ. Press, 1985), p. 325.

[3]From Manilius 4.1-118 as cited in Luck, *Arcana Mundi,* p. 340.

[4]Luck, *Arcana Mundi,* p. 349.

[5]Franz Cumont, *Oriental Religions in Roman Paganism* (New York: Dover, 1956), p. 181.

[6]An entire book has been devoted to the theme of magic and astrology: Hans Georg Gundel, *Weltbild und Astrologie in den griechischen Zauberpapyri, Münchener Beiträge zur Papyrusforschung und Antiken Rechtsgeschichte 53* (München: Beck, 1968).

[7]*PGM* 7.284-99.

[8]*PGM* 4.2891ff.

[9]*PGM* 4.2940.

[10]*PGM* 7.686-93.

[11]On the background and usage of both of these expressions, see Clinton E. Arnold, *Ephesians: Power and Magic. The Concept of Power in Ephesians in Light of Its Historical Setting,* Society for New Testament Studies Monograph 63 (Cambridge: Cambridge Univ. Press, 1989), pp. 52-56, 65-68.

[12]This view will be argued in much more detail in my forthcoming monograph on the background of Colossians. Perhaps the greatest obstacle to a more

widespread acceptance is that some scholars have felt that this interpretation of *stoicheia* is contextually inappropriate to Galatians. Suffice it to say here: (1) The *stoicheia* in Galatians 4:3 are set parallel to the personal "guardians and tutors" of 4:2, thus pointing to a personal interpretation of *stoicheia*. (2) The next reference to the *stoicheia* (Gal 4:9) is prefaced by the comment that the readers had been in bondage to "beings that by nature are no gods." This appears to be an idea similar to what Paul expressed regarding heathen religion in 1 Corinthians 8:5—there are many entities "called gods" in heaven and on earth to whom food is offered. He subsequently identifies the demons as the recipients of these sacrifices. (3) The *stoicheia* are thus not equivalent to the law, but should be regarded as evil spirits who have exploited the law and led people astray from following its divinely intended function.

[13]*PGM* 39.18-21.

[14]Some scholars question the use of the *Testament of Solomon* for illuminating the New Testament on the basis of its uncertain date (possibly postdating the New Testament) and the possibility of Christian interpolations into the text of the Testament. Most scholars believe that it is likely, however, that the demonology of the Testament reflects widespread Jewish beliefs both prior to and during the New Testament period. Furthermore, it is doubtful that this usage of the terms *kosmokratores* and *stoicheia* originated with Paul.

Chapter 4: Judaism

[1]See the excursus on "Lilith" in John D. W. Watts, *Isaiah 34—66*, Word Biblical Commentary 25 (Waco: Word, 1987), pp. 13-14; see also David Aune, "Night Hag," in *The International Standard Bible Encyclopedia*, vol. 3 (Grand Rapids: Eerdmans, 1986), p. 536.

[2]Targum Pseudo-Jonathan on Numbers 6:24-26 as cited in Watts, *Isaiah 34—66*, p. 13.

[3]C. H. Gordon, "Two Magic Bowls in Teheran," *Orientalia* 20 (1951):310.

[4]The NIV interprets these words as referring to other animals, thus the Hebrew terms are understood as "desert creatures," "owls," "wild goats" and "night creatures." The RSV takes the last two terms as demonic; it translates them as "satyr" and "night hag." The Greek Old Testament merely summarizes the Hebrew terms under the Greek terms *daimonia* ("demons") and another word signifying some kind of evil spirit *(onokentauros)*. For support for the demonological interpretation, see Watts, *Isaiah 34—66*, p. 13.

[5]See Francis Brown, S. R. Driver and C. A. Briggs, *A Hebrew and English Lexicon of the Old Testament* (1953; reprint ed., Oxford: Clarendon, 1978), p. 972.

[6]On this topic, see David Aune, "Magic; Magician," in *The International Standard Bible Encyclopedia*, vol. 3 (Grand Rapids: Eerdmans, 1986), pp. 214-16.

[7]For a full discussion of this topic, see David E. Aune, "Divination," in *The International Standard Bible Encyclopedia*, vol. 1 (Grand Rapids: Eerdmans, 1979), p. 971-74.

[8]C. F. Keil and F. Delitzsch, "Joshua," in *Commentary on the Old Testament* (reprint ed., Grand Rapids: Eerdmans, 1980), p. 365, observe that " 'an evil

spirit' is not merely 'an evil disposition,' but an evil demon, which produced discord and strife, just as an evil spirit came upon Saul. . . . [It was] not Satan himself, but a supernatural spiritual power which was under his influence."

[9]Gordon J. Wenham, *Genesis 1—15,* Word Biblical Commentary 1 (Waco: Word, 1987), pp. 73, 88.

[10]See E. Stauffer, *Theology,* p. 64. For a popular presentation of this view, see C. Fred Dickason, *Angels: Elect and Evil* (Chicago: Moody, 1975), pp. 127-37.

[11]See Gerhard von Rad, "διάβολος," in *Theological Dictionary of the New Testament,* vol. 2, ed. Gerhard Kittel (Grand Rapids: Eerdmans, 1964), p. 74.

[12]The Hebrew text actually reads, "sons of Israel." The Septuagint translation of the phrase has been strengthened by the discovery of a Hebrew version of Deuteronomy 32:8 at Qumran that reads, "sons of God."

[13]D. S. Russell, *The Method and Message of Jewish Apocalyptic* (Philadelphia: Westminster Press, 1964), p. 248. See his excellent discussion of "the guardian angels of the nations" (pp. 244-49).

[14]The Theodotian version of Daniel uses *archōn* while the Septuagint version uses *stratēgos* ("commander of an army," "general").

[15]See Russell, *Apocalyptic,* pp. 237-38.

[16]Note especially the following lines from the scroll: "The holy angels shall be with their hosts [the armies of the people of God]" (1QM 7.6); "The host of His spirits is with our foot-soldiers and horsemen" (1QM 12.8-9); "And the Prince of Light Thou hast appointed from ancient times to come to our support" (1QM 13.10); "[Satan] girds himself to come to the aid of the sons of darkness" (1QM 16.11); "[God] will send eternal succor to the company of His redeemed by the might of the princely Angel of the kingdom of Michael" (1QM 17.6).

[17]See Russell, *Apocalyptic,* pp. 254-57, for a detailed discussion of the variety of Jewish traditions regarding the existence of evil spirits prior to the flood.

[18]J. Maier, "Geister (Dämonen)," in *Reallexikon für Antike und Christentum,* vol. 9, ed. T. Klauser (Stuttgart, 1975), cols. 680-87.

[19]There is some uncertainty as to the precise dates of these documents. To complicate the matter further, some scholars think that the Testaments received Christian interpolations and redaction. In 1976, James Charlesworth summarized the scholarship on the Testaments in this way: "The Testaments probably obtained a form recognizably similar to that which we know around 100 B.C. The Testaments are apparently based upon an ancient core. . . . These twelve Testaments were probably redacted by a later Jew, perhaps in the first century B.C. . . . and were certainly interpolated and infrequently reworked by 'Christians' over a period of centuries, beginning around A.D. 100 because of the dependence upon the Gospel according to John. . . . No scholar now affirms that the Testaments were written near the end of the second century A.D. and were composed by a Christian, as M. de Jonge once suggested" *(The Pseudepigrapha and Modern Research with a Supplement* (Chico, Calif.: Scholars Press, 1981), pp. 212-13. Since Charlesworth made these comments, no new scholarship has appeared that would radically alter this assessment. Because the role of angels and evil spirits are

at the heart of the conceptual world of the testaments, it is appropriate to use them as one means of unveiling first century A.D. Jewish ideas about angelology and demonology.

[20]P. S. Alexander, "Incantations and Books of Magic," in E. Schürer, *The History of the Jewish People in the Age of Jesus Christ*, vol. 3, rev. ed., ed. G. Vermes, F. Millar, M. Black and M. Goodman (Edinburgh: T. & T. Clark, 1987), p. 342.

[21]E. R. Goodenough, *Jewish Symbols in the Greco-Roman Period*, vol. 2 (New York: Pantheon, 1953), pp. 153-295.

[22]Alexander, "Incantations," p. 345.

[23]Alexander, "Incantations," pp. 373-74, argues for an early version of the Testament appearing in the first century and contends that it "can surely be used to throw light on early Jewish demonology."

[24]For a full discussion of this topic, see James H. Charlesworth, "Jewish Interest in Astrology during the Hellenistic and Roman Period," *Aufstieg und Niedergang der Römischen Welt* II.20.2 (Berlin: Walter de Gruyter, 1987), pp. 926-56.

Chapter 5: The Teaching of Jesus

[1]R. T. France, *Matthew*, Tyndale New Testament Commentary (Grand Rapids: Eerdmans, 1985), p. 98.

[2]The order of the last two temptations is reversed in Matthew's Gospel.

[3]France, *Matthew*, p. 99.

[4]See Joseph A. Fitzmyer, *The Gospel According to Luke I—IX*, Anchor Bible 28 (New York: Doubleday, 1981), p. 529, and I. Howard Marshall, *Commentary on Luke*, New International Greek Testament Commentary (Grand Rapids: Eerdmans, 1978), pp. 177-78.

[5]Susan R. Garrett, *The Demise of the Devil* (Minneapolis: Fortress Press, 1989), pp. 45-46, argues convincingly that Jesus' conquering of the strong man in Luke 11:21-22 took place not only in the exorcisms, but primarily at his death and resurrection.

[6]Ethelbert Stauffer, *Theology of the New Testament*, 5th ed. (New York: Macmillan, 1955), p. 124.

[7]Garrett, *Demise*, p. 45.

[8]Raymond E. Brown, *The Gospel According to John I—XII*, Anchor Bible 29 (New York: Doubleday, 1966), p. 477.

[9]Brown, *John XII—XXI*, p. 714.

[10]A much closer connection between demons and sickness was perceived in the New Testament world than is commonly believed to be true in Western society today. This is why Jesus could simultaneously be accused of being "out of his mind" and being possessed by Beelzebub (Mk 3:21-22; see also Jn 10:20: "Many of them said, 'He is demon-possessed and raving mad.' "). While the various opportunities of the disciples may have involved the simultaneous need to deal with an evil spirit, it goes beyond the evidence of the Gospels to suggest that healing and exorcism were necessarily and inextricably linked.

[11]With regard to Luke's account, Marshall, *Luke*, p. 350, notes, "Luke wished to record how the Twelve, who figure prominently in Acts as witnesses and missionaries, were already called by Jesus and experienced a prefigurement of their later ministry."

[12]Marshall, *Commentary on Luke*, p. 351.

[13]Fitzmyer, *Luke X—XXIV*, p. 860. The passage is therefore not to be connected with Satan's ouster from heaven described in Revelation 12:7-13, an event that is yet future. Cf. also Robert H. Mounce, *The Book of Revelation*, New International Commentary on the New Testament (Grand Rapids: Eerdmans, 1977), p. 240, who interprets Satan's removal from heaven in Revelation 12 as "the cosmic prelude to the consummation."

[14]See Marshall, *Luke*, p. 429.

[15]Stauffer, *Theology*, p. 286, note 397.

[16]Fitzmyer, *Luke X—XXIV*, p. 860.

[17]Similarly, Graham Twelftree, *Christ Triumphant: Exorcism Then and Now* (London: Hodder & Stoughton, 1985), p. 86, concludes, "But insofar as exorcism, the defeat of Satan and the coming of the new Kingdom are interconnected, and that Jesus sent his disciples out to proclaim the coming of the Kingdom, then we can assume both that Jesus intended the disciples to be exorcists and that in fact they were exorcists." His focus on exorcism, however, is too restrictive in understanding the disciples' authority over the evil powers.

Chapter 6: What Are the Powers?

[1]There is one exception. The Theodotian text of Daniel 7:27 uses *archai* to translate the Hebrew word for "rulers."

[2]Years ago, R. H. Charles pointed to this text as important for understanding the source of Paul's vocabulary for the powers; see R. H. Charles, *The Apocrypha and Pseudepigrapha of the Old Testament*, vol. 2 (Oxford: Clarendon, 1913), pp. 180, 226-27. In more recent times, Matthew Black, *The Book of Enoch or 1 Enoch*, Studia in Veteris Testamenti Pseudepigrapha 7 (Leiden: Brill, 1985), p. 234, notes that "these words are still regarded by commentators and others as our main ancient authority for these New Testament terms, e.g., 'the principalities and powers'."

[3]Charles, *Apocrypha and Pseudepigrapha*, p. 441, remarks that these are exactly the same terms used by Paul.

[4]For a discussion of the use of these terms in magic and astrology, see Clinton E. Arnold, *Ephesians: Power and Magic. The Concept of Power in Ephesians in Light of Its Historical Setting*, Society for New Testament Studies Monograph 63 (Cambridge: Cambridge Univ. Press, 1989), pp. 51-69.

[5]See Edwin M. Yamauchi, *Pre-Christian Gnosticism*, 2d ed. (Grand Rapids: Baker, 1983); see also his article, "Pre-Christian Gnosticism, the New Testament and Nag Hammadi in Recent Debate," *Themelios* 10 (1984):22-27.

[6]For a more complete discussion of this issue, see my *Ephesians: Power and Magic*, pp. 7-13.

[7]The best introduction to the various Gnostic systems of thought is provided

in Kurt Rudolph, *Gnosis: The Nature and History of an Ancient Religion* (San Francisco: Harper & Row, 1987).

[8]For a detailed study of this issue, see Wendell L. Willis, *Idol Meat in Corinth: The Pauline Argument in 1 Corinthians 8 and 10*, SBL Disseration Series 68 (Chico, Calif.: Scholars Press, 1985).

[9]Gordon Fee, *The First Epistle to the Corinthians*, New International Commentary on the New Testament (Grand Rapids: Eerdmans, 1987), p. 359, contends that this is the basic issue throughout 1 Corinthians 8—10.

[10]On this point I am convinced by the arguments of Gordon Fee, *Corinthians*, pp. 359-63, who sees this as a separate issue from eating sacrificial meat in another context, such as in the home of a non-Christian. My understanding of 1 Corinthians 8—10 is greatly indebted to his superb treatment of this passage in his commentary.

[11]Ibid., p. 373.

[12]J. Murphy-O'Connor as cited in Fee, *Corinthians*, p. 381.

[13]See chapter four, "Judaism."

[14]For numerous other texts illustrating this widespread Jewish belief, see Hermann L. Strack and Paul Billerbeck, *Kommentar zum neuen Testament aus Talmud und Midrasch*, vol. 3, 6th ed. (Munich: C. H. Beck, 1975), pp. 47-60.

[15]Translation by H. W. Hollander and M. de Jonge in *The Testaments of the Twelve Patriarchs*, Studia in Veteris Testamenti Pseudepigrapha 8 (Leiden: Brill, 1985), p. 225.

[16]Ibid., p. 301.

[17]Fee, *Corinthians*, p. 388, note 62.

[18]Stauffer, *Theology*, p. 66.

Chapter 7: The Defeat of the Powers at the Cross

[1]Ironically, earlier in his ministry, when Jesus spoke of his impending death, Peter tried to deter him from the necessity of the cross, and Jesus replied, "Out of my sight, Satan!" (Mt 16:23). It appears that the powers of Satan were confused with regard to how God would accomplish his salvific purposes through Christ. Nevertheless, as the time for Jesus' passion drew near, it is clear that Satan sought Jesus' physical death.

[2]*BAGD*, p. 417.

[3]Most recently this view has been argued by Gordon D. Fee, *The First Epistle to the Corinthians*, New International Commentary on the New Testament (Grand Rapids: Eerdmans, 1987), pp. 101-7. Fee thinks that the word *rulers* refers not only to the people responsible for the crucifixion, but also to the leaders of this age in a broader sense, including the "wise ones" of 1:20 and 2:6.

[4]For this observation, I am indebted to Otto Everling, *Die paulinische Angelologie und Dämonologie* (Göttingen: Vandenhoeck & Ruprecht, 1988), p. 13.

[5]English translation by J. B. Lightfoot, *The Apostolic Fathers* (Grand Rapids: Baker, 1978), p. 153.

[6]I would distinguish this interpretation from that of Oscar Cullmann, who contends that Paul intended a dual reference, both human authorities and

angelic powers, in his use of the word *ruler*. The word itself only has one referent in a context, and here the context points to demonic rulers. The outcome of my interpretation, at least in this passage, is actually not far from that of Cullmann's. See Oscar Cullmann, *Christ and Time* (London: SCM Press, 1951), pp. 191-210 and *The State in the New Testament* (London: SCM Press, 1957), pp. 95-114.

[7]*BAGD*, p. 173.

[8]E. F. Scott, *The Epistles of Paul to the Colossians, to Philemon, and to the Ephesians* (London: Hodder & Stoughton, 1930), p. 189.

[9]For an insightful study of this motif, see L. Williamson, "Led in Triumph: Paul's Use of Thriambeuo," *Interpretation* 22 (1968):317-22.

[10]Eduard Lohse, *Colossians and Philemon*, Hermeneia (Philadelphia: Fortress Press, 1971), p. 112.

[11]For a detailed study of this passage, see Clinton E. Arnold, *Ephesians: Power and Magic* (Cambridge: Cambridge Univ. Press, 1989), pp. 52-56, 70-85.

[12]See David M. Hay, *Glory at the Right Hand: Psalm 110 in Early Christianity* (Nashville: Abingdon, 1973).

[13]On this passage, see the excellent treatment of J. Ramsey Michaels, *1 Peter*, Word Biblical Commentary 49 (Waco: Word, 1988), pp. 194-222. Michaels sees Peter's reference to Christ making proclamation to the spirits in refuge as "Peter's way of dramatizing concretely the universality of Christ's lordship, which he will make explicit in v. 22: 'with angels and authorities and powers in subjection to him' " (p. 206).

[14]See my discussion of this passage in *Ephesians: Power and Magic*, pp. 56-58.

Chapter 8: A New Kingdom and Identity for Believers

[1]Ethelbert Stauffer wrote one of the few New Testament theologies that brings this aspect out with clarity and forcefulness (see his *New Testament Theology*, 5th ed. [New York: Macmillan, 1955, pp. 146-49]).

[2]Josephus *Antiquities* 12.149.

[3]Donald Guthrie, *New Testament Theology* (Downers Grove: InterVarsity Press, 1981), p. 648.

[4]J. B. Lightfoot, *Saint Paul's Epistles to the Colossians and to Philemon* (Grand Rapids: Zondervan, 1977), p. 227. For further detailed discussion on the "head-body" imagery, see my *Ephesians: Power and Magic. The Concept of Power in Ephesians in Light of Its Historical Setting*, Society for New Testament Studies Monograph 63 (Cambridge: Cambridge Univ. Press, 1989), pp. 79-82.

[5]G. Münderlein, "Die Erwählung durch das Pleroma," *New Testament Studies* 8 (1962):264-76. For further discussion, see my *Ephesians: Power and Magic*, pp. 82-85.

[6]Gordon D. Fee, *The First Epistle to the Corinthians*, New International Commentary on the New Testament (Grand Rapids: Eerdmans, 1987), p. 603.

[7]Ibid., p. 605. Fee argues that the baptism and drinking clauses are parallel and convey the same content. He sees them as referring to the believers' common experience of conversion and not to some second experience of

the Spirit separate from conversion.

[8]See Cleon L. Rogers, "The Dionysian Background of Ephesians 5:18," *Bibliotheca Sacra* 136 (1979):249-57. This interpretation has received a number of endorsements, including, most recently, that of Jacob Adai, *Der Heilige Geist als Gegenwart Gottes in den einzelnen Christen, in der Kirche und in der Welt*, Regensburger Studien zur Theologie (Frankfurt am Main, Bern, New York: Peter Lang, 1985):222-23.

[9]James D. G. Dunn, *Romans 1—8*, Word Biblical Commentary 38a (Waco: Word, 1988), p. 513.

Chapter 9: The Influence of the Powers on Believers

[1]Oscar Cullmann, *Christ and Time*, tr. Floyd V. Filson (Philadelphia: Westminster Press, 1949), pp. 139-43.

[2]A. M. Hunter, as cited in J. Christian Beker, *Paul the Apostle* (Philadelphia: Fortress Press, 1980), p. 159.

[3]John R. W. Stott, *The Message of Ephesians*, The Bible Speaks Today (Downers Grove: InterVarsity Press, 1979), p. 73.

[4]For a helpful description of the nature of "the world" and "this age" as evil and how it influences social order, see Stephen C. Mott, *Biblical Ethics and Social Change* (Oxford: Oxford Univ. Press, 1982), chapter 1: "Biblical Faith and the Reality of Social Evil," pp. 3-21.

[5]*BAGD*, p. 823.

[6]J. Armitage Robinson, *St. Paul's Epistle to the Ephesians* (London: Macmillan, 1907), p. 112.

[7]For additional Jewish parallels and discussion on this verse, see my *Ephesians: Power and Magic*, p. 65.

[8]See Ralph P. Martin, *2 Corinthians*, Word Biblical Commentary 40 (Waco: Word, 1986), p. 351.

[9]Ibid., pp. 306-7.

[10]This is true whether one interprets the "we" to refer only to Jewish Christians or to Jewish and Gentile Christians together.

[11]F. F. Bruce, *The Epistle to the Galatians*, New International Greek Testament Commentary (Grand Rapids: Eerdmans, 1982), p. 202.

[12]Ibid., p. 30.

[13]Contra John Wimber, *Power Healing* (San Francisco: Harper & Row, 1987), p. 272, note 15, who thinks that Paul's "thorn in the flesh" was a reference to his opponents at Corinth. As Martin, *2 Corinthians*, p. 415, notes, the most telling point against such an interpretation is the fact that Paul prayed three times that God might take "the thorn" away from him (12:8). It is quite unlikely that, in principle, Paul would have prayed to be spared from opposition and persecution. This was more an assumption of his ministry for which he would have prayed that the gospel would overcome and prevail. It is far more likely, however, that Paul would have asked God to spare him from some annoying physical ailment he perceived had slowed him down and hindered him in his ministry.

[14]Martin, *2 Corinthians*, p. 415.

[15]Gordon Fee, *The First Epistle to the Corinthians,* The New International Commentary on the New Testament (Grand Rapids: Eerdmans, 1987), p. 209.

[16]For a detailed defense of this position, see Fee, *Corinthians,* pp. 210-13.

[17]Gordon D. Fee, *1 and 2 Timothy, Titus,* New International Biblical Commentary (Peabody, Mass.: Hendrickson, 1988), p. 83.

Chapter 10: Christ and No Other

[1]I am currently engaged in a monograph-scale research project on the background of the Colossian conflict. Many of the nuances and details of my perspective on the Colossian conflict cannot be explained or supported with the precision I would like within the space constraints of this brief presentation. I will refer the reader to the near-future publication of my research on the background of the problem at Colossae.

[2]For more details on the ancient city of Colossae, see my entry on Colossae in the *Anchor Bible Dictionary,* ed. David Noel Freedman (New York: Doubleday, forthcoming 1992).

[3]Sir William M. Ramsay, "The Mysteries in their Relation to St. Paul," *Contemporary Review* 104 (1913):198-209, especially 205; *The Teaching of Paul in Terms of the Present Day* (London: Hodder & Stoughton, 1914), pp. 283-305. Eduard Lohse, *Colossians and Philemon* (Philadelphia: Fortress Press, 1971), p. 114, suggests the translation: "Let no one condemn you, who takes pleasure in readiness to serve and in worship of angels, *as he has had visions of them during the mystery rites* (italics mine), puffed up without reason by his earthly mind." The case has most recently been argued by Randall A. Argall, "The Source of Religious Error in Colossae," *Calvin Theological Journal* 22 (1987):6-20.

[4]I have attempted to support this interpretation in two scholarly papers delivered to the Society of Biblical Literature ("Hellenistic Magic: A New Key for Understanding the Colossian Heresy," presented to the New Testament Epistles Section of the Pacific Coast Region of the Society of Biblical Literature, March 25, 1988) and to the Evangelical Theological Society ("Magic, Mystery Religions, and the Epistle to the Colossians," presented to the annual meeting of the Evangelical Theological Society, Wheaton, Illinois, November 18, 1988).

[5]The interpretation of the phrase "worship of angels" has been a point of significant controversy among interpreters. Many other views have been asserted, but among the most prominent is the view that understands the phrase in the sense of "worshiping with the angels" and assumes a setting around the heavenly throne of Yahweh. In this interpretation, the overall characteristics of the Colossian heresy are described more in terms of a Jewish mystical asceticism. See Peter T. O'Brien, *Colossians, Philemon,* Word Biblical Commentary 44 (Waco: Word, 1982), pp. xxx-xli, 142-43.

[6]Numerous books and articles have been written on hymnic character of this passage. For a good bibliography of sources, see O'Brien, *Colossians,* pp. 31-32.

[7]N. T. Wright, *Colossians and Philemon,* Tyndale New Testament Commentary

(Grand Rapids: Eerdmans, 1986), p. 103.

Chapter 11: Spiritual Warfare

[1]See Richard E. Oster, "Ephesus as a Religious Center under the Principate I. Paganism before Constantine," *Aufstieg und Niedergang der Römischen Welt* II.18.2 (Berlin: Walter de Gruyter, forthcoming), pp. 1661-1728.

[2]See Clinton E. Arnold, *Ephesians: Power and Magic. The Concept of Power in Ephesians in Light of Its Historical Setting*, Society for New Testament Studies Monograph Series 63 (Cambridge: Cambridge Univ. Press, 1989).

[3]John R. W. Stott, *The Message of Ephesians*, The Bible Speaks Today (Downers Grove: InterVarsity Press, 1979), p. 280.

Chapter 12: Christ's Final Defeat of the Powers

[1]Hans Dieter Betz, *Galatians*, Hermeneia (Philadelphia: Fortress Press, 1979), p. 205.

[2]Ibid., p. 205.

[3]English translation by H. W. Hollander and M. de Jonge, *The Testaments of the Twelve Patriarchs*, Studia in Veteris Testamenti Pseudepigrapha 8 (Leiden: Brill, 1985), p. 121. They provide many further references illustrating the Jewish belief that the devil and his spirits will be destroyed at the end of times (p. 125).

[4]See I. Howard Marshall, *1 and 2 Thessalonians*, New Century Bible Commentary (Grand Rapids: Eerdmans, 1983), p. 204.

[5]See C. K. Barrett, *The First Epistle to the Corinthians*, Harper's New Testament Commentary (San Francisco: Harper & Row, 1968), p. 358.

[6]Joachim Gnilka, *Der Kolosserbrief*, Herders theologischer Kommentar zum Neuen Testament (Freiburg: Herder, 1980), p. 75 (translation mine). Likewise, Ralph Martin, in *Reconciliation: A Study of Paul's Theology* (Atlanta: John Knox Press, 1981), p. 119, contends that in this context " 'reconciliation' takes on the meaning of harmony and peace within the cosmic order."

[7]Eduard Lohse, *Colossians and Philemon*, Hermeneia (Philadelphia: Fortress Press, 1971), p. 59.

Chapter 13: Reality or Myth?

[1]On this topic, see John Dillenberger, *Protestant Thought and Natural Science* (1960; reprint ed., Notre Dame: University of Notre Dame Press, 1988).

[2]Rudolf Bultmann, "New Testament and Mythology," *Kerygma and Myth: A Theological Debate*, vol. 1 (London: SPCK, 1964), p. 10.

[3]For example, J. C. Beker, *Paul the Apostle* (Edinburgh: T. & T. Clark, 1980), p. 189. Bultmann also spoke of the influence of the redemption myths of Gnosticism. Most scholars today question whether there was, in fact, a coherent Gnostic redeemer-myth and discount the possibility that this could have influenced the New Testament writers.

[4]Bultmann, "Mythology," p. 10. For a critique of Bultmann's thought with regard to the powers, see Peter T. O'Brien, "Principalities and Powers: Op-

ponents of the Church," *Biblical Interpretation and the Church* (Nashville: Thomas Nelson, 1984), pp. 112-17.

[5]Ched Myers, *Binding the Strong Man: A Political Reading of Mark's Story of Jesus* (Maryknoll: Orbis, 1988), p. 165.

[6]Myers, *Binding,* p. 452. He contends that the best means to the end is not through armed resistance, nor through Marxist theory and practice, but through a type of Gandhian nonviolence that he sees in Mark.

[7]See Kees W. Bolle, "Myth," in *The Encyclopedia of Religion,* vol. 10, ed. Mircea Eliade (New York: Macmillan, 1987), p. 261. See also Mircea Eliade, *Myth and Reality* (New York: Harper & Row, 1963), p. 5.

[8]See Paul Ricoeur, "Myth and History," in *The Encyclopedia of Religion,* vol. 10, ed. Mircea Eliade (New York: Macmillan, 1987), pp. 273-74.

[9]Carl G. Jung, "The Shadow," in *The Collected Works of C. G. Jung,* vol. 9.2 (Princeton: University Press, 1959), pp. 8-10. In his "The Definition of Demonism," in *The Collected Works of C. G. Jung,* vol. 18 (Princeton: University Press, 1976), p. 648, Jung describes demon possession as "a state of mind" in which certain psychic contents "take over the control of the total personality in place of the ego, at least temporarily, to such a degree that the free will of the ego is suspended." He classifies demonism partly as a psychogenic neurosis and partly as schizophrenia.

[10]I am indebted to Jeffrey Burton Russell, *Mephistopheles: The Devil in the Modern World* (Ithaca and London: Cornell Univ. Press, 1986), pp. 226-35, for his rich analysis of the thought of Freud and Jung on the topic of evil.

[11]Walter Wink, *Naming the Powers: The Language of Power in the New Testament* (Philadelphia: Fortress Press, 1984), pp. 104-5.

[12]W. Pannenberg, "Myth in Biblical and Christian Tradition," in *The Idea of God and Human Freedom* (Philadelphia: Westminster, 1973), p. 67; Anthony C. Thiselton, *The Two Horizons: New Testament Hermeneutics and Philosophical Description* (Grand Rapids: Eerdmans, 1980), p. 290.

[13]Pannenberg, *Idea of God,* pp. 67-69.

[14]Ibid., pp. 14-15.

[15]Thiselton, *The Two Horizons,* p. 289.

[16]Pannenberg, "Myth," p. 67.

[17]Thiselton, *The Two Horizons,* p. 439. Also on this hermeneutical issue, with reference to the powers, see O'Brien, "Principalities," pp. 128-33.

[18]Marcus Borg, *Jesus: A New Vision* (San Francisco: Harper & Row, 1987), pp. 63-64.

[19]Walter Wink, *Naming the Powers* (Philadelphia: Fortress Press, 1984), p. 4.

[20]See, for example, John Goldingay's comments on the angelic princes in the book of Daniel in his recent commentary, *Daniel,* Word Biblical Commentary 30 (Dallas: Word, 1989), especially pp. 312-14.

[21]Bultmann, "Mythology," p. 5.

[22]Russell, *Mephistopheles,* p. 21.

[23]Graham Twelftree, *Christ Triumphant: Exorcism Then and Now* (London: Hodder & Stoughton, 1985), pp. 152-56.

[24]T. K. Oesterreich, *Possession: Demoniacal and Other Among Primitive Races, in*

Antiquity, the Middle Ages, and Modern Times (London: Kegan Paul, Trench, Trubner & Co., 1930), p. 378, cited in Twelftree, *Christ Triumphant*, p. 154.

[25]Twelftree, *Christ Triumphant*, p. 156.

[26]Russell, *Mephistopheles*, p. 301.

[27]O'Brien, "Principalities and Powers," p. 130.

[28]Paul Hiebert, "The Flaw of the Excluded Middle," *Missiology: An International Review* 10 (1982):35-47.

[29]Gordon Fee, *The First Epistle to the Corinthians*, New International Commentary on the New Testament (Grand Rapids: Eerdmans, 1987), p. 472, note 49.

[30]This point is very well documented by Russell in *Mephistopheles* and by Mircea Eliade, "The Occult and the Modern World," in *Occultism, Witchcraft, and Cultural Fashions* (Chicago: University of Chicago Press, 1967), pp. 47-68.

[31]I. M. Lewis, *Religion in Context: Cults and Charisma* (Cambridge: Cambridge Univ. Press, 1986), p. 48.

[32]The papers and responses were published in C. Peter Wagner and F. Douglas Pennoyer, *Wrestling with Dark Angels: Toward a Deeper Understanding of the Supernatural Forces in Spiritual Warfare* (Ventura: Regal, 1990).

[33]Hans Küng, *Theology for the Third Millennium* (New York: Doubleday, 1988).

Chapter 14: The Powers and People

[1]I appreciate Paul Hiebert's balanced explanation of these two aspects of demonstrating the power of God. See his article, "Power Encounter and Folk Islam," in *Muslims and Christians on the Emmaus Road*, ed. J. Dudley Woodberry (Monrovia, Calif.: Missions Advanced Research & Communications Center, 1989), pp. 45-61.

[2]C. S. Lewis, *The Screwtape Letters: With Screwtape Proposes a Toast*, rev. ed. (New York: Macmillan, 1982).

[3]Tamara Jones, " 'Fun' Killers Now Paying Devil's Dues," in *Los Angeles Times* (Thursday, October 20, 1988), cover story.

Chapter 15: The Powers and Society

[1]For a more complete discussion of this topic, see my *Ephesians: Power and Magic* (Cambridge: Cambridge Univ. Press, 1989), pp. 44-51, 129-34, and Peter T. O'Brien, "Principalities and Powers: Opponents of the Church," *Biblical Interpretation and the Church* (Nashville: Thomas Nelson, 1984), pp. 119-25, and his "Principalities and Powers and Their Relationship to Structures," *Evangelical Review of Theology* 6 (1982):50-61.

[2]The two most influential books written from this perspective are by Heinrich Schlier, *Principalities and Powers in the New Testament* (Freiburg: Herder, 1961), and Hendrik Berkhof, *Christ and the Powers* (Scottdale: Herald Press, 1977). Schlier originally wrote between the two world wars and Berkhof just after World War 2. Three more recent writers, emphasizing the social and political interpretation of the powers, have wielded a significant influence on the evangelical community: John Howard Yoder, *The Politics of Jesus*

(Grand Rapids: Eerdmans, 1972), especially chapter eight: "Christ and Power"; Richard Mouw, *Politics and the Biblical Drama* (Grand Rapids: Eerdmans, 1976); and Ronald J. Sider, *Christ and Violence* (Scottdale: Herald Press, 1979). The most recent evangelical work emphasizing a structural interpretation of the powers is Robert Webber's *The Church in the World* (Grand Rapids: Zondervan, 1986).

[3]Sider, *Christ and Violence*, p. 51. Sider does not deny the actual existence of evil spirits, but when he applies the biblical text to a contemporary context he appears to focus exclusively on the social and political structures.

[4]Webber, *Church*, pp. 14-15.

[5]Ibid., p. 44.

[6]Ibid, p. 35.

[7]See above for full bibliography.

[8]Schlier, *Principalities and Powers*, p. 31.

[9]See my *Ephesians: Power and Magic*, pp. 59-62.

[10]*PGM* 1.179-80; 4.2699; 101.39.

[11]For a full defense of this view, see my *Ephesians: Power and Magic*, pp. 62-64.

[12]See Walter Wink, *Naming the Powers* (Philadelphia: Fortress Press, 1984); *Unmasking the Powers* (Philadelphia: Fortress Press, 1986); *Engaging the Powers* (Philadelphia: Fortress Press, forthcoming).

[13]Wink, *Naming*, p. 5.

[14]See, for example, the article by Lowell Nobel, "Stage III: In Search of a Theology of Society," *Faculty Dialogue* 12 (1989):116, where he adopts Wink's view of the powers as the starting point for his understanding of social evil in the context of a theology of society.

[15]See my *Ephesians: Power and Magic*, pp. 48-51, 129-34.

[16]Wink, *Naming*, p. 5.

[17]Ibid., see especially pp. 133-48, for an explanation of his concept of myth.

[18]Ibid., pp. 61-63, 104. I give a detailed critique of this view in my *Ephesians: Power and Magic*, pp. 48-51, 130-34.

[19]Wink, *Naming*, p. 39.

[20]See James Barr, *Semantics of Biblical Language* (Oxford: Oxford Univ. Press, 1961), pp. 217-18.

[21]See, for example, Wink, *Naming*, pp. 126-34.

[22]Ibid., p. 127.

[23]Webber, *Church*, p. 29.

[24]E. Earle Ellis, *Pauline Theology: Ministry and Society* (Grand Rapids: Eerdmans, 1989), pp. 22-23. For additional helpful discussion on this topic, see chapter five, "Pauline Christianity and the World Order."

[25]Ibid., pp. 23-24.

[26]Walter Wink comes very close to this understanding when, with regard to the "angels of the nations," he comments, "They are not 'out there' or 'up there' but within" (*Unmasking the Powers* [Philadelphia: Fortress Press, 1986], p. 93). However, since he regards the powers as the invisible spirituality of a person or a nation, he fails to give adequate recognition to their independ-

ent existence.

[27]On Paul's concept of world, see Herman Ridderbos, *Paul: An Outline of His Theology* (Grand Rapids: Eerdmans, 1975), pp. 92-93.

[28]Stephen C. Mott, *Biblical Ethics and Social Change* (New York and Oxford: Oxford Univ. Press, 1982), p. 10.

[29]Ibid., p. 16.

[30]Ibid., p. 15.

[31]Frank E. Peretti, *This Present Darkness* (Westchester, Ill.: Crossway, 1986).

[32]On the interface between Christianity and the cult of Artemis, see Richard Oster, "The Ephesian Artemis as an Opponent of Early Christianity," *Jahrbuch für Antike und Christentum* 19 (1976):24-44. See also his more recent work "Ephesus as a Religious Center Under the Principate, I. Paganism Before Constantine," *Aufstieg und Niedergang der römischen Welt* II.18.2 (Berlin: Walter de Gruyter, forthcoming), pp. 1661-1728. (My thanks to Professor Oster for providing me with a prepublication proof of the article.)

[33]See my *Ephesians: Power and Magic*, pp. 20-28.

[34]See Oster, "Ephesus," pp. 1711-13.

Select Bibliography

Historical Background Works

Aune, David E. "Magic in Early Christianity." In *Aufstieg und Niedergang der römischen Welt.* II.23.2, pp. 1507-57. Berlin: Walter de Gruyter, 1980.

_____ . "Magic." In *International Standard Bible Encyclopedia.* 3:213-19. Grand Rapids: Eerdmans, 1986.

Betz, Hans Dieter, ed. *The Greek Magical Papyri in Translation.* Vol. 1: *Text.* Chicago: University of Chicago Press, 1986. This represents a fairly comprehensive collection of Greek and Demotic magical papyri that have been translated into English. It also contains an excellent introduction to the magical papyri by Professor Betz.

Charlesworth, James H., ed. *The Old Testament Pseudepigrapha.* 2 vols. New York: Doubleday, 1983, 1985.

Cramer, Frederick H. *Astrology in Roman Law and Politics.* Memoirs of the American Philosophical Society 37. Philadelphia: American Philosophical Society, 1954.

Cumont, Franz. *Astrology and Religion Among the Greeks and Romans.* 1912. Reprint. New York: Dover, 1960.

_____ . *The Oriental Religions in Roman Paganism.* New York: Dover, 1956.

Goodenough, E. R. *Jewish Symbols in the Greco-Roman Period.* 12 vols. New York: Pantheon, 1953.

Grant, Robert M. *Gods and the One God.* Philadelphia: Westminster Press, 1986.

Johnston, Sarah Iles. *Hekate Soteira: A Study of Hekate's Roles in the Chaldean Oracles and Related Literature.* American Philological Association. American Classical Studies 21. Atlanta: Scholars Press, 1990.

Langton, Edward. *Essentials of Demonology.* London: Epworth, 1949.

Luck, Georg. *Arcana Mundi: Magic and the Occult in the Greek and Roman Worlds.*

Baltimore: Johns Hopkins University Press, 1985.

Martin, Luther H. *Hellenistic Religions.* Oxford: Oxford University Press, 1987.

Russell, D. S. *The Message and Method of Jewish Apocalyptic.* Philadelphia: Westminster Press, 1964. See especially chapter nine: "Angels and Demons."

Schürer, Emil. *The History of the Jewish People in the Age of Jesus Christ.* Revised and edited by Geza Vermes, Fergus Millar and Martin Goodman. Vol. 3, Part 1. Edinburgh: T. & T. Clark, 1986. See especially chapter seven: "Incantations and Books of Magic."

Smith, Jonathan Z. "Hellenistic Religion." In *Encyclopaedia Britannica.* 8:749-51. Chicago: Encyclopaedia Brittanica, 1979.

Works Treating the Theme of Principalities and Powers

Anderson, Neil T. *Victory over the Darkness: Realizing the Power of Your Identity in Christ.* Ventura, Calif.: Regal Books, 1990.

——————. *The Bondage Breaker.* Eugene, Ore.: Harvest House, 1990.

Arnold, Clinton E. *Ephesians: Power and Magic. The Concept of Power in Ephesians in Light of Its Historical Setting.* Society for New Testament Studies Monograph 63. Cambridge: Cambridge University Press, 1989.

——————. "Principalities and Powers." *Anchor Bible Dictionary.* New York: Doubleday, forthcoming.

——————. " 'Principalities and Powers' in Recent Interpretation." *Catalyst* 17.2 (1991):4-5.

Berkhof, Hendrik. *Christ and the Powers.* Tr. J. H. Yoder. Scottdale: Herald Press, 1977.

Bubeck, Mark. *The Adversary.* Chicago: Moody, 1975.

——————. *Overcoming the Adversary.* Chicago: Moody, 1984.

Bufford, Rodger K. *Counseling and the Demonic.* Resources for Christian Counseling 17. Dallas: Word, 1988.

Caird, G. B. *Principalities and Powers.* Oxford: Clarendon, 1956.

Dickason, C. Fred. *Demon Possession and the Christian: A New Perspective.* Westchester, Ill.: Crossway, 1987.

Garrett, Susan R. *The Demise of the Devil: Magic and the Demonic in Luke's Writings.* Minneapolis: Fortress Press, 1989.

Green, Michael. *I Believe in Satan's Downfall.* Grand Rapids: Eerdmans, 1981.

Hiebert, Paul. "Power Encounter and Folk Islam." In *Muslims and Christians on the Emmaus Road,* pp. 45-61. Edited by J. Dudley Woodberry. Monrovia, Calif.: Missions Advanced Research & Communications Center, 1989.

Kraft, Charles H. *Christianity with Power: Your Worldview and Your Experience of the Supernatural.* Ann Arbor: Vine Books, 1989.

Leivestad, Ragnar. *Christ the Conqueror: Ideas of Conflict and Victory in the New Testament.* London: SPCK, 1954.

Mott, Stephen C. *Biblical Ethics and Social Change.* New York/Oxford: Oxford University Press, 1982.

O'Brien, Peter T. "Principalities and Powers: Opponents of the Church." In *Biblical Interpretation and the Church, 110-50.* Nashville: Thomas Nelson, 1984.

Russell, Jeffrey Burton. *Mephistopheles: The Devil in the Modern World*. Ithaca and London: Cornell University Press, 1986.

Schlier, Heinrich. *Principalities and Powers in the New Testament*. Freiburg: Herder, 1961.

Stauffer, Ethelbert. *New Testament Theology*. 5th ed. New York: Macmillan, 1955.

Stewart, J. S. "On a Neglected Emphasis in New Testament Theology." *Scottish Journal of Theology* 4 (1951):292-301.

Twelftree, Graham. *Christ Triumphant: Exorcism Then and Now*. London: Hodder & Stoughton, 1985.

Webber, Robert. *The Church in the World*. Grand Rapids: Zondervan, 1986.

Williams, Don. *Signs, Wonders, and the Kingdom of God*. Ann Arbor: Vine, 1989.

Wimber, John, and Kevin Springer. *Power Evangelism*. San Francisco: Harper & Row, 1986.

——————————— . *Power Healing*. San Francisco: Harper & Row, 1987.

Wink, Walter. *Naming the Powers*. Philadelphia: Fortress Press, 1984.

——————————— . *Unmasking the Powers*. Philadelphia: Fortress Press, 1986.

——————————— . *Engaging the Powers*. Philadelphia: Fortress Press, forthcoming.

Author Index

Index of Biblical Passages Cited

Old Testament

Subject Index